Memorandoms
by James Martin

Memorandoms by James Martin

An Astonishing Escape from Early New South Wales

Edited and introduced by
Tim Causer

Warning: Aboriginal and Torres Strait Islander readers should be aware that this book contains the images and names of deceased persons.

First published in 2017 by
UCL Press
University College London
Gower Street
London WC1E 6BT

Available to download free: www.ucl.ac.uk/ucl-press

Text © Tim Causer, 2017
Images © University College London and copyright holders named in captions, 2017

A CIP catalogue record for this book is available from The British Library.

This book is published under a Creative Commons Attribution Non-commercial Non-derivative 4.0 International license (CC BY-NC-ND 4.0). This license allows you to share, copy, distribute and transmit the work for personal and non-commercial use providing author and publisher attribution are clearly stated. Attribution should include the following information:

Tim Causer (ed.), *Memorandoms by James Martin: An Astonishing Escape from Early New South Wales*. London, UCL Press, 2017. https://doi.org/10.14324/111.9781911576815

Further details about CC BY licenses are available at http://creativecommons.org/licenses/

ISBN: 978–1–911576–83–9 (Hbk.)
ISBN: 978–1–911576–82–2 (Pbk.)
ISBN: 978–1–911576–81–5 (PDF)
ISBN: 978–1–911576–84–6 (epub)
ISBN: 978–1–911576–85–3 (mobi)
ISBN: 978–1–911576–86–0 (html)
DOI: 10.14324/111.9781911576815

Acknowledgements

Working with UCL Press has been a pleasure and I would like thank everyone involved. In particular I am grateful to Lara Speicher, Jaimee Biggins and Alison Major for their guidance and their faith in this book. Catherine Bradley has been a terrifically efficient and thorough editor, and improved the text in innumerable ways. I would also like to thank Pauline Hubner for collating the images reproduced here and for navigating the intricacies of securing the required permissions. I am grateful to my two anonymous referees for so generously giving their time and expertise, and for providing such warm yet rigorous feedback. Their comments and advice were invaluable.

Thanks go to the Arts and Humanities Research Council, under whose funding much of the research for this book was carried out, and I am very grateful for their support of our ongoing work on Jeremy Bentham's writings on Australia. I would also like to thank the AHRC and the Andrew W. Mellon Foundation's Scholarly Communications programme for past support of the award-winning *Transcribe Bentham* initiative; this also facilitated the digitisation of the Bentham Papers, many of which are reproduced here.

No work is produced in isolation, and I owe a great debt to Bentham Project colleagues past and present. Professor Philip Schofield, Dr Michael Quinn, Dr Louise Seaward, Dr Oliver Harris, Katy Roscoe and Chris Riley provided a never-ending supply of advice and encouragement, and have put up with my fascination with the *Memorandoms* for several years. I promise that I will stop talking about it now! Various versions of the introduction have been read and commented upon by Professor Schofield, Dr Quinn, Dr Seaward, Katy Roscoe and former colleagues Dr Kris Grint, Dr Zoe Hawkins and Dr Hazel Wilkinson. Iterations of my transcription of the *Memorandoms* have been checked by Professor Schofield and Dr Wilkinson. Katy Roscoe provided advice on Dutch translation. Dr Grint's expertise was invaluable in producing a TEI schema to publish, in 2014 on the Bentham Project website, a first attempt at an edition of the *Memorandoms*. I am grateful to Babette Smith for encouragement and for reading the introduction, as well as advice on tracking down the escapees and checking some Australian records. I am in awe of the scholarship of Mollie Gillen and Michael Flynn, as demonstrated in their respective biographical dictionaries of the people of the First and Second Fleets. These were invaluable resources, while the magnificent *Proceedings of the Old Bailey, 1674–1913* and the National Library of Australia's *Trove* continue to be indispensable research tools. Needless to say, any remaining errors of fact and interpretation are mine and mine alone.

In attempting to identify the Indigenous peoples encountered by the escapees on their voyage, I have made use of the Australian Institute of Aboriginal and Torres Strait Islander Studies' *Map of Indigenous Australia*, created by David Horton (http://aiatsis.gov.au/explore/articles/aiatsis-map-indigenous-australia). I am grateful to Dr Kristyn Harman for her advice on this topic.

I would like to thank the following institutions for permission to reproduce images of items held in their collections: Bauer Media; the Beinecke Rare Book and Manuscript Library, Yale University; the British Library; the David Rumsey Map Collection; the National Portrait Gallery, London; the National Library of Australia; the Natural History Museum, London; the State Library of New South Wales; the State Library of Queensland; The National Archives of the United Kingdom; the Tasmanian Archives and Heritage Office; UCL Art Museum; and Vrije University, Amsterdam.

Special thanks, as always, go to Gill Furlong and her colleagues at UCL Special Collections for their continued support of the work of the Bentham Project, and for permission to reproduce images and transcripts of the Bentham Papers. These images were captured by Raheel Nabi and Tony Slade of UCL Digital Media Services.

My sincere thanks go to everyone who has had the patience to put up with me during the last 18 months or so, in what has been an extremely difficult and unpleasant period. In particular, there is a well of gratitude which will never run dry for my dear friend Laura.

Finally, thank you to my family, who support me in everything that I do.

Tim Causer
March 2017

Picture credits

The publishers would like to thank the following for permission to reproduce the images in this book: Map: Courtesy of the David Rumsey Map Collection, www.davidrumsey.com; Fig. 1: Mitchell Library, State Library of New South Wales (Safe 1/14, no.9); Fig. 3: National Library of Australia, Canberra (NK815); Fig. 4: Tasmanian Archive and Heritage Office, Hobart; Fig. 5: National Library of Australia, Canberra (NK2040); Fig. 7: Mitchell Library, State Library of New South Wales (ZMB2 811.17/1788/1); Fig. 8: Mitchell Library, State Library of New South Wales (Safe 1/14, no.11); Fig. 9: © The Trustees of the Natural History Museum, London (Watling Drawing no. 41); Fig. 10: © The Trustees of the Natural History Museum, London (Watling Drawing no. 21); Fig. 11: The National Archives of the United Kingdow, Kew (HO 201/6/88); Fig. 12: John Oxley Library, State Library of Queensland; Fig. 13: Vrije University Library, Amsterdam (LL.05606gk); Fig. 14: Mitchell Library, State Library of New South Wales (Safe 1/14, no. 28b); Fig. 15: Mitchell Library, State Library of New South Wales and courtesy of the owner of the original work (FMS/650); Fig. 16: British Library, London; Fig. 17: © National Portrait Gallery, London; Fig. 18: The National Archives of the United Kingdom, Kew (HO 13/9); Fig. 19: Beinecke Rare Books and Manuscript Library, Yale University, New Haven; Fig. 20: Beinecke Rare Books and Manuscript Library, Yale University, New Haven; Fig. 21: Retrieved 3 February 2017, from http://nla.gov.au/nla.news-article47510555. National Library of Australia, Canberra. Courtesy The Australian Women's Weekly/Bauer Media; Fig. 22: UCL Art Museum (5588), University College London; Fig. 23: © National Portrait Gallery, London; Fig. 24: Courtesy of UCL Special Collections; Fig. 25: Mitchell Library, State Library of New South Wales (Safe 1/15, no.4).

All images of the manuscript of *Memorandoms by James Martin* are Courtesy UCL Special Collections.

'New Holland, Asiatic isles', 1814. This map by John Thomson shows the Australian continent, the Pacific region, Timor and the south-eastern end of Maritime South-East Asia.

This book is for William Allen, Samuel Bird, Samuel Broom, Mary Broad/Bryant, William Bryant, Charlotte Bryant, Emanuel Bryant, James Cox, Nathaniel Lillie, James Martin and William Morton. It is, after all, their story.

Contents

List of illustrations	xiii
List of abbreviations	xv
A note on the ages of the escapees	xvi
Introduction	1
Memorandoms by James Martin	73
A note on the presentation of the text	73
Fair copy of **Memorandoms**	127
Notes	149
Bibliography	173
Index	181

List of illustrations

Fig. 1 'Botany Bay. *Sirius* & Convoy going in: *Supply* & Agents Division in the Bay. 21 Jan[ry] 1788' by William Bradley, c.1802.   2

Fig. 2 'Arthur Phillip', taken from Louis Becke and Walter Jeffery, 1989. *Admiral Phillip: The Founding of New South Wales*. London: T. Fisher Unwin.   3

Fig. 3 'The *Discovery*. Convict-Ship (lying at Deptford)', unknown artist, 1829.   5

Fig. 4 'David Collins', unknown artist, 1804.   8

Fig. 5 'Vice-Admiral John Hunter, Governor of New South Wales' by William Mineard Bennett, c.1812.   9

Fig. 6 'Cap[t]. Bligh' from William Bligh, 1792. *A Voyage to the South Sea*. London: George Nicol.   10

Fig. 7 'Sketch & description of the settlement at Sydney Cove Port Jackson in the County of Cumberland taken by a transported Convict on the 16th of April, 1788, which was not quite 3 Months after Commodore Phillips's [sic] Landing there', attributed to Francis Fowkes.   13

Fig. 8 'First interview with the Native Women at Port Jackson New South Wales' by William Bradley, c.1802.   21

Fig. 9 'Native name Ben-nel-long, as painted when angry after Botany Bay Colebee was wounded' by 'Port Jackson Painter', 1790 or 1797(?).   21

Fig. 10	'A View of Sydney Cove – Port Jackson March 7th 1792' by 'Port Jackson Painter'.	23
Fig. 11	'Description of Convicts who have absconded from Sydney', 5 November 1791.	24
Fig. 12	'H.M.S. *Pandora* in the act of foundering' by Lt-Col. Batty, after a sketch by Peter Heywood, from John Barrow, 1831, *The Eventful History of the Mutiny and Piratical Seizure of H.M.S Bounty*. London: John Murray.	31
Fig. 13	'Vue de l'isle et de la ville de Batavia appartenant aux Hollandois, pour la Compagnie des Indes', *c*.1780.	33
Fig. 14	'Batavia and Onrust in Batavia Bay' by William Bradley, *c*.1802.	34
Fig. 15	'Captain Watkin Tench, Royal Marines, 1787', unknown artist.	35
Fig. 16	'Building plan of Newgate Prison' by Charles Dance, 1800.	37
Fig. 17	'James Boswell' by Sir Joshua Reynolds, 1785.	38
Fig. 18	Pardon for Mary Bryant, 1793.	39
Fig. 19	Mary Bryant's mark at the end of her brother-in-law Edward Puckey's letter to James Boswell, 16 February 1794.	42
Fig. 20	'Leaves from Botany Bay used as Tea', belonging to James Boswell.	49
Fig. 21	Publicity stills for *The Hungry Ones*, 10 July 1963. *The Australian Women's Weekly* (1933–82), p.17.	57
Fig. 22	'Jeremy Bentham', oil, *c*.1790.	58
Fig. 23	'Samuel Bentham' by Henry Edridge, *c*.1795–1800.	60
Fig. 24	Plan of Bentham's proposed panopticon prison by Willey Revely.	61
Fig. 25	'The Kangaroo' by Arthur Bowes Smyth, *c*.1787–9.	67

List of abbreviations

ADB	*Australian Dictionary of Biography*
b.	born
bap.	baptised
BRBML	Beinecke Rare Book and Manuscript Library, Yale University
Bowring	*The Works of Jeremy Bentham*, published under the superintendence of John Bowring, 1843
c.	circa
CW	The *Collected Works of Jeremy Bentham*
d.	died
HRA	*Historical Records of Australia*, Series I
ML	Mitchell Library, State Library of New South Wales, Sydney
nd.	no date
OBP	*Old Bailey Proceedings Online*
ODNB	*Oxford Dictionary of National Biography*
SLNSW	State Library of New South Wales
SRNSW	State Records Authority of New South Wales, Sydney
TAHO	Tasmanian Archive and Heritage Office, Hobart
TNA	The National Archives of the United Kingdom, Kew
UC	Bentham Papers, UCL Special Collections. Roman numerals refer to boxes in which the papers are placed, Arabic to the leaves within each box.

A note on the ages of the escapees

Recording with precision the ages of those transported to Australia – particularly of those sent early in the convict period – can be a difficult task. There is often disagreement between primary sources as to how old the transportees were, and convicts themselves may have had reason to conceal their true ages from the authorities. A number of sources consulted in the preparation of this give differing accounts of the ages of the nine transportees at the heart of this work. As a result, unless there is definite proof of when one of the group was born or baptised, a range of dates are provided when giving their years of birth, for example William Bryant (b.c.1758–61, d.1791).

The sources consulted for the ages of the escapees were:

- Governor Phillip to Lord Grenville, 5 November 1791, enclosure no.4, 'Description of Convicts who have absconded from Sydney'. CO 201/6/88, TNA.
- HO 26/1, p.106, TNA. Criminal Register, Middlesex, 5 July 1792, p.3.
- James Boswell. 'Draft of a Petition for the Botany Bay Prisoners – 14 May 1793' in *Boswell the Great Biographer, 1789–1795*. 1989. Yale Edition of the Private Papers of James Boswell, vol.13. Marlies K. Danziger and Frank Brady, eds. London: Yale University Press and William Heinemann, pp.217–19.
- Mollie Gillen. 1993. *The Founders of Australia: a Biographical Dictionary of the First Fleet*. Sydney: Library of Australian History.
- Michael Flynn. 1993. *The Second Fleet: Britain's Grim Convict Armada of 1790*. Sydney: Library of Australian History.

Introduction

At dawn on Sunday 13 May 1787 an unusual convoy of 11 ships departed from Portsmouth. Within a few hours they had sailed into the Channel, intending to run down the western coasts of France and Spain, and to then head out into the Atlantic. The convoy's final destination had long been a mirage in the European imagination, a land so odd that the ancient Greeks (only half-jokingly) believed its inhabitants walked on their hands.[1] The First Fleet, as it became known, reached Tenerife on 3 June 1787, then sailed on to Rio de Janeiro. It arrived there in early August and remained for a month to take on supplies, reaching the Cape of Good Hope on 13 October 1787, five months to the day after leaving England.

However, when it departed from the Cape a month later the Fleet and its passengers headed out into the unknown. There would be nothing to see for weeks on end but the emptiness of the Indian and Southern Oceans, until the ships rounded the southern tip of Van Diemen's Land (Tasmania) and continued north, up the eastern coast of the Australian continent, until they reached Botany Bay on 18 January 1788 (Fig.1). Eight days later the Fleet relocated to Sydney Cove in Port Jackson – described by Governor Arthur Phillip (Fig.2)[2] as 'the finest harbour in the world'[3] – and began to disembark its cargo of people.[4] Among these people were officials, headed by Phillip, a force of marines and approximately 750 to 775 male and female prisoners, sent to serve out their sentences on an unfamiliar shore.[5] The indigenous people of the region, the Eora, had seen European ships come and go, but now boat-loads of *myall* – strangers – had landed in their Country and remained. The initial encounters between the Eora and this fresh group of incomers were often marked by mutual 'goodwill and friendliness' and fascination, though the violence and killing would come soon enough.[6]

A number of the First Fleet's officers kept journals or wrote and published accounts of the penal colony's first few years.[7] However, no narrative written by a convict transported by the First Fleet is known to be extant.

Fig.1   'Botany Bay. *Sirius* & Convoy going in: *Supply* & Agents Division in the Bay. 21 Jan[ry] 1788' by William Bradley, *c*.1802

Nothing, that is, save for a few pages in the archive of one of Britain's great philosophers, Jeremy Bentham,[8] one of the earliest and most implacable enemies of transportation to New South Wales and the colony itself. Somewhat incongruously, amid the philosophical treatises in the voluminous Bentham Papers in UCL Library's Special Collections,[9] is the earliest Australian convict narrative, *Memorandoms by James Martin*. This document also happens to be the only first-hand account of the most famous, and most mythologised, escape from Australia by transported convicts.

The Bryant party's escape and convict absconding in early New South Wales

Among those transported by the First Fleet was the supposed author of the *Memorandoms*, James Martin of Ballymena, County Antrim.[10] At the Cornwall Assizes of 20 March 1786 he had been sentenced to seven years' transportation for stealing 11 iron screw bolts valued at two shillings and sixpence, and other goods valued at two shillings, from Powderham Castle.[11] Given that Martin was a bricklayer and stonemason by trade, it is a reasonable supposition that this was a workplace theft.

Fig.2 'Arthur Phillip', taken from Louis Becke and Walter Jeffery, 1899. *Admiral Phillip: The Founding of New South Wales*. London: T. Fisher Unwin

He was subsequently detained on the *Dunkirk* prison hulk at Plymouth, where his conduct was described as 'tolerably decent and orderly', before being embarked, on 11 March 1787, upon the *Charlotte* for transportation to New South Wales.[12] In a return of escaped convicts sent to England by Governor Phillip in November 1791, Martin was described as standing at five feet and seven inches (170 cm), having a dark complexion and of 'lisp[ing] in his speech'.[13]

By what seems a remarkable coincidence, convicted on the same day at the same assizes as Martin was a future confederate in escape, Mary Broad of Fowey, Cornwall.[14] Broad had, together with Catherine Prior[15] and Mary Hayden *alias* Shepherd,[16] robbed and violently assaulted Agnes Lakeman on a road in Plymouth – 'putting her in corporal fear and danger of her life', as the assize record puts it. Broad, Fryer and Hayden stole from Lakeman a silk bonnet valued at 12 pence and other goods valued at £1 and 11 shillings.[17] All three were condemned to death, but on 13 April 1786 this sentence was commuted to transportation for seven years. On 26 September 1786 Broad was detained in the *Dunkirk* hulk where her behaviour, like that of Martin, was described as 'tolerably decent and orderly'. Broad was about three months pregnant when she was embarked upon the *Charlotte* on 11 March 1787. She gave birth to a daughter on 8 September 1787, not long after the ship had left Rio de Janeiro, and the child was baptised Charlotte Spence[18] at Cape Town on 28 September.[19] It has not been possible to identify Charlotte's father. In the 1791 return of escaped convicts, Mary Broad was described as being 'marked with the small pox'. She was 'of a middle stature', walked 'with one knee bent inwards, but is not lame', and spoke 'with the strong west country accent'. Her height was not recorded in this document, but the Newgate criminal register for 1792 noted that she was five feet and four inches (162 cm) tall.[20]

In a further coincidence, also transported aboard the *Charlotte* was Mary Broad's future husband, the Cornishman William Bryant, described in the 1791 return of absconders as being five feet seven inches (170 cm) in height and of a dark complexion.[21] He had been committed at Bodmin by the Mayor of St Ives for 'personating and assuming the names' of two Royal Navy sailors 'and in their names feloniously receiving' some of their wages. Bryant was convicted at the Cornwall Assizes of 20 March 1784 and sentenced to death, subsequently commuted on condition of his being transported to America for seven years.[22]

Yet America had not been a viable destination for Britain's convicts for almost a decade. Between 1615 and 1776 some 50,000 men, women and children were transported from the British Isles to the North American colonies, though only in significant numbers after the passage of the Transportation Act of 1717. The shipping of convicts to America was privately contracted to merchants who received, as the Transportation Act put it, 'Property in their Service'; the contractors duly sold this 'Property' as indentured labour to colonists.[23] After the prisoner's period of indentured servitude expired he or she was then released. Despite the American Revolutionary Wars (1776–83) putting a stop to convicts being sent there, British courts continued to pass sentences of transportation. Convicts so sentenced were held in gaols or prison hulks – decommissioned warships moored on the Thames, at Portsmouth and at Plymouth – while the government looked for an alternative place to which prisoners could be transported (Fig.3).[24] The government experimented in 1781 and 1782 with sending around 200 convicts to Senegambia, a British slaving outpost on the west African coast. In the first instance they were dragooned as soldiers into the so-called 101st and 102nd 'Independent Companies' to fight the Dutch and serve the interests of the Company of Merchants Trading to Africa; a later group was sent as labourers. In both cases the mortality rate was ferocious, and the idea of sending more convicts there was abandoned.[25]

William Bryant was one of the convicts left languishing in the hulks before the decision was taken to found the New South Wales penal colony. He spent just a few weeks short of three years on board the *Dunkirk* hulk at Plymouth, and it may indeed have come as something of a relief to leave it behind and board the *Charlotte* on 11 March 1787.

The *Charlotte* also carried the carpenter James Cox to New South Wales.[26] By the time he left England Cox had been sentenced to death, and reprieved from it, twice. He was brought before the bar at the Old Bailey on 11 September 1782 and indicted for 'feloniously and burglariously breaking and entering the dwelling-house' of Henry and Francis Thompson, haberdashers on Oxford Street, London, and for stealing 12 yards of thread lace valued at £4 and two pairs of cotton stockings valued at four shillings. In evidence Francis Thompson recalled how, at ten in the evening on 27 July, he heard the smashing of glass. Upon checking one of the shop's windows, he found it broken and cleared of stock. In the shop at the time were George Baily and Mr Dickey, who rushed out into the street and dragged Cox – who was 'dabbing his hands' with a handkerchief, having 'cut the fleshy part of his hand and all his knuckles' while apparently thrusting his hand through the window – back inside. Though

Fig.3   'The *Discovery*. Convict-Ship (lying at Deptford)', unknown artist, 1829

Thompson had Cox literally red-handed, he admitted to the court that none of his property was found on Cox's person.

In his defence, Cox stated that he had been on his way to Wapping and had merely 'stopped to look at some buckles in a window' when he was suddenly seized by several people who 'used me very ill'. Only Dickey swore to seeing Cox steal the goods. No-one saw him palm them off to anyone else, and though Francis Thompson admitted to having seen other people pass by at the time of the theft, he admitted: 'I had not the presence of mind to lay hold of them.' Cox was found guilty and sentenced to death, subsequently commuted to transportation for life. On 10 September 1783 he was sent to a hulk on the River Thames.[27]

Cox was one of 179 prisoners who, on 26 March 1784, were embarked upon the *Mercury*, the dispatching of which was, as historian Emma Christopher suggests, the second part of a 'madcap attempt to resume convict transportation to America'.[28] During the previous year the then Home Secretary Lord North[29] had contracted the London merchant George Moore to ship prisoners to America in return for £500 and the profit of selling the convicts' indentures. Moore had already dispatched one shipload of prisoners in an endeavour covered in subterfuge: his ship, the *George*, had been renamed the *Swift*, the convicts were described in the departure notices as indentured servants and the *Swift*'s destination was listed as Nova Scotia. When it put to sea, however, the captain made instead for Baltimore, where George Salmon, Moore's business partner, was to organise the sale.

However, shortly after passing out of the Thames in August 1783 the *Swift* was seized by a group of convicts. They had been allowed on deck, out of their irons, by the captain in consideration of their health. The ship was run aground at Rye in Sussex and, although about one-fifth of the convicts escaped into the countryside, most were subsequently recaptured.[30] A similar fate befell the *Mercury* when, early on the morning of 8 April 1784, some of the prisoners – who had smuggled on board small saws and nitric acid to remove their irons – seized control of the ship near the Scilly Isles. In this case bad weather forced the mutineers to put in at Torbay in Devon on 13 April, where 66 mutinous convicts were apprehended on board the *Mercury* by the crew of HMS *Helena*. A further 24, including Cox, were later arrested in locations throughout Devon.[31]

A Special Commission was held at Exeter Castle on 24 May 1784, chaired by John Heath,[32] to try the convict mutineers. Under the Transportation Act of 1768 there was a reward of £20 per head for any individual who apprehended a person 'at large within this Kingdom' while under a sentence of transportation and was subsequently convicted of returning from transportation.[33] As the crew of the *Helena* had captured 66 convicts, they stood to share quite a windfall.[34] However, Mr Justice Heath refused to try these 66 since, having been captured aboard the *Mercury* at sea, they 'could not be said to be at large within the kingdom'; the convicts were simply ordered to remain on their previous sentences. A local journalist covering the trial expressed sympathy towards the *Helena*'s crew for having been deprived of their 'merited reward'.[35] For the 24 convicts arrested on land, there was no such exemption. All were sentenced to death for returning from transportation, though all were later reprieved and two were eventually acquitted. Cox, now under a second sentence of transportation for life, was sent to the *Dunkirk* hulk at Plymouth, where he behaved 'remarkably well' until being embarked on the *Charlotte* on 11 March 1787.[36] In the 1791 return of absconders, Cox was described as being five feet eight inches in height (172 cm), of a dark complexion and with black hair.[37]

The other First Fleeter who would later join the escapees was the waterman Samuel Bird.[38] He had been sentenced to transportation for seven years at the Surrey Assizes on 20 July 1785 for stealing 1000lbs (453 kg) of saltpetre from a warehouse in Wandsworth. He was convicted with a James Bird, who may have been an elder brother or cousin.[39] On 24 October 1785 Samuel Bird was sent onto the *Justitia* hulk at Woolwich before being embarked on the *Alexander* on 6 January 1787. In the return of absconders of November 1791 he was said to be five feet seven inches (170 cm) in height, 'a stout man of a dark complexion' and with dark hair.[40]

* * *

From the earliest establishment of the penal colony of New South Wales, transportees sought to devise ways to escape from it. Escape could take many forms and need not involve physical departure: a convict could attempt to evade work by feigning sickness or by breaking their tools, or seek metaphorical escape through recreation, like the prisoners of the Norfolk Island penal station during the late 1840s, for example, who sought escapism in the penny magazines of the Island's well-stocked library.[41] But it was through absconding, the removing of one's self from the place of lawful confinement – if 'confinement' is the correct term for the situation of convicts in a continent-sized open gaol – that prisoners made their greatest challenge to the authority of the convict system. Punishments for absconding, particularly in New South Wales's early years, could be savage. On 5 June 1788 Edward Cormick[42] took to the bush and remained at large for 18 days, subsisting on – according to Judge-Advocate Lieutenant David Collins (Fig.4)[43] – 'what he was

Fig.4   'David Collins', unknown artist, 1804

able to procure by nocturnal depredations among the huts and stock of individuals'. Cormick surrendered, half-starved, on 23 June; he was tried the next day and hanged the day after that.[44] John 'Black' Caesar absconded to the bush in May 1789, a fortnight after being convicted at the Sydney Criminal Court of theft and receiving a second sentence of re-transportation for life. He was recaptured on 6 June and sent to work in irons on Garden Island in Sydney Harbour.[45]

Exemplary punishments had a limited effect. The authorities in New South Wales were well aware that the availability of even a glimmer of hope of getting away successfully was a significant encouragement to convicts to attempt it. This was a particular problem in a place where, if they were so minded, a transportee could simply wander off into the bush, notwithstanding the dangers that posed. For example, many scoffed at the ignorance of Irish convicts for believing that there was a society of free white people living several hundred miles south of Sydney, on the other side of the Blue Mountains, where there was no need to work and plenty of food. Governor John Hunter (Fig.5)[46] took the effect of these rumours seriously, however, particularly when a 'depraved set of transports' from Ireland attempted to drive stolen cattle overland to this far-off country.[47]

During January 1798 around 20 Irish convicts were arrested when they gathered to set out for the 'fancied paradise, or to China', armed with two pieces of paper as their guide: one contained written directions,

Fig.5 'Vice-Admiral John Hunter, Governor of New South Wales' by William Mineard Bennett, c.1812

while on the second someone had drawn a picture of a compass. Hunter was aghast at the 'obstinacy and ignorance' of these people, and though a number of them were flogged he thought that 'nothing but experience' would ever convince the Irish of the falsity of their belief. Out of 'humanity, and a strong desire to save these men, worthless as they are, from impending death' in attempts to escape, Hunter included four Irish convicts in an exploration party led by John Wilson, named Bun-bo-e by the Dharug people.[48] He hoped that first-hand accounts from such an expedition would put paid to belief in this far-off Arcadia.[49] The soldiers and three of the four convicts turned back when the party reached the Mount Hunter district, approximately 43 miles (70 km) from Sydney. Wilson, the remaining convict and Governor Hunter's servant John Price continued; they travelled as far as the Wingecarribee river, about 80 miles (130 km) to the south-west of Sydney, before turning back. However, as David Levell points out, the Irish convicts regarded the expedition as a 'transparent' ploy on Hunter's part, believing that 'the results of his authorised bush escapade' were 'not worth waiting for'. They, and others, continued to escape, whether in search of the mythical land or simply somewhere – anywhere – that was not New South Wales.[50]

Colonial officials such as Hunter regularly characterised convict escapes such as these as impulsive, quixotic, doomed plunges into the darkness of the bush or the violent waters of the Pacific. This was a reflex response even when the authorities had no idea what actually happened to absconders, and one which was still evident 40 years after

James Martin and company left New South Wales. In 1830 the *Sydney Gazette* reassured its concerned readers that 11 men who stole a boat and escaped from Norfolk Island – almost 1000 miles (1600 km) east of Sydney – had undoubtedly perished; they must either have drowned or met death 'in a more terrific form...either from being destroyed by the cannibals of New Zealand, or from starvation in being driven about the wide ocean at such a season'.[51] Yet this strategy could be undermined by even the most imprecise and vague of rumours. The Van Diemonian colonist David Burn[52] recounted a story that one of this group of escapees from Norfolk Island had been 'elected Chief' by the 'natives' of Pleasant Island (present-day Nauru), but had been expelled owing to his having committed 'murders and barbarities'. The last Burn had heard of this unnamed man was of his being 'worked in irons at Manila'.[53]

Contrary to public declamations of stupidity, historian Grace Karskens notes that 'convicts were not as geographically ignorant as their superiors liked to believe'.[54] They knew of James Cook's[55] exploration of the Pacific through popular literature and newspapers, and of the extraordinary survival of Captain William Bligh of HMS *Bounty* (Fig.6).[56] Bligh had sailed from England in December 1787 with a commission to transport breadfruit and other crops from the Pacific to the West Indies, where

Fig.6   'Capt. Bligh' from William Bligh, 1792. *A Voyage to the South Sea.* London: George Nicol

they were to be introduced and cultivated as food for plantation slaves. At the end of October 1788 the *Bounty* reached Tahiti, where it took on board 1000 young breadfruit plants. The ship departed for the Caribbean at the start of April 1789. On 28 April part of the crew, led by Fletcher Christian,[57] mutinied. Bligh and the crew members who remained loyal to him were set adrift in the ship's 23-foot launch. They managed to travel around 3200 miles (c.5000 km) to Kupang in West Timor in little more than two months, and suffered only one death among them – a tribute to Bligh's exceptional navigational skills.[58] As Captain Watkin Tench of the Marines, who travelled to New South Wales on the First Fleet, put it, after Bligh's survival 'no length of passage, or hazard of navigation, seemed above human accomplishment'.[59]

Some transportees were more than accomplished, bringing to New South Wales skills both vital to the fledgling colony and in themselves useful for absconding.[60] Among those transported by the First Fleet were stonemasons, weavers, carpenters, farmers and blacksmiths, as well as sailors and fishermen – people who had worked the seas and currents for much of their adult lives. In addition, given the demographics of the colony, skilled convicts were of necessity appointed to positions of responsibility. Judge-Advocate Collins complained of having to place 'a confidence in these people', but 'unfortunately, to fill many of those offices to which free people alone should have been appointed in the colony, there were none but convicts'. Though some transportees had given 'proofs, or strong indications of returning dispositions to honest industry', there were others 'who had no claim to this praise'.[61] Among those for whom Collins had no praise was William Bryant, whose seamanship and fishing skills, learnt in his native Cornwall, saw him placed in charge of managing the colony's fishing enterprise. This was a job of particular importance in the colony's early years when food was scarce: the ration in the colony was subjected to repeated reductions to the point where, in April 1790 all hands were placed upon a subsistence ration. As Collins put it, the dire state of the colony's food stores meant that 'it was determined to reduce still lower what was already too low'.[62]

Bryant's role gave him and his family a relatively privileged position. He and Mary Broad had married on 10 February 1788 and they, together with young Charlotte, were provided with the privacy of their own hut. Bryant was also allowed to keep some of his catch by way of an incentive, but he was caught abusing this indulgence: on 4 February 1789 he was brought before magistrates Collins and Augustus Alt[63] and charged with 'secreting and selling large quantities of fish'.[64] The main witness for the prosecution was the convict Joseph Paget,[65] who worked in Bryant's fishing boat and acted as a sort of servant to his family. Bryant would use Paget as an intermediary to pass on fish in exchange for spirits or other services rendered. For the defence, John White[66] – who, as surgeon aboard the *Charlotte*, had employed Bryant to issue rations to the other convicts – testified as to Bryant's honesty, but to no avail. Bryant was found guilty.[67] Theft of provisions was often punished with particular ferocity at this time: for example, on 27 March 1789 Marine Privates Richard Askew, James Baker, James Brown, Richard Dukes or Lukes, Thomas Jones and Luke Hines or Haines were hanged for having repeatedly plundered the government store.[68] By comparison Bryant got away lightly (though it undoubtedly did not feel that way to him): he received 100 lashes from the cat o'nine-tails and was dismissed from his post. In addition he and his family were also evicted from their accommodation. Bryant did continue to work in the colony's fishing boats, however, though he was no longer in charge of their operation and was (theoretically) under close supervision. As Collins acidly put it, 'notwithstanding his villainy, [Bryant] was too useful a person to part with and send to a brick cart'.[69]

In her study of successful convict escapes, Karskens found that such endeavours were 'overwhelmingly a collective rather than an individualist enterprise'; they were 'carefully organised' and setting out to sea offered the greatest chance of getting away.[70] The escape led by William Bryant perfectly fits the Karskens model, though a precedent for escaping by sea had been set by others. Collins reported on a 'desertion of an extraordinary nature' on 26 September 1790, when five men working at the government farm at Rose Hill, around 12 miles (20 km) from Sydney, rowed undetected down the Parramatta river in a small boat. Once in Sydney they stole a larger and more seaworthy vessel with a sail, apparently aiming for Tahiti.[71] Led by the 'daring, desperate' John Turwood,[72] the group of men – George Lee, George Connoway,[73] John Watson[74] and Joseph Sutton[75] – sailed out of Port Jackson and disappeared.

Demonstrating the automatic response to a convict escape, Collins comforted himself in thinking that 'from the wretched state of the boat wherein they trusted themselves, [it] must have proved their grave'.[76] He was wrong: the men were driven ashore at Port Stephens, around 130 miles (210 km) to the north of Sydney. There they lived among the Worimi people until 26 August 1795, when Turwood, Lee, Connoway and Watson – Sutton having died in the meantime – were picked up by Captain William Broughton[77] of HMS *Providence*. They were returned to Sydney, where David Collins described their telling 'a melancholy tale of their sufferings in the boat' to the 'crowds both of black and white people which attended them their adventures in Port Stephens'. Turwood and company described 'in high terms' the 'pacific disposition and gentle manners of the natives' and spoke of the ceremonies which granted them tribal names. They were 'allotted' wives and 'one or two had children', though Collins mocked their 'ridiculous story, that the natives appeared to worship them' and believed them to be 'the ancestors of some of them who had fallen in battle and had returned from the sea to visit them again'.[78]

There is no record of any of the Turwood group having been punished for absconding. Though Bryant and the others could not have known the fate of this party when they escaped in March 1791, the very fact that it had been possible to sail unchallenged out of the harbour could only have been an encouragement to Bryant and the others (Fig.7).

We might well add to the Karskens model the importance of trust and comradeship, and in this respect the Turwood group was also a prototype for Bryant's. All five of Turwood's party were transported to New South Wales by the Second Fleet: Sutton arrived in the *Surprize* on 26 June 1790 and Watson in the *Neptune* a day later, while the core of the

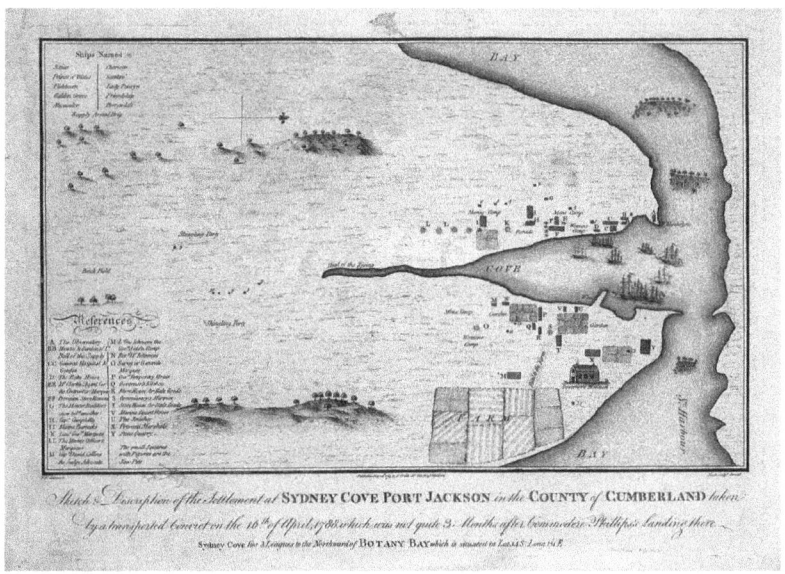

Fig.7 'Sketch & description of the settlement at Sydney Cove Port Jackson in the County of Cumberland taken by a transported Convict on the 16th of April, 1788, which was not quite 3 Months after Commodore Phillips's [sic] Landing there', attributed to Francis Fowkes

group, Lee, Connoway and Turwood himself, arrived in the *Scarborough* on 28 June. It is not outside the realms of possibility that the three shipmates formed an association during the *Scarborough*'s journey south. The ties between Lee and Connoway ran even deeper. They, along with Alexander Seaton, had been sentenced to death together at the Old Bailey on 30 August 1786 for stealing two bullocks, valued at £20, at Poplar.[79] Sutton had already made a vain attempt to leave New South Wales in August 1790 by stowing away on the *Neptune*; he was discovered hiding under a pile of firewood, and it was only as part of a collective that he successfully got away.[80] Turwood and Lee evidently learned the lesson of co-operation when they and several others put into action their plan to hijack successfully the government boat *Cumberland* on 5 September 1797, while it was ferrying goods between Sydney and the Hawkesbury river farms. Though Governor Hunter sent an armed whaleboat in pursuit of the pirates, the *Cumberland* – and those who seized it – were never heard of again.[81]

Similarly, a core of the Bryant party spent a good deal of time in the same place. James Martin and Mary Bryant were convicted at the same assizes and they, along with William Bryant and James Cox, were all confined in the *Dunkirk* hulk at Plymouth. In due course all four were transported to New South Wales by the *Charlotte*. While it can only be an assumption that they knew each other closely or were – as writer Judith Cook supposed, 'close friends' – it is not unlikely that the four had at least met or knew of one another prior to landing in New South Wales, particularly during the eight months spent in the *Charlotte*'s floating community.[82] In addition, as we shall see, three more members of Bryant's party arrived in New South Wales in 1790 in the same ship. Familiarity, in this instance, may have contributed to members of the group being comfortable with and trusting in one another.

We do not know when William Bryant determined to make his escape, though it might be reasonably supposed that the flogging he endured in February 1789 focused his mind. As to why he sought to escape, David Collins thought that since in March 1791 Bryant's 'term of transportation, according to his own account, had recently expired' he may have felt entitled to take his leave, since the government was not about to provide a return voyage for him.[83] According to the London newspapers, at the Bow Street hearing of 30 June 1792 the surviving escapees stated that they absconded owing to the entire colony being put on short rations for an extended period, and from fear of 'being starved to death' decided to 'risk their lives on the sea, [rather] than drag out a miserable existence on an unhospitable shore'.[84] This was no idle fear: by mid-April 1790 there was only enough salt pork and beef in New South Wales to last another four and a half months, enough rice and peas for five months and enough flour and biscuit for eight months. On top of that, the quantity of barley and wheat sown that year was insufficient to meet the colony's needs. The harvest had failed to meet expectations and some crops had to be retained for sowing in the following season. In short, New South Wales was clinging on, in desperate need of supplies.[85] Collins remarked on the effects of 'the miserable allowance' of food upon the health of the labouring convicts and was particularly struck by the fate of one unnamed elderly prisoner who, on 12 May 1790, fainted with hunger at the government store while waiting for his daily ration. The man, 'unable with age to hold up any longer', was carried to hospital where he died the following morning. Here, after an autopsy, 'his stomach was found quite empty'. Collins noted that the man had no cooking utensils of his own; he either gave away part of his ration in return for use of a pan or, failing that, ate his rice raw.[86]

During this 'season of general distress' Collins found that even the most severe punishments failed to dissuade people from committing robberies. 'While there was a vegetable to steal', he wrote, 'there were those who would steal it.'[87] Supplies had, in fact, been sent from England in mid-1789 in the *Lady Juliana* and the *Guardian*, but the latter ship – carrying about three times as much in the way of provisions as the former – struck an iceberg near Marion Island, some 1000 miles (1700 km) from Port Elizabeth on Christmas Eve 1789. It took a crew of 60 men, including 21 convicts, to steer the floundering *Guardian* towards the Cape of Good Hope, where it was towed into Table Bay, condemned and broken up.[88] The arrival of the *Lady Juliana* at Port Jackson on 3 June 1790 did bring some provisions, and 221 female convicts, but Governor Phillip admitted that the loss of the *Guardian* and the 'very liberal supplies' it carried had 'thrown the settlement back' in a very severe manner.[89] Within three weeks the colony's situation took an even more serious turn.

Though the colonists were overjoyed at the arrival of the store-ship *Justinian* on 20 June 1790, following close behind were three convict ships – the *Surprize*, the *Neptune* and the *Scarborough*, the remainder of the Second Fleet – bringing hundreds more prisoners to the colony. Those who watched the disembarkation of the ships were horror-struck at the state of the convicts brought ashore. Of the 1017 prisoners embarked aboard the three transports in England, 267 – just over one-quarter – died during the voyage; according to Governor Phillip, a further 488 required immediate medical treatment on being landed.[90] Collins described the 'lean and emaciated' condition of the sick: 'both the living and the dead exhibit[ed] more horrid spectacles than had ever been witnessed in this country'.[91] Perhaps the most harrowing account of the Second Fleet's arrival was given by Reverend Richard Johnson, the colony's chaplain who had travelled to New South Wales with the First Fleet.[92] He recorded how some of the deceased were 'thrown into the harbour, and their dead bodies cast upon the shore, and were seen laying naked upon the rocks', while

> The landing of these people was truly affecting and shocking; great numbers were not able to walk, nor to move hand or foot; such were slung over the ship side in the same manner as they would sling a cask, a box, or anything of that nature. Upon their being brought up to the open air some fainted, some died upon deck, and others in the boat before they reached the shore. When come on shore many were not able to walk or stand, or to stir themselves in the least, hence some were led by others. Some creeped upon their hands and knees, and some were carried upon the backs of others.

Hospital tents were erected, and Johnson saw 'unexpressible' suffering as the sick endured scurvy, fever and dysentery, 'covered over almost with their own nastiness, their heads, bodies, cloths, blanket, all full of filth and lice'. It was a sight, in summary, 'truly shocking to the feelings of humanity'.[93]

How had this horror come to pass? The government had contracted the fitting out of the Second Fleet to the London shipping and slaving firm of Camden, Calvert and King, and the whole endeavour was marked by corruption and wilful neglect. The *Neptune*, for instance, had the greatest number of deaths of any convict ship sent to Australia – nearly one in three of the prisoners died on the voyage – and it appeared that rations were withheld and the prisoners routinely kept in irons below decks by the ship's master, Donald Trail.[94] Such was the hunger aboard the *Neptune* that the convicts had been driven to eating the ship's five cats.[95] The treatment of the Second Fleet's prisoners drove Governor Phillip into a fury. He placed the blame firmly with Camden, Calvert and King and the convict transports' masters for crowding the ships with too many prisoners and denying them access to fresh air on deck. He also turned his anger towards the government for paying no attention to who was being transported, being merely concerned with 'sending out the disordered and helpless' and clearing out the gaols. Should this course be maintained, Phillip declared, he expected that New South Wales would 'remain for years a burthen to the mother country'.[96]

An inquiry into the Second Fleet commenced in London during November 1791. Witnesses testified that Trail and the *Neptune*'s first mate, William Ellerington,[97] had not only kept the convicts on short rations, but had also opened a shop in Sydney to sell to colonists, at an inflated price, the convict provisions they had stockpiled. At some point in the proceedings Trail absconded, presumably to escape prosecution, but he was apprehended. Trail and Ellerington were brought to trial in June 1792, charged with having murdered Andrew Anderson, a sailor on the *Neptune*, and John Joseph, the ship's cook, in a private prosecution brought by the lawyer Thomas Evans.[98] Though further damning evidence of the conditions aboard the *Neptune* emerged, including floggings, wanton disregard for the prisoners' health and an incident in which Trail punched the convict Jane Haly[99] full in the face, the jury took three hours to clear both defendants of murder.[100] Trail later resumed service in the Royal Navy and held commercial interests at the Cape of Good Hope. When he died he had amassed considerable wealth – most likely acquired from his dealing in slaves and convicts.[101]

The arrival of the Second Fleet, and the illness, chaos and misery which it brought, may have been an additional spur to William Bryant and his fellows to put their escape plan into action. If they had intended to leave during mid-1790, the plan may have been somewhat complicated by the arrival of William and Mary Bryant's son Emanuel,[102] who was baptised in Sydney on 4 April 1790. The prospect of absconding with a babe in arms and a mother recovering from childbirth was far from ideal. Collins hypothesised that Bryant only planned to take his wife (and, by inference, the children) with him as a result of his 'dread of her defeating his plan by discovery if she was not made personally interested in his escape'. Collins reported that Bryant 'had been frequently heard to express, what was indeed the general sentiment among the people of his description [i.e. convicts], that he did not consider his marriage in this country as binding'. In Collins' view, this belief was so widespread that Governor Phillip issued a government order stating that no expiree would be allowed to depart from New South Wales if in so doing they left behind a family incapable of supporting themselves.[103] Collins' explanation as to why the escape did not take place in mid-1790 is not all that convincing, and there is a far more prosaic reason as to why the group did not abscond in the wake of the arrival of the Second Fleet: they had simply not yet acquired the necessary equipment or expertise.

Much of this missing expertise was provided by four Second Fleet survivors who were recruited into Bryant's gang. Not the least of these was William Allen of Kingston-upon-Hull,[104] an experienced mariner who was aged about 54 when he arrived in New South Wales. He claimed to have served in 'both [of] the last wars in His Majesty's fleet under Captain Moutray[105] in the *Ramilies* and after she was broke Captain Marotter[106] and Admiral Graves'.[107] John Moutray had received command of the *Ramilies* in March 1779, and Allen was aboard in July 1780 when Moutray was ordered to escort a sizeable convoy of merchant ships and their valuable cargo to America and the East and West Indies. Early on in the voyage Moutray ignored a reported sighting of sails, and on 8 August the *Ramilies*, the *Thetis* and the *Southampton* sailed right into the entire Franco-Spanish fleet then blockading Gibraltar. The loss to the merchant fleet's insurers was an astonishing £1,500,000. Moutray was court-martialled at Jamaica during January 1781 and removed from his command, though he later resumed service.[108] Allen also served under Rear-Admiral Thomas Graves, presumably when Graves was the commander-in-chief of the North American Squadron during 1781. Allen was again aboard the *Ramilies*, the flagship of Graves's fleet, in September 1782 when the squadron was hit by a severe storm off the coast of Newfoundland while escorting to Britain a convoy of merchantmen, French prizes and damaged British ships in need of repair. Several ships and many lives were lost, and the foundering *Ramilies* was dismasted and set alight by its crew, who escaped to the *Belle*, one of the merchant ships. Allen was presumably aboard the *Belle* when it reached Cork on 10 October 1782.[109]

Allen was firmly back on dry land when he was convicted at the City of Norwich Assizes on 30 July 1787 of stealing 49 linen handkerchiefs, valued at 35 shillings, from a shop owned by Leyson Lewis and James Hayward. He was found not guilty of stealing privately in a shop – a capital offence – but guilty of theft, and was sentenced to seven years' transportation.[110] He was held in Norwich Castle until mid-October 1787 when he was sent to the *Stanislaus* hulk at Woolwich, transferring in April 1788 to the *Lion* hulk at Portsmouth. Allen was embarked upon the *Scarborough* on 29 November 1789, and in New South Wales became the assigned servant of Captain James Campbell.[111] He was described in the 1791 return of absconders as being a shoemaker by trade, of five feet and nine inches (175 cm) in height, of a dark complexion and with dark hair, and 'was ruptured'.[112]

Also transported on the *Scarborough* was Samuel Broom.[113] He had been convicted at the Shropshire Assizes on 26 July 1788 of stealing three pigs belonging to John Asprey on 19 April 1788.[114] Broom was sentenced to seven years' transportation, and by mid-August 1788 was aboard the *Fortune* hulk at Langstone Harbour in Portsmouth. In May

1789 a report described him as infirm but fit enough to be transported, and he was embarked upon the *Scarborough* on 30 November 1789.[115] He was described in the 1791 return of absconders as being six feet (182 cm) tall, of a fair complexion, and that 'he walks lame'.[116]

Joining Allen and Broom aboard the *Scarborough* was the weaver Nathaniel Lillie[117] who, at around one in the morning on 11 January 1788, burgled the house of Benjamin Summerset, a baker in Sudbury. From here he took, among other things, a silver-cased watch, two silver tablespoons and a fishnet. Lillie was convicted at the Suffolk Assizes on 19 March 1788 and sentenced to death, subsequently commuted to transportation to life. In August 1788 he was sent to the *Lion* hulk at Portsmouth, and on 29 November 1789 was embarked aboard the *Scarborough*.[118] Lillie was described in the 1791 return of absconders as being five feet six inches (167 cm) in height, of a dark complexion, and, like Allen, 'was ruptured'.[119]

Rounding out the Second Fleet quartet was William Morton[120] who, as the navigator of the escapees' boat, was perhaps the most important member of the group.[121] Morton was convicted of obtaining money by false pretences at the Newcastle-upon-Tyne Quarter Sessions on 24 April 1789. He was sentenced to transportation for seven years and sent to the *Justitia* hulk on the River Thames on 4 July. From here he was embarked on the *Neptune* on 12 November 1789 for transportation to New South Wales.[122] The 1791 return described Morton as being five feet and nine inches (175 cm) in height, 'a thin man of a dark complexion'; it also noted that he had served as second mate aboard an East India Company ship.[123]

William Bryant chose extremely well in recruiting his crew. David Collins' grudging recognition that Morton knew 'something of navigation' was a masterful piece of understatement, given the boat's safe passage to Timor with the survival of all on board.[124] Mary Bryant, who grew up in the fishing community of Fowey and whose father was a mariner, could presumably handle a boat. Bird 'knew perfectly well how to manage a boat', according to Collins, and Allen, as we have seen, had significant naval experience. Again according to Collins, James Cox had 'endeavoured to acquire such information on the subject [of navigation] as might serve him whenever a fit occasion should present itself'.[125] Cox's carpentry and Lillie's weaving skills would also have been useful in effecting repairs to the boat, sails and the escapees' clothing. It is also worth noting that the escapees were all above the average height of transported convicts: five feet and six inches (167 cm) for men and five feet and one inch (156 cm) for women between 1724 and 1789.[126] At six feet tall, Samuel Broom in particular would have towered over most other transportees.

During late February 1791 the escape plan was clearly well advanced. So well advanced, in fact, that it had already been brought to the attention of the authorities. Collins wrote that Bryant had been 'overheard consulting in his hut after dark, with five other convicts, on the practicability of carrying off the boat in which he was employed'.[127] This was reported to Governor Phillip, who ordered that Bryant should be 'narrowly watched, and any scheme of that nature counteracted'. This observation smacks of being wise after the event; surely Bryant would have been put under rather closer surveillance than the evidently inadequate level of observation to which he was subjected? However, the day after the plot was reported to Phillip, Bryant had an accident while burdened with a full catch when returning from the fishing grounds. According to Collins, 'the hook of the fore tack' gave way in 'a squall of wind, the boat got stern-way, and filled, by which the execution of his project was for the present prevented'.[128] A sister of the Eora warrior Bennelong,[129] Carangarang,[130] and three of her children were in the boat when it was swamped (Figs 8 and 9). All reached the shore safely, with Carangarang apparently 'swimming to the nearest point with the youngest child upon her shoulders'. Several Eora, seeing the accident, 'paddled off in their canoes, and were of great service in saving the oars, mast etc' of Bryant's boat and helping to tow it to shore.[131]

While the presence of Carangarang and her children in the boat was never adequately explained by Collins, modern authors have seized upon it to make a number of unsupported claims. It is variously suggested that the Bryants were close friends with Bennelong and his family, that both families taught each other their respective fishing techniques and that Bennelong even assisted Bryant and company in getting out of Port Jackson.[132] For instance, author Judith Cook asserted that the Bryants 'continually made contact with the natives', claiming that Bennelong and his family paid frequent visits to the Bryants' hut and that Carangarang and her sister 'would take their children to play with Charlotte Bryant and the two native women would sit and do their best to communicate with Mary'.[133] This is only one example of the unevidenced embroidering and embellishment of the historical record when it comes to telling the story of this escape, to be discussed more fully later in this introduction.

The accident may or may not have delayed the convicts' flight, but it certainly proved fortuitous, possibly lulling the watching authorities into a false sense of security. Certainly it gave Bryant and company the opportunity and cover to repair and modify the boat for a sea journey without arousing too much suspicion.[134] In the event they waited only

Fig.8 'First interview with the Native Women at Port Jackson, New South Wales' by William Bradley, *c.*1802

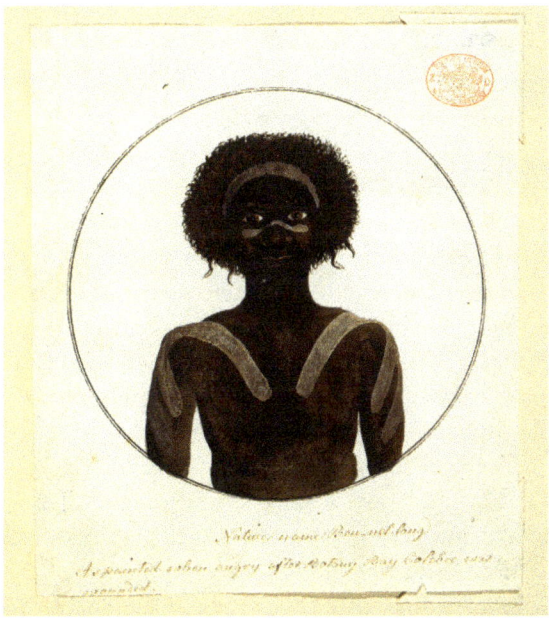

Fig.9 'Native name Ben-nel-long, as painted when angry after Botany Bay Colebee was wounded' by 'Port Jackson Painter', 1790 or 1797(?)

a few weeks before putting their plan into operation. On 22 March 1791 the *Supply* sailed for Norfolk Island, and on the morning of 28 March the Dutch snow *Waaksamheyd* also departed Port Jackson.[135] There was now no ship in the harbour capable of outrunning the fishing boat. Under cover of darkness on the night of 28 March, Bryant and his comrades loaded the vessel with supplies and rowed their way out of the harbour and into the Pacific Ocean (Fig.10). They were long gone by the time the alarm was raised the following morning.[136]

The extraordinary degree of preparation on the part of Bryant and company thoroughly undermined the assumption that convict absconders were unprepared fools. They had dug out cavities underneath the floorboards of the Bryants' hut, which the family had presumably been allowed back into by the authorities, in which to store equipment they had acquired from Detmer Smit,[137] master of the *Waaksamheyd*. Smit had sold Bryant a compass, quadrant, map and information about the journey north, all of which were vital for the navigator William Morton; it seems that funds were raised by Bryant having returned to selling fish illicitly.[138] In addition they had stockpiled provisions, with Private John Easty reporting that they had gathered 'a large quantuty of Carpinters tools of all Sorts for Enlargeing the Boat with beds', bedding, sails, firearms and ammunition, material to effect repairs to the boat when needed and a fishing net.[139] It is stated in the *Memorandoms* that when the party sailed they had with them a hundredweight of flour and rice, 14 pounds of pork and eight gallons of water, which almost precisely matches the account given in newspaper reports after the survivors returned to England.[140] When the escapees told their story at Bow Street in June 1792, one newspaper report stated that William Bryant and the others had made all of these preparations without telling Mary, and that Bryant only 'acquainted his wife his determination' to escape a few days before they absconded.[141] Given that the provisions would have taken some time to collect, and were stored underneath the Bryants' hut, this seems unlikely to say the least.

Private Easty believed that the escapees intended to sail for 'Bativee' – Batavia, present-day Jakarta. Easty's description of the absconders in his diary was sympathetic: he thought it a 'very Desparate attempt to go in an open Boat for a run of about 16 or 17 hundred Leags and in pertucalar for a woman and 2 Small Children', and believed that they must have been driven to it by 'the thoughts of Liberty from Such a place as this is Enoufh to induce any Convicts to try all Skeemes to obtain it'. Easty considered convicts to be 'the Same as Slaves all the time thay are in this Country', and that even if their sentences had expired 'by Law thare is no difference between them and a Convict that is jest Cast for transportation'.[142] Easty was, of course, incorrect about the absconders' intended destination. Collins had it right, though, when conjecturing that there was 'little reason to doubt their [successfully] reaching Timor', providing 'no dissension prevailed among them, and they had but prudence to guard against the natives wherever they might land'.[143] Collins even eschewed the usual assumptions about the fate and skill of escapees, betraying here an implicit respect for the seamanship of Bryant, Morton and the others – a respect he did not have for the group led by John Turwood.

Bryant and his company left behind consternated colonial officials, and a note from James Cox to his partner and fellow convict Sarah Young.[144] The letter has not survived but Collins saw it, and described how Cox impressed upon Young the importance of

> relinquish[ing] the pursuit of those vices which, he told her, prevailed in the settlement, leaving her what little property he did not take with him, and assigning as a reason for his flight the severity of his situation, being transported for life, without the prospect of any mitigation, or hope of ever quitting the country, but by the means that he was about to adopt.[145]

Fig.10 'A View of Sydney Cove – Port Jackson. March 7th 1792' by 'Port Jackson Painter'

The journey to Timor and the escapees' recapture

Within two days of putting to sea – so on or around 30 March 1791 – the escapees (Fig.11) reached a small inlet approximately 138 miles (222 km) to the north of Sydney, which they named Fortunate Creek. There they found a 'Quantity of fine Burn^g Coal', a 'Varse Quantty of Cabage tree' and 'avarse Quantity of fish'.[146] Bryant and his companions also had their first encounter of the journey with Indigenous Australians, to whom they gave some 'Cloaths & other articles and they went away very much satisfied'.[147] Warwick Hirst suggests that 'Fortunate Creek' was Glenrock Lagoon, south of present-day Newcastle, and that to the escapees 'can be attributed the discovery of coal in Australia'.[148] It was a discovery which impressed William Bligh, who had returned to Timor in 1792, in rather less straitened circumstances than on his previous visit. He was now in command of HMS *Providence*, having again been employed to transport breadfruit from Tahiti to the West Indies. The Governor of Kupang, Timotheus Wanjon,[149] presented Bligh with William Bryant's written account of his party's voyage, entitled 'Rem[ark]^s on a Voyage from

Fig.11 'Description of Convicts who have absconded from Sydney', enclosure no.4 in Governor Arthur Philip to Lord Grenville, 5 November 1791. This report carried a physical description of those convicts who had absconded from New South Wales and who were, as far as Phillip knew, still at large

Sydney Cove New South Wales to Timor'. Bligh's brief summary of the journal closely corresponds with the account given in the *Memorandoms*, and on the subject of the coal Bligh quoted Bryant:

> Walking along shore towards the entrance of the Creek we found several large pieces of Coal – seeing so many pieces we thought it was not unlikely to find a Mine, and searching about a little, we found a place where we picked up with an Ax as good Coals as any in England—took some to the fire and they burned exceedingly well.[150]

This quotation is the only occasion on which we can read William Bryant's own words, as his apparently rather lengthy account of the escape has not survived. (In 1814, when Kupang was under British control, the records held in the government archives were used to make paper bullet cartridges prior to an expedition against the rajah of Amanuban – pieces of Bryant's journal may have ended up being fired from British rifles.)[151] Bligh thought that Bryant's account was important, if only for the 'Circumstance of the Coals being found', and recorded this paragraph in the hope that someone might be able to identify the location of the seam. Bligh wrote that he was too ill, suffering from a 'violent head ach' and a recurring fever which left his brain feeling 'as if in a state of boiling', to copy the entire journal himself. Though he paid a copyist to do it for him, this man 'did not get a fourth part through it'.[152] Bligh did, however, find the journal 'clear and distinct', and thought that Bryant 'must have been a determined and enterprising man'.[153] George Tobin,[154] third lieutenant of the *Providence*, also saw Bryant's 'interesting account of his various distresses and escapes from the natives'. He, too, remarked upon the escapees' discovery of the coal, but in 'what latitude [it was found] I cannot charge my memory'.[155]

The escapees left Fortunate Creek and put out to sea again on or around 1 April. They proceeded north until, on approximately 3 April, they entered a 'very fine harbour Seeming to Run up they Country for Many miles'.[156] Hirst suggests that this was Port Stephens, a harbour of some 51 square miles (134 sq. km) where the Myall and Karuah rivers meet.[157] Here the escapees took on fresh water and made repairs to their leaking boat during the day, but at night they were 'Drove of by they Natives – which meant to Destroy us'. They continued up the coast in search of a safe haven, and were about to put ashore when 'there Came they natives in Varse numbers with Spears and Sheilds &c'.[158]

Several of the escapees – exactly who is not indicated in the *Memorandoms* – attempted to approach and tried 'By signes to pasifie them But they not taking they least notice according[ly] we fired a Musket thinking to afright them', but this had no effect.[159] As the Aboriginal people advanced towards the shore, the escapees felt 'forsed to take to our Boat and to get out of their reach as fast as we Could'.[160] The party then rowed a further 10 miles (16 km) up the harbour until they reached a 'little white Sandy Isl[d]'. Here they were able to land and repair the boat's hull without any 'Interup[on] from they Natives'.[161] The party remained on this islet for two days, before continuing their journey north.

On or around the night of 6 April the wind forced the boat 'Quite out of sight of Land'. Although they managed to struggle close to land again during the following day, the ocean was so rough that Bryant and his companions were unable to make landfall for almost three weeks. They were left 'much Distress[d] for water and wood' during this time. When the seas finally calmed on or around 28 April, an attempt by two of the escapees to get some fresh water and wood was interrupted by the appearance of a group of Indigenous people on the shore.[162]

The escapees were now also struggling to keep the leaking boat above water. They were relieved to find and enter a small river, which enabled them to put ashore for the first time in weeks and set about repairing the seams of the boat. The group returned to sea on or around 30 April, travelling a further 20 miles (32 km) north in search of a 'Harbor to get some Refreshment', but were unable to find anywhere to put in. Next their survival was imperilled by an oncoming storm.[163] With the 'Sea Breaking over us Quite Rapid', the party found themselves 'Oblidged to trow all our Cloathing over Board they Better to lighten our Boat' and prevent it from being swamped. They managed to reach a bay during the night, but the darkness and the violence of the sea made them fearful of 'Staving our Boat to Pieces' if they attempted to land. They laid anchor in the hope of riding out the storm, but disaster struck at around two in the morning of approximately 1 May when the anchor cable snapped. The *Memorandoms* records that: 'we were drove in the Middle of the Surf Expecting every Moment that our Boat wou'd be Staved to Pieces & every Soul Perish but as God wou'd have we Got our Boat save on Shore without any Loss or Damage' – apart from the loss of an oar.[164]

Fortunate to have survived this terrifying storm, and now safe on land, the soaked party eventually got a fire going, caught some shellfish for food and topped up their water supplies. They were taken a little by surprise when 'the Natives Came down in great Numbers', but 'we Discharged a Musquet over their Heads & they dispersed immediately & we saw no more of them'. The escapees stayed for a further two days and two nights and returned to sea on or around 3 May. They endured two or three days of further heavy weather, 'our Boat Shipping many heavy Seas, so that One Man was always Employed in Bailing out the Water to keep her up'.[165]

The party next made landfall at a place they named 'White Bay', which Hirst suggests was Moreton Bay.[166] They sailed down the Bay for around six to nine miles (10 to 14 km) and found a suitable landing place, where they spotted 'two [Indigenous] Women & 2 Children with a Fire Brand' on shore. The escapees landed, but the two women 'being Frightened Ran away but we made Signs that we wanted a Light which they Gave us Crying at the same Time in their Way'.[167] The Bryant party then spent the night undisturbed in two of these huts, but at about 11 the following morning 'a great Number of the Natives Came towards us'. The escapees once again fired their musket into the air, and the Indigenous people disappeared into the woods.[168]

The escapees departed White Bay on or around 9 May. That night they were driven out to sea by a strong gale and expected 'every Moment to go to the Bottom'. When daylight finally came they could see nothing but the sea 'running Mountains high'. Though they employed a drogue (a piece of equipment used in a storm) throughout the day and following night to keep the boat upright, that did not stop those on board from expecting 'every Moment to be the Last the sea Coming in so heavy upon us every now & then that two Hands was Obliged to keep Bailing out'. They hauled landward throughout the following day but the coastline remained stubbornly out of view, the boat was too sodden to light a fire and they had nothing to eat but raw rice. The *Memorandoms* left it to the reader 'to Consider what distress we must be in the Woman & the two little Babies was in a bad Condition'. On or around 12 May they found salvation, landing on a small Island about '30 Leagues' – or about 103 miles (165 km) from the mainland, having concluded that if they 'kept out to Sea that we shou'd every Soul Perish'.[169]

According to Hirst, this was Lady Elliot Island. The vague description in the *Memorandoms* seems to confirm this, although Lady Elliot Island is only approximately 53 miles (85 km) from the Australian mainland. The island was described as being about 'one Mile in Circumference' and surrounded by a beach and a coral reef, and was populated by 'very fine Large Turtles'. By the time the escapees left the island on or around 18 May they had killed 12 of these turtles, and dried the meat to sustain them during the next stage of the voyage.[170]

The escapees made the mainland that evening, passing by 'a great Number of Small Islands' – possibly those in and around the vicinity of the Great Barrier Reef, though the imprecise description makes it impossible to be certain. They were disappointed in their search for more turtles on these islands, and though the 'great Quantity of Shell Fish did not look particularly appetising 'being very Hungred we were glad to Eat them & Thank God for it'. Had it not been for these shellfish and the remainder of the dried turtle meat, then the escapees would most likely have starved.[171]

Fairly soon afterwards the party rounded Cape York Peninsula and entered the Gulf of Carpentaria. Though the shallow Gulf stretches for 366 miles (590 km) at its mouth – from Cape York in the east to Cape Arnhem in the west – the escapees seem to have sought initially to take a longer, theoretically safer, route by hugging the coastline. At one point they saw on shore 'several of the Natives in two Canoes'. They steered towards these men who appeared 'very Stout & fat & Blacker [than] they were in other Parts we seen before', noticing that 'there was One which we took to be the Chief with some Shells Around his Shoulders'. These people were most likely Torres Strait Islanders and they 'seemed to stand in a posture of Defence' against the escapees. Though one of the party resorted to the tried-and-trusted tactic of firing their musket into the air, the Torres Strait Islanders 'began Firing their Bows & Arrows', causing the escapees hurriedly to hoist their sails and row away as quickly as possible.[172]

After escaping from this group and travelling further along the coast, the party spotted 'a small Town' comprised of about 20 huts, with a fresh water supply nearby. Since there was no-one around the escapees took the chance of landing to fill up their water casks, but did not tarry for long, being 'Afraid of Staying on Shore for fear of the Natives'. Instead they spent the night at anchor a few miles offshore.[173] Bryant and the others had planned to return to the village in the morning to collect more water, but the sight of two large canoes heading their way caused them to reconsider. There were about '30 or 40 Men in each Canoe', and when one hoisted its sails and made to give chase the escapees promptly determined to take what water they had and to cross the Gulf in an attempt to outrun their pursuers.[174]

The escapees were successful on both counts. They managed to shake off their pursuers, no mean feat given the seamanship for which Torres Strait Islanders were renowned, and to cross the Gulf in four and a half days. They then took on more water and set out for Timor, crossing the Arafura and Timor Seas inside three days with no further recorded incident. They reached West Timor on 5 June 1791, after a 69-day voyage. Every one of the party had survived the punishing journey from Port Jackson.

When they put in at Kupang, the main Dutch settlement in the west of Timor, the escapees were greeted by Governor Wanjon. According to William Bligh, Bryant 'represented himself as a Mate of a Whale Fisher that was lost', and his 'very ingenuous [sic] account of their misfortunes' during the voyage 'gained them protection'.[175] Bligh described Bryant's missing journal as an 'account of everything as it really happened' on the voyage, and learnt from Wanjon how Bryant had apparently adapted it to form the tall tale which deceived the Dutch authorities.[176] As is described in the *Memorandoms*, they were taken to Wanjon's home where he 'behaved extremely well to us filld our Bellies & Cloathed Double with every[thing] that was wore on the Island'.[177]

Though the group were now at liberty of a sort, they were constrained by their lie to Wanjon and had to watch their step. They gained employment to support themselves and, according to a later newspaper report, Martin earned $200, of which he gave $56 to Wanjon for subsistence.[178] However, after two months of living in relative freedom in Kupang their precarious existence came to an abrupt end. According to the *Memorandoms*, William Bryant 'had words with his wife went and Informed against himself wife & Children and all of us', and they were immediately arrested and confined in 'the Castle'.[179] It seems hard to believe that after everything Bryant would have given up himself, his family and his shipmates so willingly. Carolly Erickson speculates that William and Mary Bryant had become estranged, based on David Collins' observation that transportees such as William Bryant did not consider their marriages in New South Wales 'as binding', and that he may have been seeking his independence through such a drastic manoeuvre.[180] This is not a convincing explanation, given that Bryant must have known that returning from transportation was a capital offence. Erickson (and others) invented narratives of marital strife between the Bryants, based upon nothing more than a few sentences written by Collins and the mention in the *Memorandoms* of there having been 'words' between the Bryants. The most egregious example of this concoction is from Judith Cook, who observes that William Bryant had become tired 'of the esteem in which [Mary] was held by his colleagues'; he had 'always believed that women should know their place, and Mary had got well above hers', so planned to find a berth on a ship away from Kupang and leave his family behind.[181] There is no evidence whatsoever that Bryant held this attitude, and against such speculation might be set historian Alan Atkinson's suggestion that

William and Mary Bryant's escaping together was 'a dramatic demonstration of married love'.[182] Moreover, according to Lieutenant George Tobin, William Bryant wrote admiringly in his lost journal that while at sea his wife 'bore their sufferings with more fortitude than most among them'.[183]

The available primary sources provide other, conflicting explanations of the discovery of the escapees' true identities. William Bligh was told by Governor Wanjon that one unnamed member of the group spitefully informed on the rest as a result of 'not being taken so much notice of as the next', which again might be considered sceptically given the potential penalty for being at large.[184] David Collins, writing at some distance, physically and temporally, suggested that the escapees' inherent criminality must have given them away; by 'practising the tricks of their former profession, [they] gave room for suspicion', were arrested and, under questioning, 'their true characters and the circumstances of their escape were divulged'.[185]

Perhaps the most plausible explanation was that given by Watkin Tench. He knew the escapees – some better than others, having travelled to New South Wales aboard the *Charlotte* with William and Mary Bryant, James Cox and James Martin – and later encountered some of them again aboard HMS *Gorgon* on the voyage back to Britain (see pp.34–6). It is entirely possible that Tench's account was derived from speaking with the surviving escapees aboard the *Gorgon* on the return voyage to Britain. Tench described how the Dutch received Bryant and his companions 'with kindness and treated them with hospitality', but that their behaviour gave rise to suspicion. They were put under surveillance 'and one of them at last, in a moment of intoxication' betrayed the secret'.[186] Modern writers have named William Bryant as the one who drunkenly blabbed the truth, but Tench does not, and there is no evidence for claiming this beyond the statement in the *Memorandoms* about Bryant having 'words with his wife'.[187]

Whatever the truth of it, the escapees had been imprisoned for several weeks when, on 16 September 1791, a group of genuine shipwreck survivors pulled into Kupang in four open boats. They were led by Captain Edward Edwards[188] who, in August 1790, had been commissioned by the Admiralty to travel to the South Pacific in HMS *Pandora*; he was to search for and arrest any surviving *Bounty* mutineers he could find and return them to Britain for trial. The *Pandora* reached Tahiti in March 1791, where Edwards and his crew captured 14 of the mutineers; he had them confined in irons in the ship's temporary prison, otherwise known as '*Pandora*'s Box'. After spending another five months fruitlessly searching the region for the *Bounty* and the remaining mutineers, the

Pandora set out again for Britain, but on 28 August the ship struck an outcrop of the Great Barrier Reef and quickly sank (Fig.12). The survivors of the shipwreck, 89 crewmen and 10 mutineers, fled to the *Pandora*'s four boats. Like Bligh and the Bryant party before them, they began the long voyage to Kupang.[189]

One of the survivors was George Hamilton, the *Pandora*'s surgeon,[190] and his account provides yet another explanation of how the escapees' identities were discovered. Hamilton claimed that when the survivors of the wrecking of the *Pandora* appeared, a 'Captain of [a] Dutch East Indiamen' went to the Bryant party to proclaim 'the glad tidings of their captain having arrived'. One of the escapees – unnamed, of course – started up 'in surprise, [and] said "What Captain! Dam'me, we have no Captain;" for they had reported that the Captain and the remainder of the crew had separated from them at sea in another boat'. The reaction led to 'a suspicion of their being impostors', and Hamilton added that Mary Bryant and one of the men 'fled into the woods; but were soon taken'. They then 'confessed they were English convicts, and that they had made their escape from Botany Bay'.[191] Hamilton's story cannot be true (although several present-day writers have accepted it as so.

Fig.12 'H.M.S. *Pandora* in the act of foundering' by Lt-Col. Batty, after a sketch by Peter Heywood, from John Barrow, 1831, *The Eventful History of the Mutiny and Piratical Seizure of H.M.S Bounty*. London: John Murray

Presumably the colourful detail of Mary Bryant's bold dash for freedom was too seductive to resist).[192] As the *Memorandoms*, Bligh's log and other primary sources make clear, the escapees had already confessed their true identities to Wanjon; they had been arrested and imprisoned for about a month before the bedraggled survivors of the *Pandora* arrived in Timor. The *Memorandoms* does state that in the period between being imprisoned and Edwards' arrival they were allowed 'out of the Castle 2 at a time' each day, but there is no mention there, or elsewhere, of any of the group making a run for it.[193]

Edwards took formal charge of the prisoners on 5 October 1791.[194] The following day the escapees, the *Bounty* mutineers and the surviving crew of the *Pandora* were embarked upon the *Rembang*, a Dutch East India Company (VOC)[195] ship contracted by Edwards to carry them to Batavia.[196] The voyage proved calm enough until 12 October when, according to Surgeon Hamilton, 'a tremendous storm arose'. Within 'a few minutes every sail of the ship was shivered to pieces; the pumps [were] all choked, and useless', and the ship was driven towards shore. The storm was 'attended with the most dreadful thunder and lightning we had ever experienced'. Possibly succumbing to patriotic prejudice, Hamilton described how the terrified Dutch sailors rushed below decks, and that the *Rembang* was only 'preserved from destruction by the manly exertion of our English tars, whose souls seemed to catch redoubled ardour from the tempest's rage'. Hamilton did add, however, that he did not mean to 'throw any stigma on the Dutch, who I believe would fight the devil, should he appear in any other shape to them but that of thunder and lightning'.[197]

The *Rembang* reached Batavia on 7 November 1791, a place at which Captain James Cook had advised visitors to make their stay 'as short as possible, otherwise they will soon feel the effects of the unwholesome air of Batavia, which, I firmly believe, is the Death of more Europeans than any other place upon the Globe of the same extent'.[198] When the *Rembang* arrived many of those on board were evidently already sick, and Surgeon Hamilton's 'first care' was to send to hospital the 'sickly remains of our unfortunate crew'. He remarked upon how several corpses, having flowed 'down the canal struck our boat, which had a very disagreeable effect on the minds of our brave fellows, whose nerves were reduced to a very weak state from sickness'. Hamilton may not have held out much in the way of hope for the ailing, memorably describing Batavia as a 'painted sepulchre, this golgotha of Europe, which buries its whole settlement every five years' (Fig.13). He did not blame the climate for the fearful mortality there, but the 'letch a Dutchman has for stagnant mud';

Fig.13 'Vue de l'isle et de la ville de Batavia appartenant aux Hollandois, pour la Compagnie des Indes', c.1780

Hamilton hoped his readers would 'pardon my spleen, when I tell them professionally, that all the mortality of that place originates from marsh effluvia, arising from their stagnant canals and pleasure-grounds'.[199]

'Golgotha' soon claimed more victims. The Bryant party were imprisoned in irons on a hulk but, on 1 December, barely three weeks after arriving, little Emanuel Bryant died in the VOC hospital, five months short of his second birthday.[200] It is stated in the *Memorandoms* that 'we lost the Child' first, and that six days later William Bryant was 'taken Bad'.[201] He died on 22 December, and father and son were buried together in Batavia.[202] Though the description of their deaths in the *Memorandoms* is very matter-of-fact, the use of 'we lost' is revealing, perhaps indicative of the bonding experience of the voyage and the pain that the loss of the two male Bryants inflicted upon the group – none more so than upon Mary Bryant. It is a rather dark irony that the group all survived the perilous journey from Port Jackson to Timor, only suffering deaths among their number when back in British custody.

Edwards had in the meantime secured a passage to the Cape for those in his charge, and they were embarked upon three Dutch ships. Edwards, some of his crew and the ten *Bounty* mutineers travelled on the *Vreedenberg*. Surgeon Hamilton, more of the *Pandora*'s crew and half of the escapees went on the *Horssen*, while the remainder of the crew and the escapees were embarked on the *Hoornwey*.[203] This leg of the voyage was described by Surgeon Hamilton as 'tedious', though it was marked by 'great death and sickness going through the Straits of Sunda' (Fig.14).[204] The Bryant party lost another member when, between the islands of Java and Sumatra, James Cox either drowned after falling overboard (according to Captain Edwards) or 'jumped overboard in the night, and swam to the Dutch arsenal at Honroost' (according to Hamilton).[205] Cox may have twice escaped the gallows, but it seems unlikely that he would have survived falling into the sea while in chains. Either way Cox was never heard of again: the *Memorandoms* simply states 'James Cox Died'.[206] Samuel Bird and the navigator William Morton, without whom the escapees would probably never have made it safely to Kupang, also died aboard the *Hornwey* before it reached the Cape.[207]

Edwards and his rag-tag group reached the Cape on 18 March 1792. Here they found HMS *Gorgon* under anchor, having recently arrived from Sydney en route for Britain. The surviving escapees were put on board the *Gorgon* for the voyage home. They found that the ship carried a detachment of the Marines who gone to New South Wales with the First Fleet and, as is recorded in the *Memorandoms*, 'we was known well by all the marine officers which was all Glad that we had not perished at sea'.[208]

Fig.14 'Batavia and Onrust in Batavia Bay' by William Bradley, c.1802

One of these officers was Watkin Tench (Fig.15), who was evidently amazed to be travelling with 'this little band of adventurers' again:

> I confess that I never looked at these people, without pity and astonishment. They had miscarried in a heroic struggle for liberty; after having combated every hardship, and conquered every difficulty. The woman [Mary Bryant] and one of the men [James Martin], had gone out to Port Jackson in the ship which had transported me thither [the *Charlotte*]. They had both of them been always distinguished for good behaviour. And I could not but reflect with admiration, at the strange combination of circumstances which had again brought us together, to baffle human foresight, and confound human speculation.[209]

The *Gorgon* left the Cape for Britain during early April 1792. However, there was to be one more death among the group on this final leg of the voyage. During early May Lieutenant Ralph Clark[210] wrote of the deaths of several of the soldiers' children, noting that they were 'going very fast- the hot weather is the reason of it'. On 6 May Clark recorded that 'the child beloning [sic] to Mary Broad the convict woman who went a way in

Fig.15 'Captain Watkin Tench, Royal Marines, 1787', unknown artist

the fishing Boat from Port Jackson last year died about four oClock'. The body of four-year-old Charlotte Bryant, who had spent much of her short life at sea, was 'committed...to the deep' that same day.[211]

The *Gorgon* reached Portsmouth on 18 June 1792. According to the *Memorandoms* William Allen, Samuel Broom (now seemingly adopting the alias of 'John Butcher'), Mary Bryant, Nathaniel Lillie and James Martin were first taken to Purfleet. From there they were 'Conveyed by the Constables to Bow st office London' and were then 'taken before Justice Bond and...fully committed to Newgate'.[212]

Back in Britain: James Boswell and the fate of the surviving escapees

The *Memorandoms* ends here, but the fates of the survivors can be pieced together from other sources, at least up to a point. On 30 June 1792 they were brought before the Bow Street Police Magistrate Nicholas Bond,[213] where they told their story of hardship, escape and recapture. When they were finished, Bond remarked that he had 'never experienced so disagreeable a task as being obliged to commit them to prison, and assured them as far as [it] lay in his power he would assist them'.[214] The prisoners declared that 'they would sooner suffer death than return to Botany Bay' and, as the *London Chronicle*'s reporter put it, 'His Majesty, who is ever willing to extend his mercy, surely never had objects more worthy of it' than these escapees from New South Wales. After the hearing some in the crowd collected and gave money to the 'destitute' prisoners.[215] They appear to have been admitted to Newgate on 5 July and were brought to the bar at the Old Bailey two days later. No doubt they would have been relieved when the judge ordered them to 'remain on their former sentence, until they should be discharged by due course of law', rather than being taken to the gallows or potentially being re-transported.[216] The escapees were then returned to Newgate to serve out their respective terms (Fig.16)[217] – all but Lillie, who had been transported for life, were under seven year sentences.

While Allen, Broom, Bryant, Lillie and Martin languished in Newgate, a well-known figure began to make intercessions on their behalf. The lawyer and biographer James Boswell[218] had taken an interest in their case (Fig.17), and in August 1792 he wrote to the Home Secretary, Henry Dundas,[219] imploring his former schoolmate to ensure that 'nothing harsh shall be done to the unfortunate adventurers from New South Wales, for whom I interest myself, and whose very

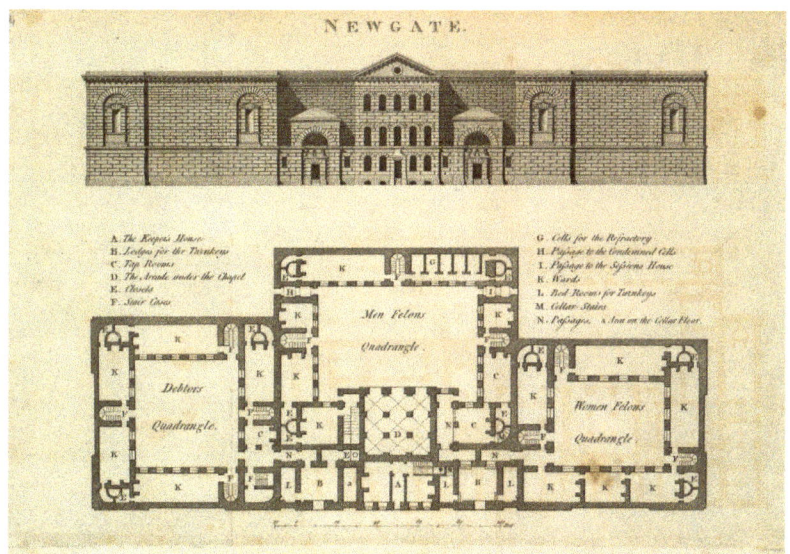

Fig.16 'Building plan of Newgate Prison' by Charles Dance, 1800

extraordinary case surely will not found a precedent'.[220] Boswell also visited the influential Evan Nepean[221] at the Home Office during November 1792 to discuss the 'poor people who escaped from Botany Bay', an interview in which Nepean apparently told Boswell that the 'Government would not treat them with harshness, but at the same time would not do a kind thing to them, as that might give encouragement to others to escape'.[222] Encouragement and precedent were precisely what concerned David Collins when he recorded that 15 convicts had absconded, in two separate groups, from Sydney by sea during September and October 1797.[223] Collins believed that had the Bryant party

> instead of meeting with the compassion and lenity which were expressed in England for their sufferings, been sent back and tried in New South Wales, for taking away the boat, and other thefts which they had committed, it was probable that others might have been deterred from following their example.[224]

Those in New South Wales fully expected the weight of the law to be brought to bear upon the escapees. When the news of their arrest in Timor and subsequent despatch to England reached Sydney in June 1792, Private John Easty thought it 'Likely thay will be all Excuted'.[225]

The caution called for by Nepean meant that the group had to wait for their freedom. Mary Bryant was the first to be released, receiving

INTRODUCTION 37

Fig.17 'James Boswell' by Sir Joshua Reynolds, 1785

an unconditional pardon on 2 May 1793 – although her sentence had expired in March – and she moved into lodgings in Titchfield Street.[226] It is worth remarking on the fact that Mary Bryant was pardoned and released, but the others remained in gaol. There is no evidence of an outpouring of sympathy or a concerted press campaign on behalf of Mary Bryant after she was sent to Newgate, contrary to the impression given in the modern literature. The newspapers carried no updates on her condition in gaol, and it appears that she and the others were forgotten, as the press does not appear to mention them again until Mary Bryant was pardoned in May 1793 (Fig.18).

When the pardon did come, the reports were perfunctory, indicating a residual interest in the case, but nothing approaching a sensation. As was noted in the London *St James's Chronicle* of 14 May 1793, 'His Majesty has granted a free pardon to Mary Bryant, who accompanied by several male convicts, escaped from Botany Bay, and traversed upwards of 3000 miles by sea in an open boat, exposed to tempestuous weather'.[227] This notice was repeated verbatim in a number of regional newspapers.[228] One slightly longer exception, which treated Mary Bryant's story in gendered terms, was the wildly unreliable report of her release in the *Dublin Chronicle* of 4 June 1793. She was referred to dismissively, without name, as 'The female convict who made her escape from Botany Bay'. The author of the account invented a story that Mary Bryant's pardon had been secured one day by 'a gentleman of high rank in the army', who returned to Newgate the following day 'with his carriage, and took the

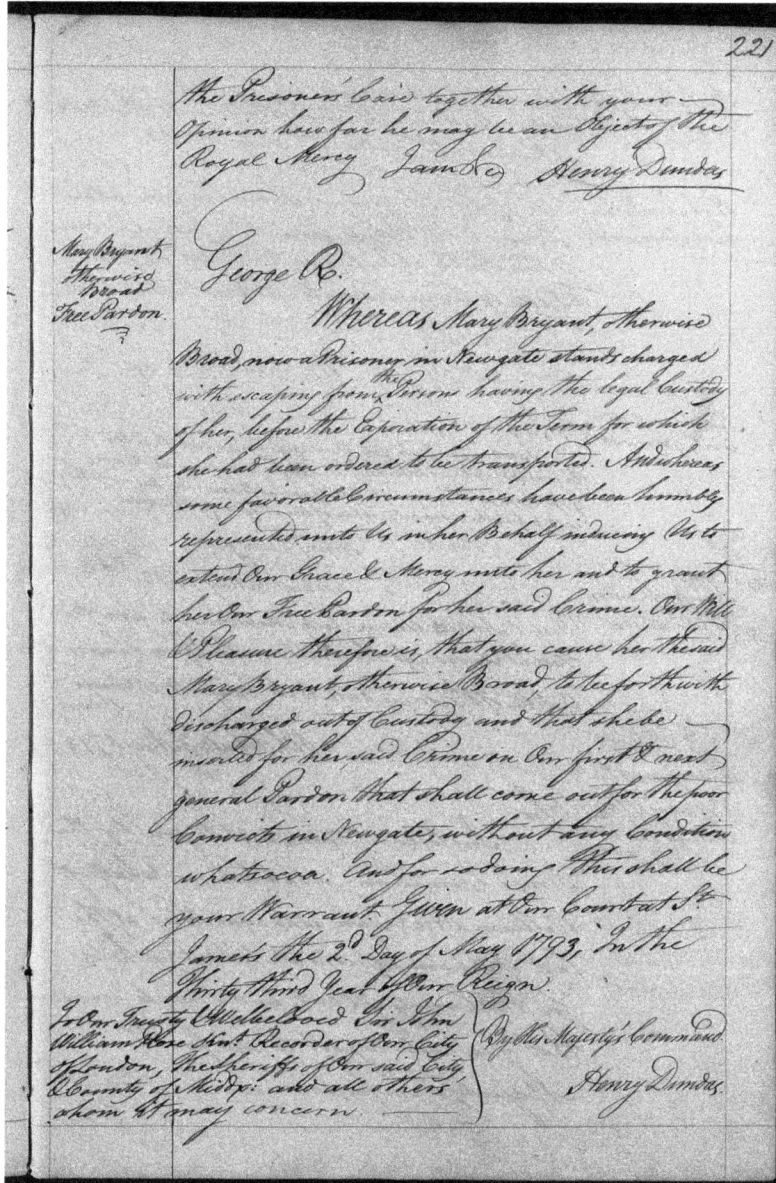

Fig.18   Pardon for Mary Bryant, 1793

poor woman, who almost expired with the excess of gratitude'.[229] It has not been possible to determine why Mary Bryant alone received a pardon, or whether Boswell's lobbying was the determining factor in one being granted.

Boswell had heard from Mary Bryant's family by mid-1793, and on 14 August he wrote a letter on her behalf to her sister, Elizabeth Puckey:

> Your sister Mary is much gratified by the contents of your letter to me and she will be happy to return to her native place and be among her relations, since she has the satisfaction to know that she will be received kindly. In the meantime, she will be much obliged to you, if you will again write to me, mentioning how her Father is and how many of the Family are alive in your neighbourhood. She desires me to mention to you that she one day met her brother Joseph who now resides in London, but as he had used her ill, she did not speak to him. She sends her love to you all, and you may be assured that she is well.[230]

Four days later Boswell was approached by a Mr Kestle, 'a native of Fowey' who claimed to know 'all the relations of Mary Broad very well, and had received a letter from one of them directing him to me'. Kestle claimed that a ludicrously large sum of money – 'no less than three hundred thousand pounds' – had been left to Mary Bryant's father, though Boswell was rightly suspicious of this fanciful story and warned her not to put much store in it. Kestle's acquaintance with Mary Bryant's family was genuine, however: he brought Mary's sister Dolly and they had an emotional reunion at her lodgings where Dolly 'cried and held her sister's hand'.[231] Overcome with gratitude for how he had cared for Mary, Dolly promised Boswell that if 'she got money as was said, she would give me a thousand pounds'.[232]

Boswell arranged for Mary Bryant's voyage back to Fowey and her family, paying for her passage aboard the *Ann and Elizabeth* which sailed from London on 13 October 1793. He refused two invitations to dinner on the previous night to ensure that he could accompany her on 12 October to Beal's Wharf, Southwark, where the boat was moored. Earlier that day, with Mary's direction, he had written 'two sheets of paper of her curious account of the escape from Botany Bay' – but, like the journal of her late husband, they have not survived. Boswell stayed with Mary for two hours at the pub on the wharf, sharing a bowl of punch with her and the landlord and the captain of the *Ann and Elizabeth*. Despite the prospect of returning to her family, Boswell found that 'her spirits were low; she was sorry to leave me; [and] she was sure her relations would not treat her well'. As they parted Boswell promised Mary a gift of £10 per year 'as long as she behaved well, being resolved to make it up to her myself in so far as subscriptions should fail'.[233] He did attempt to raise a public subscription for this allowance, and made enquiries through his friend William Johnson Temple[234] about potentially securing donations in Cornwall. Temple thought there was not much prospect of success for that after he discovered that the family of Boswell's 'heroine' were considered 'eminent for *Sheep-stealing*' in the area.[235] Nor were Boswell's fund-raising attempts in London necessarily any more successful. When he called upon Baron Thurlow,[236] the former Lord Chancellor, in December 1793, Boswell asked him 'to give something to Mary Broad'. Thurlow replied, 'Damn her blood, let her go to a day's work'. But when Boswell 'described her hardships and heroism, he owned I was a good advocate for her, and said he would give something if I desired it'.[237] In the end Boswell paid for the allowance himself until his death, sending it to her through the Reverend John Baron of Lostwithiel.[238]

Although the enormous inheritance – an approximate £17 million in today's money – described by the mysterious Mr Kestle did not exist, it appeared there was at least the prospect of a more modest, but still substantial sum. This had been left to Mary Bryant's brother-in-law Edward Puckey, who lived in Fowey; he sent a letter to Boswell in February 1794 about this money, but unravelling the matter is far from straightforward, owing to Puckey's terrible handwriting, apparently limited literacy and idiomatic expression. He told Boswell that a notice in the *London Chronicle* of 19–22 March 1791 announced that there were 44 unreceived dividends in the Bank of England in the name of the late Isaac Barrett, a wax chandler who lived at Haymarket in London.[239] According to Puckey this money belonged to the Popes, 'of wich we are of the same famely'. Puckey had found the will of James Pope, which stated that Pope had given 'most of his welth to yong barett', a relation of the deceased Isaac Barrett and a nephew of his wife Elizabeth, and that if the younger Barrett should die 'befor he Came of age it [the money] was to return to his family the poopes'. A Mr Redstone had 'goot all perticklers and all the Regesters Concening this matter' and had given the Puckeys 'ever incougment we Could wish for and has provd James poope to be our Relation'. Since both Barretts were now dead, there was apparently hope that the Puckeys might be due the money. As far as it can be understood from the confusing letter, a Mr Rosewear had the relevant documents to prove that the younger Barrett had died aged seven, but he 'now daylays' and the Puckeys had not heard from him for five months. Mr Redstone had also disappeared. The Puckeys were suspicious and Edward implored Boswell to 'see us rited if possepel you Can'.[240]

It is little wonder that, in reply, Boswell stated that Puckey's story was 'not distinct enough to enable me to be of any service to you'. However, he did offer, with typical kindness, that if Puckey let him know of 'any person of the profession of the Law with whom I can converse or correspond on the subject you may depend on my best assistance'.[241] There is no subsequent reply from Puckey to Boswell, nor does there appear to be any record of whether or not the family were successful in

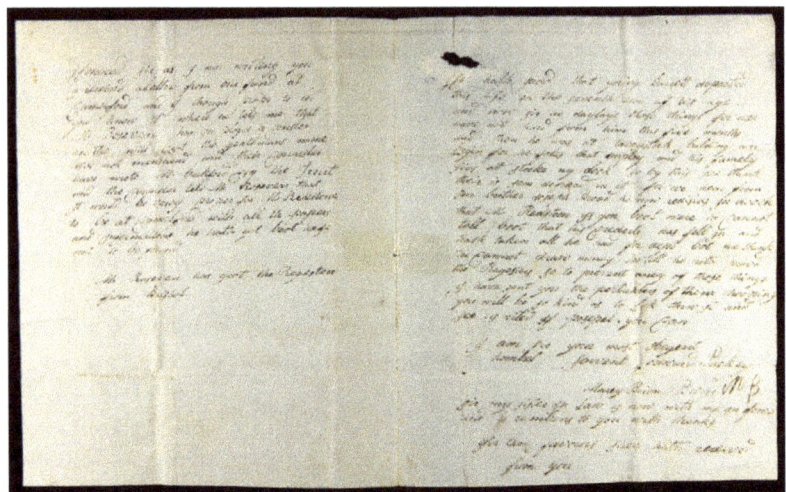

Fig.19   Mary Bryant's mark at the end of her brother-in-law Edward Puckey's letter to James Boswell, 16 February 1794

tracking down this dividend or if Mary Bryant stood to gain any money by it – or indeed whether Puckey's story should even be believed.

Puckey's letter ended on a happier note. 'Sir my sister in law is now with me,' he declared, and she 'rembers to you with thanks for the favours shee hath receved from you'. Next to his own signature Puckey had written 'Mary Brion Broad' and she had made her mark of 'M B' (Fig.19).[242] Boswell was delighted to read of her having arrived safely and finding an 'agreeable reception among her relations', and he hoped 'her behaviour will always be such as to deserve their kindness'. He had just 'received very favourable accounts' of Mary Bryant from Reverend Baron, who had sent Boswell's five pounds to her on 1 May 1794. Boswell asked Puckey to tell her of the impending arrival of the money and to 'tell her that I expect to hear from her every half year'.[243] The payment in late 1794 was the last, as Boswell died in London on 19 May 1795.

Boswell was notorious for his sexual proclivities. His journals candidly recount affairs with society ladies, actresses and innumerable encounters with prostitutes, as well as the almost inevitable suffering from painful venereal disease, complications from which are thought to have caused his death (Boswell used contraception, but evidently not frequently or successfully enough). It appears that Boswell's reputation and habits were a source of amusement to his friends, and his interest in Mary

Bryant's case saw the poet William Parsons[244] imagine her parting from Boswell on a London dock:

> Though every night the Strand's soft virgins prove
> On bulks and thresholds thy Herculean love,
> Was it for this I braved the ocean's roar,
> And plied those thousand leagues the lab'ring oar;
> Oh, rather had I stayed, the willing prey
> Of grief and famine in the direful bay!
> Or perished, whelmed in the Atlantic tide!
> Or, home returned, in air suspended died!
> For thou, relenting, shalt consent at last
> To feel more perfect joy than all the past;
> Great in our lives, and in our deaths as great,
> Embracing and embraced, we'll meet our fate:
> A happy pair, whom in supreme delight
> One love, one cord, one joy, one death unite!
> Let crowds behold with tender sympathy!
> Love's true sublime in our last agony!
> First let our weight the trembling scaffold bear,
> Till we consummate the last bliss in air…[245]

Parsons' doggerel was grossly unfair to Boswell on this occasion, and there is no evidence of a sexual relationship between him and Mary Bryant. Moreover, this was not the first occasion on which Boswell had exerted himself in the cause of someone suffering under the law. In 1774 he was unsuccessful both in defending his client, John Reid, against a capital charge of sheep-stealing at the High Court of Justiciary in Edinburgh and in preventing Reid from being hanged for the offence. Boswell's biographer Frank Brady suggests that Reid's execution was 'a naked demonstration of [Boswell's] powerlessness in a struggle with public authority', and that the failure haunted him.[246] Boswell's lobbying on behalf of Mary Bryant and the other surviving escapees was entirely in character, and his vigour in pursuing their cause may have been influenced by his having been unable to help Reid.

Though Allen, Broom, Lillie and Martin remained in Newgate when Mary Bryant sailed home, Boswell had not forgotten them. As early as 14 May 1793 he had drafted a petition to Nepean on their behalf, pointing out that:

> Not one of these poor men has been either a highwayman or a housebreaker.[247] Their offences, though justly punishable, have been

of a slighter degree of malignity. For this they have atoned: by an imprisonment before trial—by confinement on board the hulks at Portsmouth—by a severe passage to New South Wales—by servitude and almost starvation there—by a series of most distressful sufferings in the course of making their escape—by imprisonment since, in the gaol of Newgate. They did certainly in the impatience of misery subscribe a petition praying to have their wretched captivity exchanged for a situation on board His Majesty's fleet. But it is humbly submitted to Government whether, all things considered, they should not have a second chance to be good members of society and be permitted to do the best they can for themselves and their families. It should seem to be of the genius of our Constitution to act with mildness and compassion when there is no obvious call for severity. …It is therefore earnestly requested that in this extraordinary case the clemency of the Crown might be benignantly exercised.[248]

He continued to lobby Henry Dundas, even writing to Lady Jane Dundas[249] in May 1793 to beg, unsuccessfully, for her 'humane intercession with my old friend your husband in favour of four unfortunate men (by no means gross offenders) who made their escape from Botany Bay'.[250] Boswell concluded by observing that her husband was aware of the particulars of the matter, and since that was the case Lady Jane assured Boswell (somewhat curtly) that 'any intercession or interference from her would be very unnecessary & could have no effect in influencing Mr Dundas in the discharge of his public duty even if she had not laid down a rule of never mentioning those things to him'.[251]

Boswell's efforts on behalf of the men ceased for a period during June and July 1793. On the night of 5 June 1793, while walking home drunk, he was knocked down and robbed in Titchfield Street.[252] The injuries Boswell suffered were so severe that they confined him to bed for a while, but he was again well enough to visit the men in Newgate during mid-August, where he 'comforted' and 'assure[d] them personally that I was doing all in my power for them'.[253] Evan Nepean had apparently written a letter in their favour, but nothing had been done by the time Boswell addressed Nepean on 13 September 1793 to express 'great uneasiness on account of the three poor men who escaped from Botany Bay'. He reported that 'the unfortunate men who rely upon me' were 'miserable in Newgate, and I am afraid think that I have betrayed or neglected them', and requested to be informed 'by a note tonight or tomorrow morning whether the humanity of government will be shewn by pardoning them'.[254]

Matters were moving behind the scenes. Nepean received a memorandum from the government solicitor Joseph White,[255] dated 1 November 1793, which appears to have been the catalyst for the prisoners' release. White noted that the convicts themselves had 'intimat^d an intention of moving to be discharged [from Newgate] on the Ground that the time for which they were respectively transport^d is *now Expired*'. When they had been committed to Newgate the previous year, White observed, there was 'little disposition [from the government] that these People shou'd be prosecut^d'. Now that their sentences had expired White thought it 'possible that such prosec^n may not be necessary' and asked 'whether it is your pleasure we approve their being discharged?'[256] White was mistaken about their sentences: only Martin's had in fact expired. Allen's term ran until July 1794 and Broom's until July 1795, while Lillie was under a life sentence.

The convicts' 'intimation' appeared to have been made without Boswell's knowledge or assistance. On 2 November Boswell visited Newgate, and then the Mr Pollock, the first clerk in Dundas's office, to again apply on behalf of 'the men who had escaped from Botany Bay'. When he returned home he was astonished to find Allen, Broom, Lillie and Martin waiting at his front door on Great Portland Street. On 3 November Boswell discovered that they had been discharged from Newgate by proclamation, that is, a notice was issued to state that the men would go free unless anyone came forward wishing to prosecute them. No one did. Boswell met Lillie and Broom later that afternoon, but did not see Allen and Martin who 'had gone to take a walk' about town.[257] The survivors of this most remarkable of escapes were all, at last, free.

* * *

The fate of the surviving escapees, especially in the case of Mary Bryant, has been the subject of much speculation and invention. In the search for a happy ending, some writers have suggested that after returning to Fowey she later remarried. Frederick A. Pottle was the first to note that a Mary Bryant married a Richard Thomas in 1807 in the parish of St Breage in Cornwall, though he was very sceptical that this was the absconder Mary Bryant.[258] Judith Cook seemed more convinced that this was *the* Mary Bryant, but did admit that she had nothing on which to hang her supposition other than wishful thinking.[259] In his largely fictional account of the escape, Jonathan King invented the story that Mary Bryant and Richard Thomas were childhood sweethearts separated by her transportation, but reunited upon her return to Cornwall.[260] Carolly Erickson was more sceptical on the matter, with her doubts based on the fact that the Mary Bryant who married in 1807 gave birth in both 1811 and 1812; the transported Mary Bryant would have been approximately 47 years old in 1811 and, as Erickson claimed, 'most women in eighteenth- and early nineteenth-century England did not live that long, let alone bear children at such an advanced age'.[261] (According to the study of J. P. Griffin, the life expectancy of women aged 15 between 1680 and 1779 – like Mary Bryant – was 56.6 years.)[262]

Another factor to note is that we cannot be entirely sure under which name Mary Bryant lived after returning to England. The Newgate criminal register named her as 'Mary Briant *alias* Broad', but Boswell always referred to her as 'Mary Broad'. A search of subsequent criminal registers finds that a Mary Broad was committed to Newgate for trial at the Old Bailey in September 1806 and acquitted of stealing four sheets valued at 21 shillings, two table cloths valued at nine shillings, an apron valued at a shilling and a handkerchief also valued at a shilling, all the property of one Thomas Middlebrook.[263] The defendant was 40 years of age when tried, which puts her around the age of the escapee Mary Broad/Bryant. However, if this was the same woman then, although 14 years had passed, surely at least one London journalist would have recognised the supposedly famous escapee from Botany Bay? Regrettably there is no physical description of the woman in the 1806 Newgate register for comparison, so this can only be additional speculation as to the subsequent detail of Mary Bryant's life. The same can be said about the 80 year-old Mary Bryant who, according to the 1841 census, lived in the Bodmin Union Workhouse.[264] Though this woman was born in Cornwall and was approximately of the right age, the evidence that she is the woman we are looking for – like that for the assumption that the transportee Mary Bryant married Richard Thomas in 1807 – remains inconclusive.

The fate of the four male survivors is also unclear. William Allen, Samuel Broom, Nathaniel Lillie and James Martin largely disappear from the record, though Boswell's draft petition of 14 May 1793 on their behalf does at least provide some supplementary information. William Allen, then 56 according to Boswell, apparently had a wife at Beccles in Suffolk 'from whom he has heard since he came home'.[265] According to a newspaper report of their hearing before Justice Nicholas Bond, Allen was 'bred to the Sea'. He gave Boswell a hint as to his future: '"Water I must follow" are his words, but [he] would rather go where he can get most by it; viz., in a merchantman: "I have the world to begin again."'[266] Where Allen began again, we cannot be certain.

Samuel Broom *alias* John Butcher was unmarried and a husbandsman by trade.[267] He had heard from a Mr Woodward, the landlord of the Lion pub in Broom's native Kidderminster, stating that he would 'be kindly received and get his bread in his own country'.[268] Broom may have had other ideas, having sent a petition under the name of John Butcher to Home Secretary Henry Dundas on 23 January 1793, in which he stated that though he had 'suffered a great deal in going and Coming from Botany Bay', he was willing to go back to New South Wales to assist with farming there. He claimed that having been 'brought up in the thorough Knowledge of all kinds of land' he was 'Capable of bringing Indifferent Lands to perfection', and that he had received 'an offer some time ago of going to Botany Bay to endeavour to make that Land more fertile than it has ever appeared to be'. Broom expected 'Nothing for my Trouble', but hoped Dundas would 'Condescend to Indulge me with an answer'.[269] Dundas does not appear to have condescended to even answer the petition, let alone indulge his request – and nor does anyone else.

Nevertheless, a series of present-day writers have claimed that not only was the petition agreed to, but that Broom *alias* Butcher enlisted in the New South Wales Corps and returned to Sydney, where in September 1795 he was granted 25 acres of land in the Petersham Hill district.[270] Thomas Keneally even suggests that Broom *alias* Butcher was 'an early instance of an ordinary man seeing New South Wales as quite habitable under conditions of freedom', while Jonathan King claimed that he 'farmed the land [in New South Wales] for the rest of his life', married a former convict and 'together they raised a family of free children in the colony in whose future he so firmly believed'.[271] But none of this is true. It is one of the myths pertaining to the Bryant group which originate with Louis Becke and Walter Jeffery's novel, *A First Fleet Family* (1896) – myths which have become accepted through repetition. Becke and Jeffery had evidently done their research to the extent of quoting the petition in full, but the claim that Broom *alias* Butcher enlisted in the military, returned to New South Wales and 'became a flourishing settler' is entirely their embellishment.[272]

Samuel Broom *alias* John Butcher did not, and could not, have returned to the Antipodes with the New South Wales Corps. In the first instance, information in the historical record immediately draws these claims into doubt. His age and seemingly imperfect health would have precluded him from military service: he was at least 50 years old in 1793 and, as we have seen, he was described as 'infirm' prior to being transported to New South Wales, while the 1791 return of absconders reported him to be lame.[273] But the key evidence is that the only John Butcher to join the New South Wales Corps and settle in the colony was born in Bedfield, Suffolk in approximately 1764. He enlisted as a private in the Corps from the Savoy military prison, transferring from the 1st Dragoon Guards, on 11 May 1792 – a date when the escapee Broom *alias* Butcher was a prisoner aboard HMS *Gorgon*, still weeks away from returning to Britain. Private Butcher travelled to New South Wales in the *Boddingtons*. The ship sailed from Cork, with 125 male and 20 female convicts aboard,[274] on 15 February 1793, at a time when Samuel Broom *alias* John Butcher was confined to Newgate Gaol. After arriving in New South Wales, Private Butcher served in detachments at Parramatta and at the Hawkesbury river. When the 73rd Regiment arrived in 1810 to replace the New South Wales Corps, he opted to transfer to the 73rd and remain in the colony. He appears to have worked as a district constable in Sydney, and to have been granted or leased some land: the 1822 New South Wales Land and Stock Muster recorded that Butcher lived on 30 acres at Parramatta. In February 1824 Butcher married the Irish convict Eliza Stewart,[275] who had arrived in the colony in the *Woodman* the previous June. The Butchers do not appear to have had any children: the 1828 New South Wales Census listed only John and Eliza Butcher, aged about 60 and 27 respectively, living at Clarence Street in Sydney; presumably the residence at Parramatta had either been sold or the lease had ended by this time.[276] While it is not clear when the couple died, what is evident is that the escapee Samuel Broom *alias* John Butcher did not return to New South Wales. Instead he, like William Allen, simply disappears from view after being released from Newgate in November 1793.

Nathaniel Lillie was born in Sudbury in Suffolk and, according to Boswell, had a wife and four children. He had been contacted by his uncle Richard Wardel, a cabinet-maker and joiner living at Gatney Street, Pimlico and also by his brother Robert Angus, a waiter based in Old Russell Street, Bloomsbury. Boswell believed that Lillie would be supported by these relatives, who would help him 'get a livelihood by his own trade'. Lillie had already given ample evidence of his capacity for hard work by having laboured 'night and day in gaol as a net-maker to support his family', who were living in London as early as July 1792. Presumably after Nathaniel was released, he was reunited with his wife Deborah and their children.[277]

In the summer of 1813 a Nathaniel and Deborah Lilley were charged with burgling the house of Robert Andrews at Stanstead and of stealing a cotton gown, a woollen waistcoat, two silver teaspoons, and a pound note. Only Nathaniel was brought to trial: he was convicted on 12 August 1813 at the Suffolk assizes at Bury St Edmunds and sentenced to death. The sentence was commuted to transportation for life, but rather than being shipped to New South Wales he was instead sent to the *Captivity* hulk at Portsmouth.[278] Nathaniel served seven years on the hulks before receiving a free pardon on 4 November 1820.[279] The Nathaniel Lilley convicted in 1813 was 54 years of age, around the age that the escapee Nathaniel Lillie would have been in 1813, and the likelihood is that the men were one and the same. Both were burglars and both were convicted in Suffolk; they shared the same distinctive name and both had a wife named Deborah. It appears that Nathaniel Lillie had run afoul of the law once again, 22 years after escaping from New South Wales. His fate after November 1820 is unclear.

Appropriately enough we come, last of all, to James Martin, who according to Boswell was aged 36 in 1793. He reported that Martin had a wife and son in Exeter, and expected that he could earn 'a guinea a week, being a very good workman as he proved when at Botany Bay, where he worked a great deal for the settlement'. Martin had heard from his mother, brother and sister in Ireland, and was willing to return there or to seek work in London.[280] Whether he took either, or neither, of these options, or if he was ever reunited with his wife and child, will probably remain a mystery.

Aside from the *Memorandoms*, there exists another tangible remnant of the Bryant party's astonishing journey. Within James Boswell's papers, now at the Beinecke Rare Books and Manuscript Library at Yale University, is a folded piece of paper on which he wrote 'Leaves from Botany Bay used as Tea' (Fig.20). Inside were several dried wild sarsaparilla leaves, from which the escapees made tea to ward off scurvy. Boswell presumably acquired these from the five survivors and, given that he so carefully preserved their gift, they and their story had evidently made a lasting impression.[281]

* * *

When Jeremy Bentham mentioned, in passing, the escape of the Bryant party in his work on convict transportation, *Panopticon versus New South Wales*, he made a prediction:

Fig.20 'Leaves from Botany Bay used as Tea', belonging to James Boswell. It seems likely that he may have been given them as a souvenir by the surviving escapees

One of these days, as stations multiply, and the [Australian] coasts become more and more difficult to guard, we may expect to see better boats, stolen or even built, for voyages of escape to Otaheite or some other of the many shorter voyages, with the help of a seaman or two to each of them, to command it.[282]

This was remarkably prescient. In his 1822 report on New South Wales and Van Diemen's Land, Commissioner John Thomas Bigge[283] came to a similar conclusion:

The necessity of the regulations that more particularly apply to the prevention of the escape of convicts in ships, appears to me to be greater at this moment than at former periods, and will continue to increase with the trade of the colony, and until the convicts shall be entirely withdrawn from those parts of it that are frequented by merchant vessels.[284]

Though no official record had been kept of how many convicts absconded from the penal colonies, Bigge estimated that around 250 convicts had made an attempt at it before 1822, 'either by concealing themselves on board vessels, or by attempting to seize them by violence'. Of these people, 194 had been re-arrested and nine had been killed. He thought that those who stowed away on ships were aiming to reach India, while those who seized vessels sought to take the well-worn 'passage to Timor or Batavia'.[285] When Bigge's reports were published, British settlement in Australia had spread to places on the eastern coast which the Bryant party had passed three decades earlier. A penal station was opened at Coal River in 1804 (present-day Newcastle) and another at Port Macquarie in 1821; those at Moreton Bay and Norfolk Island would be established in 1824 and 1825 respectively. Each settlement opened new shipping routes to move goods and people, routes which convicts were willing and able to exploit.

Historian Ian Duffield has identified at least 60 seizures and attempted seizures of boats by male and female convicts between 1790 and 1829 in New South Wales, Van Diemen's Land and at Norfolk Island.[286] For instance, Charlotte Badger[287] and Catherine Hagerty[288] were two members of a motley crew of convicts and free people who seized the colonial brig *Venus* at Port Dalrymple in Van Diemen's Land in June 1806, and proceded to sail to the Bay of Islands in New Zealand.[289] The *Frederick* was built by convicts at Macquarie Harbour;

in January 1834 it was stolen by ten of them, who later abandoned the leaky ship off the coast of Chile.[290] Transportees did not confine their absconding to the Pacific region, as historian Clare Anderson has described: throughout the first half of the nineteenth century convicts and former convicts looked to the Indian Ocean region, escaping from the Antipodes to the Indian sub-continent and as far afield as Mauritius.[291]

Such was the ingenuity of transportees that some even fashioned an escape from convict Australia's most remote penal station at Norfolk Island. In 1848 the claim of Earl Grey,[292] Secretary of State for War and the Colonies, that 'Nature herself has rendered the island one of the securest places of detention' was nothing more than hubris; it wilfully ignored 20 years of experience.[293] In December 1826 the *Wellington*, carrying one of the earliest major shipments of prisoners to Norfolk Island, was seized by convicts en route and diverted to New Zealand.[294] At least 64 men got away from the island, having either constructed or stole boats, while at least another 88 were punished for either plotting or attempting to escape. One striking case was that of James Punt Borrit,[295] who was sent directly from England to Norfolk Island in 1840 by the *Mangles*. In an echo of William Bryant, after the island's free coxswain drowned Borritt's seafaring skills saw him given charge of Norfolk Island's whaleboat and he was employed in ferrying people and goods to and from ship to shore. He was allowed to choose his crew, selecting men including his *Mangles* shipmates William Vine (another man with sailing experience),[296] John Day[297] and William Pedder.[298] On 2 June 1841 they and five others sailed away from Norfolk Island to New Caledonia, though Borrit eventually made it back to Britain. He remained at large for 16 months before being recognised and re-transported – ironically enough – straight back to Norfolk Island aboard the *Hyderabad*.

The point of this apparent digression is that as remarkable as the Bryant party's flight was, it was an early one in a long line of escapes from Australia by sea. A clear lineage runs from the John Turwood group and the Bryant party through to Borrit and his fellows, and indeed beyond. These escape attempts saw well-prepared groups of convicts, willing to co-operate and generally with some seafaring knowledge among them, take advantage of the (ever-increasing) interconnectedness of European colonial possessions. For some transportees the sea was not merely a barrier, a vast wall between them and their former home; it was also a constant, tantalising reminder of the possibility of freedom.

The Mary Bryant 'legend' and interpretations of the story

Many people will know the tale told in the *Memorandoms* as 'the Mary Bryant story' – especially in Australia, where it has effectively become a part of the national memory. It is a story which has been told and re-told innumerable times in the last 120 years, in the form of histories, novels, plays, poetry, television series and even a musical.[299] It would be a Sisyphean task to account for every piece of Bryantiana which has been and continues to be produced, so this section will largely limit itself to the major historical accounts.[300] These are, by and large, unsatisfactory and derivative; Ian Duffield's reference to 'the (discursively) hackneyed Mary Bryant episode' is not unfair.[301] Owing to the relative paucity of records pertaining to the lives of the escapees – perhaps coupled with the fact that the manuscript versions of the *Memorandoms* have until now been inaccessible without a research trip to London – modern writers have frequently been unable to resist the temptation to depart from the historical record, substituting for it unsupported speculation and, in some cases, outright invention.

The first two book-length historical accounts of the escape were published in 1937 and 1938. Geoffrey Rawson's *The Strange Case of Mary Bryant* (1938) should not be taken seriously, as its key source material is Becke and Jeffery's novel, *A First Fleet Family* (1896). Becke and Jeffery adopted the role of the editors of the journal of Marine Sergeant William Dew, which they claimed to have received from Dew's grandson some months previously. Dew was said to have travelled to New South Wales in the First Fleet, and Becke and Jeffery claimed that his narrative expands upon the Bryant party's escape as told in 'most of the so-called histories of the Colony'.[302] William Dew was a real historical figure, a Marine private who served in Watkin Tench's detachment.[303] Historian Mollie Gillen could find no records of his life in New South Wales, and suggests that Dew left the colony in the *Atlantic* on 11 December 1792, rather than by HMS *Gorgon* as the novel claims.[304]

Dew's 'journal', however, was not real, and Becke and Jeffery embroidered the historical record so successfully that Rawson went along with most of their inventions.[305] These inventions include: the suggestion that Mary Broad and William Bryant were lovers before going to New South Wales, and that she was transported for aiding and abetting his escape from Winchester Castle (Rawson adds the detail that they switched clothes and Bryant left the gaol dressed as a woman); fighting between William Bryant, Samuel Bird and Samuel Broom in the boat during the voyage to Timor; Mary Bryant meeting her true love, one Lieutenant Fairfax, at the hulks, his having been the father of young Charlotte; and Mary and Fairfax rekindling their relationship on HMS *Gorgon* during the voyage back to England, where he procured for her a pardon and they settled in London to raise a family.[306] Rawson's book is properly consigned to the realm of romantic fiction – particularly in its imagined dialogue, and more than one lingering reference to Mary Bryant's 'dazzling bosom'.[307] Yet it is emblematic of the enduring power of Becke and Jeffery's embellishments. These have become so entangled with reality that they live on even in more recent works, such as the egregiously titled *The True Story of Mary Bryant: Escape from Botany Bay* (2003) by Gerald and Loretta Hausman, which substitutes the historical figure of Watkin Tench for the fictional Lieutenant Fairfax.[308]

Unfortunately for Rawson, his work was undermined entirely by Frederick A. Pottle's *Boswell and the Girl from Botany Bay*. This short book was based on Pottle's Presidential Address to the Elizabethan Club at Yale University. It was first published in the United States in 1937, in a print run limited to 500 copies, and was then published again in London the following year.[309] Pottle was a Boswell scholar and the first researcher to identify the Scottish lawyer's role in securing the release of the surviving escapees. His research was built upon by Charles H. Currey in *The Transportation, Escape and Pardoning of Mary Bryant* (1963), whose account was the first to use the *Memorandoms* in telling the story. The works of both Pottle and Currey are hugely valuable, and largely refrain from romanticism and supposition. In addition to these texts, readers are best served by consulting Warwick Hirst's *Great Convict Escapes in Colonial Australia* (1999) and – with a slight reservation – Carolly Erickson's *The Girl from Botany Bay* (2005). Hirst's examination of the escape is largely based upon the *Memorandoms*, and is all the better for it.[310] Erickson's, meanwhile, generally sticks to the documentary record and makes some perceptive general observations about the period. However, she does employ some artistic licence in describing conditions during voyage from Sydney to Timor, imagining Mary Bryant's state of mind and ascribing the testimony of the survivors at Bow Street to her alone.[311]

The best-known and most widely referenced of the modern accounts is undoubtedly Judith Cook's *To Brave Every Danger: the Epic Life of Mary Bryant of Fowey* (1993), yet it is one of the least satisfactory histories of the escape. Cook offers a great deal of unevidenced speculation as fact and, as the book contains no references, it is difficult to see where many of her claims originate. For instance, according to Cook, during the journey to Timor it was always Mary Bryant who took the lead: she 'organized a hunt for fresh food, saw to the replenishment of the water cask', and when William Bryant 'lost heart very quickly each time the going became tough … again and again it was left to Mary to rally and encourage the men'.[312] Given that the only first-hand account we have of the journey is the *Memorandoms*, and it does not support any of these claims, they can be fairly dismissed.

Cook's Mary Bryant was a reluctant thief, who either fell in with a 'bad lot' or decided to steal only after finding herself 'so angry at the injustice' of a period of dearth in the West Country, 'that she threw caution to the winds and embarked on a bold and dangerous venture to provide herself with funds with which to buy food to keep her family from starving' (conveniently ignoring the violence meted out by Mary Bryant, Catherine Fryer and Mary Shepherd towards the unfortunate Agnes Lakeman). Cook also claims that, during the *Charlotte*'s voyage to New South Wales, 'from time to time, [Mary] negotiated on behalf of the other women for improvements in their ration of food and water'. She also maintains that it was Mary Bryant who formulated the escape plan in Sydney, cajoled her husband into absconding and 'who came up with the idea that the best boat in which to make a substantial journey… would be the Governor's own boat' – although it was actually the colony's fishing boat, to which they had daily access, which the party stole.[313] *To Brave Every Danger* reads as though Cook was determined to create a romantic portrait of Mary Bryant, and was willing to ignore, massage or create evidence to support it.

Perhaps the most glaring example of Cook's willingness to invent is in describing how the escapees were hit by a storm after leaving 'White Bay':

> It was then that the men seemed to give up all hope of a successful outcome to the voyage, resigning themselves to their deaths. Mary simply refused to give in. Snatching up a hat belonging to one of the men, she began to bail, calling on the rest to follow suit. What was the matter with them? What kind of men were they to sit bewailing their fate while the boat sank under them, not even making an attempt to fight for their lives? … Once she had organized the bailing, she took the tiller, straining against the huge seas. She told them, as they laboured, that she had no intention of drowning and nor should they. … She was their shining light and, as Martin writes, in spite of the very real distress she must have been suffering as the condition of her 'two babies' deteriorated rapidly through the continual cold and wet, she never once gave way to her own fears.

This is total fiction. The *Memorandoms* says no such thing. Rather, it points out that everyone in the boat gave themselves up for lost, such was the violence of the storm, and the only mention of Mary Bryant was in inviting the reader to 'Consider what distress we must be in Woman & the two little Babies was in a bad Condition'.[314] Cook seems to have taken her description from the *Annual Register* for 1792, which imagined this part of journey as follows:

> At one time their anchor broke, and the surf was so great, that the men laid down their oars, in a state of despair, and gave themselves up as lost; but this Amazon, taking one of their hats, cried out, "Never fear," and immediately began to exert herself in clearing the boat of water: her example was followed by her companions, and by great labour the boat was prevented from sinking, until they got into smoother seas.[315]

Cook rightly describes the *Register*'s account of the escapees' journey as 'rather inaccurate', but was willing to believe this section since it suited her narrative purpose. It is difficult to disagree with Carolly Erickson's conclusion that Cook 'invents freely, sometimes contradicting the written records'.[316] *To Brave Every Danger* routinely enters the realm of fiction and should be read with an extremely sceptical eye.

Unlike Judith Cook, in *Mary Bryant: Her Life and Escape from Botany Bay* (2004) Jonathan King does at least admit that although the book is 'based on truth, I have embellished many parts of the story to help bring Mary to life in terms of our modern world'.[317] 'Embellished' can be taken to mean 'invented', since the book incorporates Mary Bryant's reunion and marriage to 'childhood sweetheart' Richard Thomas, romanticised encounters with Indigenous Australians and some genuinely atrocious faux Cornish-inflected dialogue ('Doan change the subject, now. Who be the lucky father, or doan the likes of you normally know such things?').[318]

Aside from Becke and Jeffery's *A First Fleet Family*, modern fictional accounts of the escape include (but are not limited to) Anthony Veitch's *Spindrift* (1980), Lesley Pearse's *Remember Me* (2003), John Durand's *The Odyssey of Mary B* (2005), Jo Anne Rey's *The Sarsaparilla Souvenir* (2005) and Laurie Sheehan's *Mary Bryant, the Convict Girl* (2006).[319] All, apart from Veitch, appear to rely heavily upon Cook's *To Brave Every Danger*, with all the issues that entails. Mary Bryant features as 'Dabby Bryant' in Timberlake Wertenbaker's play *Our Country's Good* (1988), and in the one-man show *Boswell for the Defence* – which ran in London in

1989 and 1990, and Australia in 1991 – Leo McKern played Boswell as he fought her corner.[320] As a testament to the wide interest in the tale, in 1980 Jenny Agutter suggested to an Australian magazine that she 'would like to do the story of the convict Mary Bryant'.[321] The tale was the subject of Nick Enright and David King's musical *Mary Bryant* (1988), and Enright wrote a screenplay about the Bryants, entitled *The World Underneath*, for Warner Brothers, though this film project was never realised.[322]

Two versions of the escape have, however, been produced for television. The first was *The Hungry Ones* by Rex Rienits, a ten-episode serial broadcast by the Australian Broadcasting Commission (ABC) in 1963 (Fig.21), and the fourth in as many years based upon early Australian colonial history.[323] The *Hungry Ones*, unlike its predecessors, was not terribly well received: Nan Musgrove was scathing in her review, believing that this was the first of the ABC's historical serials 'that can be dismissed with that expressive Australian word "crook"', finding that the actors 'move through their parts like well-controlled puppets' and criticising the serial for being 'inaccurate historically' and the script for its 'glaring omissions'.[324]

The second version was *The Incredible Journey of Mary Bryant* (2005),[325] a joint British and Australian production which was once the most expensive television mini-series ever made in Australia. The *Incredible Journey* takes innumerable unwarranted liberties with the story.[326] Mary Bryant is, as historian Jacqueline Wilson points out, 'gratuitously sexualized': she feigns a relationship with an infatuated British officer, then lives with him for a time solely to distract him while the other escapees make preparations to leave the colony. After the escape the officer pursues the party all the way to Timor, motivated by a combination of lust and revenge.[327] This villainous officer is named 'Ralph Clarke', and is presumably based upon a real Marine officer, Ralph Clark, who travelled to New South Wales on the First Fleet. However, the historical Clark did not have a relationship with Mary Bryant. Nor did he – or anyone else – pursue the Bryant party to Timor, or lead a party which led to William Bryant being shot dead and Mary Bryant captured by British soldiers at Kupang. The *Incredible Journey* also thins out the number of adult escapees to seven: Samuel Broom, Samuel Bird and Nathaniel Lilley are amalgamated into the figure of 'Sam Liley', while a new individual, 'Thomas Watling' is added to the group. This addition is all the more confusing as the real Thomas Watling, later known as a painter, was indeed transported to New South Wales. However, he did not arrive until October 1792, by which time over half the Bryant party were dead and the survivors were confined to Newgate.[328] Captain Edwards and James

Fig.21 Publicity stills for the ABC historical serial *The Hungry Ones*, from *The Australian Women's Weekly*, 10 July 1963, p.17. *The Hungry Ones* was first broadcast at 7.30pm on Sunday 7 July 1963 on Channel 3. It ran for 10 episodes

Boswell are written out of the story entirely, and the court scenes at the end of the second episode are extremely unrealistic. Finally, in a bizarre conclusion, James Martin chooses to return to New South Wales since it is a place where a free man 'could make of himself what he chose, without the prejudice of who he once was' – a description utterly at odds with the picture of the squalid, brutal, inequitable colony so studiously created during the first episode. The *Incredible Journey of Mary Bryant*, and the treatment of the story more generally, provides yet more proof that the truth is more often than not richer, and far more interesting, than fiction.

Jeremy Bentham, and *Panopticon versus New South Wales*

Some of the key questions about the *Memorandoms* are how, when and why the document was acquired by the utilitarian philosopher Jeremy Bentham (Fig.22). The answer to each of these questions, disappointingly, is that we simply do not know. Judith Cook's supposition that James Martin 'gave his *Memorandum* [sic] to Jeremy Bentham' is false, enticing as it is to imagine a meeting between them both.[329] Bentham did establish a direct link with Newgate Gaol, but not until late 1802 and early 1803 when he corresponded with the Reverend Doctor Thomas Brownlow Forde, Ordinary of Newgate.[330] The *Memorandoms* is not mentioned in their letters, though this is unsurprising: Forde only became Ordinary in 1798, and he and Bentham corresponded about a decade after the narrative was apparently written and the surviving escapees were released from the gaol.[331] In fact the only occasion on which Bentham refers to the escape by James Martin and his fellows is in a single line in his work on convict transportation, *Panopticon versus New South Wales* (written in 1802–3, but not published until 1812).[332]

Fig.22 'Jeremy Bentham', oil, *c.*1790

In the 'First Letter to Lord Pelham' – a composite part of *Panopticon versus New South Wales* – Bentham highlighted the falsity of the argument, put forward by proponents of transportation, that the remoteness of New South Wales would prevent convicts from ever returning. Working through David Collins' *Account of the English Colony*, Bentham calculated that approximately 89 prisoners had been permitted to leave Sydney between 1790 and 1796 after their sentences expired, and that a further 76 had absconded prior to the expiration of their sentences. 'Already', Bentham noted, clearly referring to the escape of the Bryant party and the others, 'has an open boat been known to furnish the means of escape; and that through the vast space between New South Wales and Timor'.[333] He says nothing more about the escape or the individuals involved, and we can by no means be certain that the *Memorandoms* was even in Bentham's possession at the time of writing this in 1802, as he could have easily gleaned this information from Collins or elsewhere.

We do know, however, why Bentham devoted a significant portion of his time to writing about transportation. In early 1802 Bentham was disappointed, frustrated and very angry. He had spent a great deal of time, effort and money during the previous decade in what – as had become all too apparent – proved a vain attempt to persuade the government to build a 'panopticon' prison of his design. The idea behind the panopticon, from the Greek παν- ('all') and οπτικος- ('seeing' or 'optics'), originated with Bentham's younger brother Samuel (Fig.23).[334] While working in Russia for Prince Potemkin,[335] Samuel devised the 'central inspection principle' as a solution to the problem of how to observe, and consequently regulate, the behaviour of apparently undisciplined and misbehaving skilled craftsmen, themselves supposed to be supervising and training unskilled workers.[336] Jeremy believed that Samuel's 'important, though simple, idea in architecture' could be applied to a multiplicity of institutional buildings, from poor-houses to factories to asylums and, most (in)famously to prisons.[337]

It was in this latter context that Jeremy Bentham envisaged an 'Inspection House', a circular building with the prisoners' cells arranged around the outer wall and an inspection tower occupying the centre (Fig.24). From this tower the prison's governor could look into the cells at any time; he would even be able to speak to the prisoners in their cells through an elaborate network of 'conversation tubes', though the inmates themselves would be unable to see the governor. (The governor would have been Bentham himself.)[338] Bentham expected that this 'new mode of obtaining power of mind over mind, in a quantity hitherto

Fig.23 'Samuel Bentham' by Henry Edridge, c.1795–1800

without example' would ensure that the prisoners, believing that they might be being watched at any time, would modify their behaviour in a positive manner in order to avoid the punishment that would inevitably follow any breach of the prison's discipline.[339] After serving their time in the panopticon, they would then be returned to society as useful, industrious citizens.[340] The panopticon is today best known through the analysis of the French philosopher Michel Foucault, for whom it represented the emergence of modern 'disciplinary' societies and their desire to subject their citizens to surveillance and control.[341] As Anne Brunon-Ernst notes, Foucault's 'theorisation of surveillance society' has 'turned

Bentham into the forerunner of Big Brother'.[342] These assertions would have struck Bentham as odd, since for him the panopticon was simply a mode of deterring and reforming criminals; it was cheaper and more rational, and would inflict less pain, than any other form of convict discipline. (It should be noted that no prison which strictly conformed to Bentham's plan has ever been built.)

Bentham was outraged when the government abandoned the panopticon, believing that he had been the victim of a conspiracy and that the will of parliament had been subverted. Though the Penitentiary for Convicts Act of 1794[343] authorised the construction of a penitentiary, it was never acted upon – in large part because it proved impossible to find a site on which it could be built. George Spencer, second Earl Spencer,[344] objected to the proposed location at Battersea Rise as it was near his estate, and Viscount Belgrave[345] and the Dean and Chapter of Westminster were similarly opposed to its being built at Tothill Fields. Bentham ended up purchasing a small, boggy and entirely unsuitable site on the Millbank estate. The panopticon had been thwarted, in Bentham's eyes, by venal politicians who, rather than act in the best interests of the community, were instead motivated by 'sinister interests'. He became

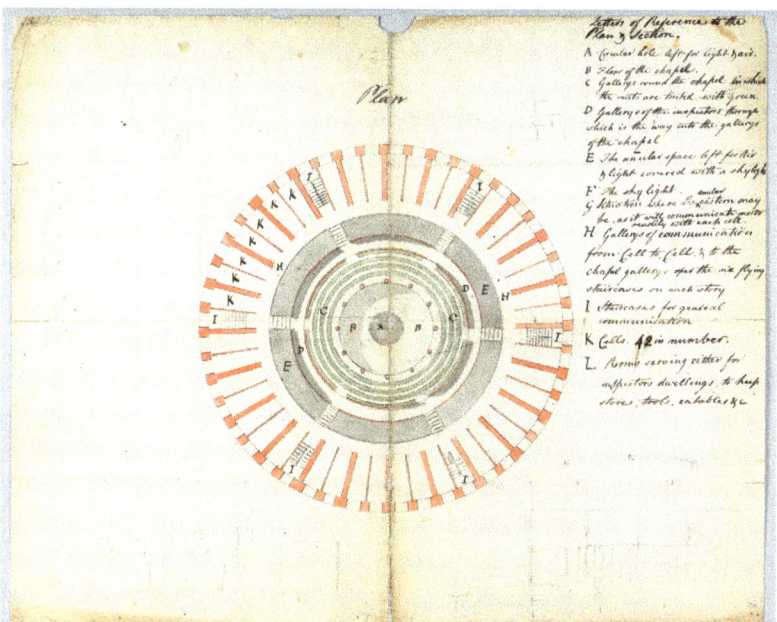

Fig.24 Plan of Bentham's proposed panopticon prison by Willey Revely (UC cxix. 120)

convinced that 'nothing worthwhile could be achieved through the existing political structure in Britain', and the final decades of his life were dominated by the effort to develop and disseminate a systematic programme of root-and-branch reform of the legal, political and ecclesiastical establishments, so that they might serve the interest of the many rather than the ruling few.[346]

The story of Bentham's protracted negotiations with the government and the failure of the panopticon scheme is told by Janet Semple in *Bentham's Prison*, and need not be recited here.[347] However, it is important to note that the experience was formative in Bentham's intellectual development. Its failure was his greatest disappointment, resulting in the 'destruction of eight years of the most valuable part of [my] life'; the government had, he continued, 'murdered my best days!'.[348] According to his literary executor John Bowring,[349] Bentham preferred not 'to look among Panopticon papers. It is like opening a drawer where devils are locked up—it is breaking into a haunted house'.[350] He believed that he had been subjected to a co-ordinated campaign of humiliation and neglect orchestrated by the underlings of ministers, as his letters went unanswered and unacknowledged for weeks and he loitered on a daily basis in Treasury corridors. He was reduced in May 1799 to chasing Charles Long,[351] junior secretary to the Treasury, into the porters' water closet in the hope of an audience.[352] (Long, for his part, felt harassed by Bentham's near constant presence at the Treasury and purposefully avoided him.)[353] All of the humiliation took its toll. After the abortive meeting with Long in the gents', Bentham told his friend Reginald Pole Carew[354] that 'I hate the sight of man [...] if I remain unshot, undrowned, unhung, it is to avoid burthening the public with Coroner's fees.' He ended the short note with: 'Given at my dog-hole this 25 day of May, 1799—Bow, wow, wow.'[355]

Though the panopticon scheme was not effectively killed off until June 1803,[356] a metaphorical noose had been round its neck for some time, and Bentham knew it. One outlet for his frustration during 1802 and early 1803 was the writing of a near-contemporary account of his experience, entitled 'A Picture of the Treasury under the Administration of the Rt. Hon. W. Pitt[357] and the Rt. Hon. H. Addington[358] with a Sketch of the Secretary of State's Office under the reign of the Duke of Portland'.[359] The 'Picture' runs to hundreds and hundreds of manuscripts, and a perusal of the 25 section titles – 'Clandestine and Perfidious Assurances to Lord Belgrave', 'Insidious Letter', and 'Official Incapacity' – gives some indication of the extent of Bentham's bitterness.[360] The only parts of the 'Picture' which were published dealt with convict transportation; though

Bentham listed them as sub-sections in his outline of the 'Picture', they subsequently took on a life of their own and morphed into the 'Letters to Lord Pelham' and 'A Plea for the Constitution', the constituent parts of *Panopticon versus New South Wales*.[361]

Bentham's first recorded opinion on New South Wales was given in May 1791. He had just come across some House of Commons papers regarding Britain's new penal colony, and thought that:

> the establishment in question presents a truly curious scene of absurdity improvidence and extravagance. The impossibility of success in every imaginable point of view stands demonstrated upon the very face of the accounts in the most glaring colours … I feel myself strongly tempted to give before the public a sketch of it as soon as I have a little leisure.[362]

It took Bentham another 11 years before he finally put pen to paper on the subject, but his low opinion of New South Wales had only hardened in the intervening period – especially after protracted negotiations with government over the cost of his panopticon. To cut a very long story short, in mid-1800 the Treasury Board decided that the panopticon, if it was to be built at all, should be an experimental prison housing 500 inmates (the original plan had been to accommodate 1000). One of the reasons given for this alteration was 'the improved state of the Colony of New South Wales', a statement Bentham was so disgusted with he would later deploy it himself, dripping in irony, in the 'First Letter to Lord Pelham'.[363]

Bentham had collected information about New South Wales during the late 1790s. At the time he had been working on a plan for a preventive police force with the London magistrate Patrick Colquhoun[364] and drafting the sections dealing with New South Wales for the report of the 1798 Select Committee on Finance.[365] He therefore had a reasonable body of material on which to draw when writing the 'Letters to Lord Pelham' and 'A Plea for the Constitution', which was supplemented by heavy use of the *Account of the English Colony in New South Wales* by its Judge-Advocate David Collins,[366] the second volume of which had, in mid-1802, just been published.

The 'First Letter to Lord Pelham' had been drafted by mid-August 1802. Bentham attempted to use it as leverage for the panopticon by sending, through the offices of his friend Charles Bunbury,[367] a two-sheet outline of the work and an introductory note to the Home Secretary, Lord Pelham.[368] Bentham wished Pelham to understand 'very distinctly, that if, within a week from this date … I were not fortunate to receive the honour of a letter in his Lordship's hand', then he would publish the text and expose both the reality of New South Wales and the machinations of government to public scrutiny and scorn.[369] Pelham's response was evasive, though he commented upon Bentham's 'present state of mind'. The inference that he had become unhinged, unsurprisingly, only aggravated Bentham further.[370]

By the end of 1802 both 'Letters to Lord Pelham' had been privately printed. Bentham gave copies to those who had interested themselves in the panopticon scheme, including Bunbury, William Wilberforce[371] and the Speaker of the House of Commons, Charles Abbot (who happened to be Bentham's step-brother),[372] as well as to potentially sympathetic MPs such as Sir John Anderson, French Laurence and William Eden.[373] 'A Plea for the Constitution', which had the more evocative original title of 'The True Bastile', soon followed, after being read and revised by Bentham's friend, the lawyer Samuel Romilly.[374] Though it was also privately printed, Bentham was far more circumspect about distributing 'A Plea for the Constitution', believing that the 'discoveries' he set out in it were so dangerous that, if they became widely known, they risked 'the setting of the whole Colony in a flame'. One such discovery, Bentham thought, was that politicians, civil servants, judges and colonial officials were all in his view liable to be 'punished with a pretty little collection of punishments called a *Premunire*: inter alia imprisonment for life with forfeiture of all their property' for violating the Habeas Corpus Act. He also condemned the fact that although convicts were theoretically sent to New South Wales for specific lengths of time, no provision was made to return them to Britain and so they were effectively, and illegally, being transported for life. Though he anticipated that a bill of indemnity would be obtained to protect those in power, it would not be before their violation of justice and the constitution had been exposed.[375]

Bentham intended to publish the 'Letters to Lord Pelham' and 'A Plea for the Constitution', but in 24 February 1803 the publisher, Messrs Brooke and Clarke turned down the works, ostensibly for their 'rather political concern'.[376] Bentham himself appears to have quickly lost interest in the texts after June 1803 when Charles Bunbury urged him not to publish 'A Plea for the Constitution', on the grounds that it would 'bring upon you Enemies irreconcileable, and procure you Friends only amongst the Malefactors of New South Wales'.[377] They are barely mentioned again in his correspondence after this time unless someone wrote to ask him for a copy. The texts were set aside until 1812 when the government's enthusiasm for panopticon was apparently, if only momentarily, rekindled. In response Bentham fully published for the first time all of his works relating to panopticon – including the 'Letters to Lord Pelham' and 'A Plea for the Constitution', unaltered apart from a new title page – in a single volume entitled *Panopticon versus New South Wales*. This complicated publication history has sometimes led to an assumption that *Panopticon versus New South Wales* was published and became available to the wider public in 1802, according to it an influence which it could not have begun to have had for another decade.[378]

The 'First Letter to Lord Pelham' is a hugely important text. It is the first theoretically and philosophically detailed critique of transportation and the penal colony of New South Wales by a major philosopher of punishment. The 'Second Letter' compares the penal colony with American penitentiaries and provides innumerable further examples of the awful conditions in New South Wales. Editorial work at UCL's Bentham Project has established the existence of an unpublished 'Third Letter to Lord Pelham', which ostensibly analyses conditions in British gaols and prison hulks but also contains a bitter attack on the hypocrisy of government ministers. 'A Plea for the Constitution' is concerned with the constitutional arrangement of New South Wales, which Bentham believed was illegally founded and whose government violated basic tenets of the British Constitution, including Magna Carta, the Habeas Corpus Act and the Bill of Rights. For instance the governor, according to Bentham, had legal authority neither to enact nor promulgate local ordinances, nor to inflict punishments for their transgressions – a dangerous argument to make about a colony whose population, at the time, consisted in the main of transportees and their gaolers.

Greatly influenced by the Italian jurist Cesare Beccaria,[379] Bentham believed that punishment would only deter criminal offending when its infliction was certain and publicly known. However, as Bentham put it, 'all punishment is mischief: all punishment in itself is evil', and so only as much punishment as was necessary to deter should be inflicted.[380] In the 'First Letter to Lord Pelham' Bentham argued that transportation was an unscientific, corrosive failure, incompatible not only with his own general theory of punishment, but also with the central principles of British justice. It violated the principle of proportionality by obliterating any distinction between sentences passed upon criminals. In effectively transporting for life all prisoners sent to New South Wales, Bentham argued that 'never did this country witness an exercise of power more flagrantly reprehensible, more completely indefensible'.[381] In addition, he considered transportation a lottery in which no-one could determine how much or how little pain would be inflicted upon the transportee, either on the journey to New South Wales or in the colony itself. The convicts' past crimes and present behaviour had little influence on how they fared in New South Wales, where exploitable skills were more important than reformed character in determining their treatment. Even if, by some stroke of fortune, the punishment in the colony was proportionate, it was inflicted so far from the general population on which it was supposed to operate, namely in Britain, that all deterrent effect was lost.[382]

Despite the claims of politicians and administrators, argued Bentham, transportation did not reform prisoners. Reformation occurred via means of education, the inculcation of good habits and through close surveillance: none of this was possible in the vast open gaol that was New South Wales, where the colonial government's only interest was in extracting as much labour as possible from its convict workers. Finally Bentham argued that transportation did not even have the saving grace of being cheap. He generally regarded colonies as a drain on the mother country; the fact that New South Wales was founded as a penal colony only exacerbated the drain on Britain's financial, military and human resources as ever-increasing numbers of convicts were transported. Bentham expected that the colony would produce little of value and, as a 'vast conservatory of military law' it was 'odious … even at that vast distance, to the sense of every true Briton'.[383]

Although grounded in his theory of punishment, *Panopticon versus New South Wales* was, as its title makes clear, written by a partisan for one mode of criminal punishment over another. There are few works in which Bentham is quite as animated or deploys all of his powers of sarcasm, irony and mockery as in the 'First Letter to Lord Pelham', a masterful work of rhetoric and propaganda for the panopticon. Bentham's use of evidence is, however, often tendentious; he cherry-picked the worst examples from Collins' *Account* and disregarded those that did not fit his argument.[384] Bentham's New South Wales was a community sinking in immorality of the darkest shades, threatened with extinction by fire, flood, famine and attacks by Indigenous Australians. It was a place awash with drink in which convicts held public office, were granted land and could generally do as they pleased; they escaped retribution for their acts, even when they burned down the colony's church and gaols. Such was Bentham's antipathy towards New South Wales that in one unpublished manuscript he even mocked the flora and fauna: he would 'not give a single barrel [of oysters] from Old Wales, for all that will ever be imported from the New', while the emu would never be 'looked upon by the fairest and best judges as any thing better than an apology for an ostrich' (Fig.25).[385]

Fig.25 'The Kangaroo' by Arthur Bowes Smyth, c.1787–9. Bentham was underwhelmed by reports of kangaroos emerging from New South Wales, sarcastically observing that the fur of 'our own hares, and rabbits, not forgetting cats – will shew to great advantage [compared] with the kangaroo and kangaroo-rats of New South Wales'. See UC cxvi. 110

Bentham's critique of transportation only briefly concerned those in government and it had relatively little immediate impact. However, his arguments regarding the ineffectiveness and uncertainty of transportation were repeated by proponents of penitentiary imprisonment during the following decades and, as John Gascoigne put it, Bentham's 'ideological legacy was instrumental in helping to bring transportation to an end'.[386] These ideas can be seen, for instance, in the work of Henry Grey Bennett in his *Letter to Viscount Sidmouth* (1819)[387] and in *Thoughts on Secondary Punishments* (1832) by Richard Whately,[388] described by Gascoigne as the 'most eminent pamphleteer against New South Wales since Bentham'.[389] Perhaps the most obvious example of Bentham's influence can be seen in the report of the Select Committee on Transportation of 1837–8, chaired by the young, dandyish, radical MP Sir William Molesworth.[390] Molesworth was an arch-Benthamite and his fellow students, according to John Ritchie, joked that Molesworth 'not only admired Bentham but also understood him'.[391] Bentham's influence ran deep, and it is striking how similar Molesworth's parliamentary reports on transportation are, stylistically, methodologically and philosophically, to *Panopticon versus New South Wales*.[392] They are key documents in the history of transportation and were responsible for shaping perceptions about the awfulness of New South Wales, Van Diemen's Land and Norfolk Island during the 1830s and well beyond.[393]

In August 1802 Bentham wrote, that armed with the 'Letters to Lord Pelham' and 'A Plea for the Constitution', when the time was right New South Wales would be his target and he would aim at 'the evacuation of that scene of wickedness and wretchedness'.[394] He came nowhere near achieving this but, though he did not live to see it, his arguments contributed prominently to the 1830s anti-transportation campaign, culminating in the abolition of transportation to New South Wales in 1840. Bentham may have lost his own battle against New South Wales, but this would have been a small victory that he might well have savoured.[395]

The Memorandoms: previous editions and the manuscripts

Three previous editions of the *Memorandoms* have been published. The first was edited by Charles Blount and published by the Rampant Lions Press in 1937.[396] The Blount edition was limited to 150 copies and access to it can be difficult: in the British Isles, according to a COPAC search, only the British Library, the National Library of Scotland and the university libraries of Trinity College Dublin, Cambridge and Oxford have copies. In Australia, according to the National Library of Australia's *Trove*, the state libraries of New South Wales, Queensland, South Australia and Victoria have copies, as do the libraries of the Australian National University and the universities of Queensland and Newcastle. On the rare occasions that a copy becomes available for sale, it typically costs upwards of £150.

Blount wrote of how, when 'working upon the Bentham Papers at University College, London, in furtherance of an object other than this, I had the good fortune to find "Memorandoms by James Martin"'.[397] (Blount was then carrying out research on the relationship between Bentham, Étienne Dumont and the Comte de Mirabeau).[398] The Blount edition's value lies chiefly in its novelty, and we are indebted to him for first bringing the *Memorandoms* to light. The transcript is reliable and the introduction is useful, though Blount's description of convict transportation is the standard one of the 1930s and his analysis of Bentham's views on the subject is somewhat superficial. The introduction also contains several factual errors. Chief among these is Blount's assumption that all of the escapees were transported by the First Fleet and that Martin must have misnamed several of his fellows. Accordingly, Blount attempted to re-identify the Second Fleeters in the Bryant party as First Fleeters. He believed, for example, that Nathaniel Lillie was really Nathaniel Lucas, an entirely different individual who was at Norfolk Island from March 1788 until April 1805, and who then remained in New South Wales until his death in 1818.[399]

The second edition of the *Memorandoms* was produced by Victor Crittenden and published by the Mulini Press in 1991.[400] Crittenden founded the Mulini Press in the late 1970s, and over the years it has published many valuable historical sources, bibliographies and works by and about early Australian authors.[401] The Crittenden edition is an 11-page pamphlet, consisting of a brief introductory note, the transcript and some brief commentary upon the text. No British library has a copy, though it is available in 13 Australian research libraries, according to the National Library of Australia's *Trove*.

Blount and Crittenden reproduced only one of two manuscript versions of the *Memorandoms*, namely the original, located in Box clxix of UCL's Bentham Papers at folios 179 to 201. These sheets are enclosed in a folder on which is written 'Journal (original) of J. Martin who in company with 12 others escaped from Botany Bay—on 28th March, 1791'. The statement is slightly erroneous, as including Martin, there were 11 escapees: nine adults and two children. The second version of the *Memorandoms* is an edited fair copy of the original, also in Box clxix and at folios 202 to 205.

The third edition of the *Memorandoms*, edited by Tim Causer, was published online on the Bentham Project website in early 2014.[402] It reproduced for the first time transcripts of both versions of the *Memorandoms*, and was accompanied by an introductory note and annotation to the text. The present work supersedes this edition.

The original version of the *Memorandoms* is written on 23 small, fragile pieces of paper. When the manuscripts were numbered for cataloguing purposes, two pages were numbered out of order: page two of the narrative is folio 181 and the third page is folio 180. On the verso of folio 197 (page 19 of the narrative) is a note about payment for a 'pair of Wheels' dated March 1791, and on the verso of folio 198 (page 20 of the narrative) is an address. The *Memorandoms* appears to have been written on whatever paper was to hand, as these two jottings have nothing to do the narrative.

The *Memorandoms* is undated, and though the *Catalogue* of the Bentham Papers compiled by Alexander Taylor Milne indicates that the manuscript was written around 1795, this is almost certainly incorrect.[403] Rather, it seems likely that it was written at some point between the survivors' hearing at Bow Street on 30 June 1792 and 2 November 1793, when the last of the surviving escapees were discharged from Newgate Gaol.

The narrative is written in three distinct hands. Charles Blount erred in his suggestion that the document was written by four individuals. He was correct that the first eight pages are the work of a single person, succeeded by the hand of a second individual on the ninth page. The first writer then briefly resumes at the top of page ten, before the second hand once again takes up the pen. Blount thought that a third hand began writing on the fourth line of page 17, but the formation of letters in this purported 'third hand' is identical to that in the preceding pages. Rather than there being a change of hand, the same writer instead appears to have either re-cut or sharpened their quill, or taken up a new one. (A similar thing occurs between the third and fourth line of page 16.) Finally, the document ends, from page 21 onwards, in a third hand; it is much less developed and the grammar deteriorates markedly. The catchwords written in the bottom right-hand corner of the pages appear to be in the hand of the person responsible for producing the fair copy; they were presumably added to aid navigation of the document.

Blount speculated that the *Memorandoms* was written by James Martin, William Allen, Samuel Broom and Nathaniel Lillie while they were in Newgate Gaol. He thought that there 'can only be one explanation of the nature of the manuscript', namely that Martin 'collected what paper he could' and 'commenced to write an account of his journey', only to grow tired and 'except for one brief attempt to resume the pen himself' dictate the remainder of the story to his fellows. Blount found it 'pleasant to think' that the *Memorandoms* was recorded in the hands of the prisoners themselves.[404] It is indeed an agreeable thought that the document is a collaborative effort between the convicts, and it is possible. Martin's name is given in the title, the narrative is written in the first person and it opens with the statement 'I James Martin'. The detail and content of manuscript closely correlates to other primary sources, such as William Bligh's summary of William Bryant's lost journal, and Watkin Tench's brief account of their escape, as well as newspaper reports of the escapees telling their story at Bow Street on 30 June 1792. Later convict records indicate whether or not transportees could read or write, but this information was not recorded as a matter of course in the early years of transportation to New South Wales, so we do not know how literate these men were. However, both Martin and Lillie were skilled tradesmen and Allen had served in the Royal Navy; it is reasonable to suppose that they had some degree of literacy. The *Memorandoms* contains a number of naval terms which may have been well-known to someone like Allen, but obscure to those with no naval background. It is also worth noting that the portion of the *Memorandoms* which Blount supposed was written by

Martin, an Irishman, reveals a certain Irish cadence in places, such as the replacement of the definite article with the colloquial 'they' ('they Country'), and in the spelling of words such as 'varse' and 'Quardrant'. Ultimately, though, there is nothing to confirm Blount's suggestion, the evidence for which is only circumstantial. It is almost certain that Mary Bryant had nothing to do with the composition of the narrative, since men and women were accommodated in separate wards in Newgate; moreover, as James Boswell noted, she could not write.[405]

The fair copy of the *Memorandoms* is written on the type of foolscap paper customarily used by Bentham himself. It is ten pages long and is written in a neat, unknown hand, with the original's idiosyncratic and colloquial grammar and spelling heavily edited. Bentham does not appear to have employed a regular amanuensis during the 1790s and it may have been the case that the original was sent out to a copyist. Yet we cannot be sure whether or not Bentham himself sent the original to be copied, and there is nothing to support Blount's suggestion that the fair copy was 'prepared for the press' by Bentham.[406] Unless some new information is found in the depths of the Bentham Papers, then the whys and wherefores of Bentham's acquisition of the *Memorandoms* will remain a subject of speculation.

Memorandoms by James Martin

A note on the presentation of the text

This edition of the *Memorandoms* has sought to reproduce, as accurately as possible, the features of the original manuscript. Accordingly the original spelling and punctuation have not been corrected, and the abbreviations, deletions, insertions and interlineations of the manuscript have been retained.

Where a word in the manuscripts is broken across a line by the penner, it has been completed in the transcription before a new line is begun.

The identifiers for the original manuscripts from which the transcript is taken appear on the right-hand side of the text. The numerals [169–179], for instance, refer to box clxix, folio 179 of the Bentham Papers in UCL Library's Special Collections. A superscript 'r' refers to the recto of the manuscript folio and a superscript 'v' to the verso.

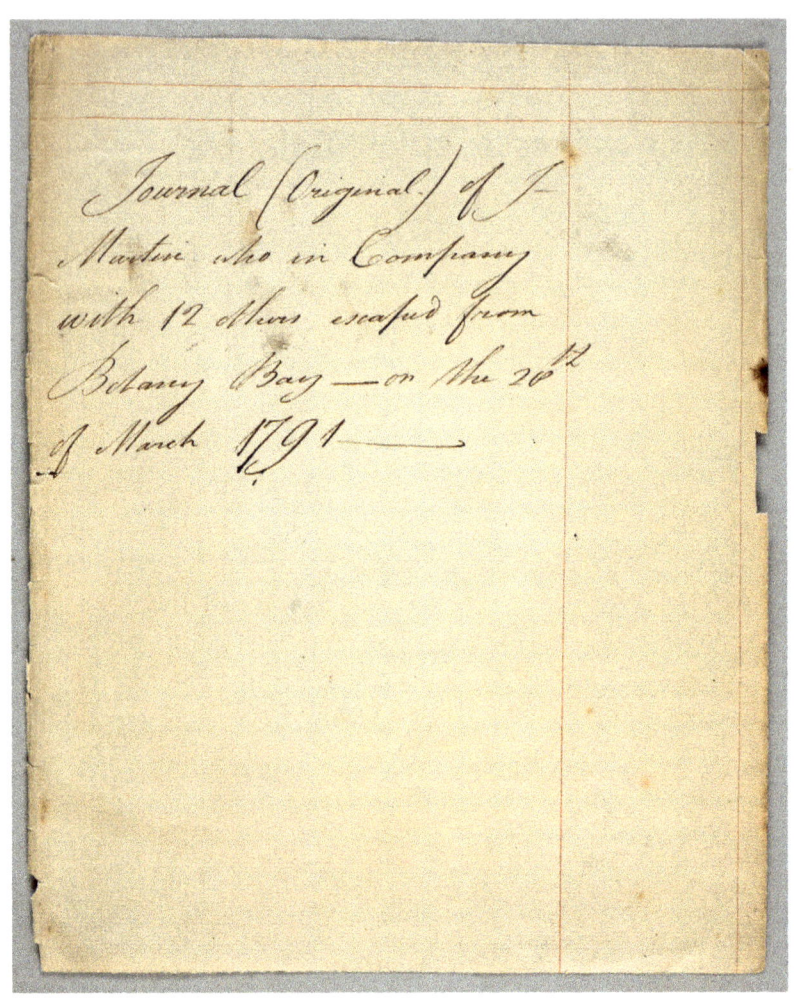

Journal (Original) of J— Martin who in Company with 12 others escaped from Botany Bay — on the 28th of March 1791 —

Journal (Original) of
J.Martin who in Company
with 12 others escaped from
Botany Bay—on the 28th
of March 1791—

Memorandoms

By James Martin

I James Martin Being Convicted at they
City of Exeter in they County of Devonshire
Being found guilty of Stealing of Stealing
16½ of old Lead and ½ of old Iron the
~~they~~ property of Lord Courtneys powderum
Cackle near Exeter — Received Sentance for to be
Transported to Botany Bay for 7 years —
Returned from they Bar to Exeter goal &
there remaind 2 months — from thence sint
on Board they Dunkirk there remaind 10 month
from thence put on Board they Charlotte got
Then Bound to Botany Bay — March 12. 1787

[169–179]

1
Memorandoms
By James Martin

I James Martin Being Convicted at they
City of Exeter in they County of Devonshire
Being found guilty of Stealing ~~of stealing~~
16/2^{lb} of old Lead and 4/2^{lb} of old Iron[407]—~~Recev^d~~
they property of Lord Courney[408] powdrum
Cacle nere Exeter[409]—Recev^d Sentence for to be
Transported to Botany Bay[410] for 7 years—
Returned from they Bar to Exeter goal &
there remaind 2 Months—from thence sent
on Board they Dunkirk[411] there remaind 10 month
from thence put on Board they Charlotte[412] Transport
Then Bound to Botany Bay—March 12 1787[413]

Saild Round to Spithead there Remaind to they
13 of May — then Sail in Copany with 10 Sail
for Batany Bay under Comandand of govoner
Philips, made they Peek of Tenreef 5 Day
of June, there Remaind 6 Days, then Saild
for they Island of Reiodegeneras burg &
on our pasage there Remaind one Month
then Sail for they Cape of good hope —
Being Eight weeks and three Days on our
pasage — then Saild for Botany Bay
Being 10 weeks on our pasage —
Came to an anchor in Port Jackson
Send on Shore in two Days — they Convicts
Being Sent on Shore So Began to work

2

Saild Round to Spithead thence Remaind to they
13 of May—then Sail in Copany with 10 Sail[414]
for Botany Bay under Comandand of govoner
Philips.[415] Made they Peek of Tenureef[416]—5 Day
of June, there Remaind 7 Days, then sail^d
for they Island of Reiodeginera,[417] being 8 wks
on our passage—there remaind one Month
then Sail^d for they Cape of good hope—
Being Eight weeks and three Days on our
pasage[418]—then Sail^d for Botany Bay
Being 10 weeks on our pacage—[419]
Came to an anchor in port Jackson
Send on Shore in two Days—they Convicts
Being Sent on Shore So Began to work[420]

~~we~~

on

on governments account on being Landed
we were Encamped — and foured in tents
of six in a tent — after we Being Encamped
We Some were Sent to Clear they ground
others Sent to Build huts — I Remaind on the
Island from January 1788 — unto March
1791 — on the 28 Day of March Made
my Escape in Compy with 7 men more one
with one woman & two Children — in an open
Six oar Boat — having of provisions on Bd.
one hundred wt. of flower & one hundd wt of
Rice 14 lb of pork and about Eight gallons
of water — having a Copass Quadrant
and Chart

3

on governments account—on being landed
we were Encamped—and fourmed in sqads
of six in a tent—after we Bing Encamped
We Some were sent to Clear they ground
Others Sent to Build huts[421]—I Remaind on the
Island[422] from January 1788—unto March
1791—on the 28 Day of <u>March</u> made
My Escape in Comp^y with 7 men more & one
with one woman & two Chil^{dn}—in an open
Six oar Boat—having of provisions on B^d
one hundred w^t[423] of flower & one hund^d w^t of
Rice 14^{lb} of pork and aBout Eight galons
of water having a Copass Quardrant
and Chart[424]—

                                                          after

after two Days sail reach a little Creek

about 2 Degrees to they Northward of port
Jackson there found a Quantity of fine Burn
Coal they Remaind 2 nights & one Day
and found a Larve Quantity of Cabage tree
which we Cut Down & procured they Cabage
Then they Natives Came Down to which
we gave Some Cloather & other articles
and they went away very much Satiosfied
They apperanance of they Land appeare
more better here than at Sidney Cove
here we got averse Quantitty of fish which
were of a great Refreshment to us
+ we call it fortunate Creek. after

4

after two Days sail reach a little Creek[425]+
aBout 2 Degrees to they Northward of port
Jackson[426] there found a Quantity of fine Burn[g]
Coal they Remaind 2 nights & one Day
and found a Varse Quantty of Cabage tree
which we Cut Down & procured they Cabage[427]
Then they Natives Came Down[428] to which
we gave some Cloaths & other articles
and they went away very much satisfied
They apperanance of they land appears
more better here than at Sidney Cove
here we got avarse Quantity of fish which
were of a great Refresment to us—
+ ⌈we call it fortunate Creek⌉

after

after our stay of 2 nights & one Day we
proceeded our Voyge to they Noothward
after 2 Days sail we Made a very fine
harbour Seeming to Run up they Country
for Many miles and Quite Comodious for
they Anchorage of Shipping — here we found
a plenty of fresh water — hawl'd our Boat
ashore to repair her Bottom being very leaky
they Better to pay her Bottom with some Bees
wax & Rossin which we had a small Quantity
Thereof — But on they Same night was Drove
of By they natives — which meant to Destroy
us — we Launch'd our Boat and Road of in they
Streme Quite out of Reach of them —
that

5

After our stay of 2 nights & one Day[429] we proceeded our Voyge to they Northward after 2 Days sail[430] we Made a very fine harbour Seeming to Run up they Country for Many miles and Quite Comodious for they Anchorage of Shipping[431]—here we found aplenty of fresh water—hawld our Boat ashore to Repair her Bottom being very leaky they Better to pay her Bottom with some Bees Wax & Resin which we had a small Quantiy Thereof—But on they Same night was Drove of By they Natives[432]—which meant to Destroy us—we Launch^d our Boat and Road of in they Strame Quite out of Reach of them

that
~~after~~

that being Sunday Monday we were obliged
Stream we Could Lower Down the give
To Land Some Miles Below — on Mondays Morn
we Attempted to land when we found a place
Convenient for to Repair our Boat we accordingly
we put Some of our things — part being ashore
there Came the natives in Vast numbers
with Spears & Shields &c we forced in parts
one party of us Made towards them they
Better By signes to pacifee them But
they not taking the least notice accordingly
we fired a Musket thinking to afright
them But they took not they least notice
thereof — on perceiving them Push more forward we were forsed to take to our Boat
 and

6

that being Sunday[433] Monday[434] we were of in y[e]
Stream we Rowed Lower Down thinging for
To Land Some Miles Below—on Monday Morn[g]
We Attempted to land when we found a place
Convenient for to Repair our Boat we accord[y]
we put Some of our things—part being ashore
there Came they natives in Varse Numbers
with Spears & Sheilds &c we formed in parts
one party of us Made towards them they
Better By Signes to pasifie them But
they not taking they least notice accordingly
we fired a Musket thinking to afright
them But they took not they least notice
Thereof—on perceving them Rush more forward
we were forsed to take to our Boat

              and

and to get out of their reach as fast as we
could — and what to Do we could not tell
But on Consulting with each other it was
Determined for to Row up they harbour which
accordingly we Rowed up they harbour 9 or 10
miles till we made a little white Sandy Isld
in they Middle of they harbour — which Landed
upon and hauld up our Boat and Repair her
Bottom with what Little materials we had
Whilst our Stay of 2 Days we had no Interrup.on
from they Natives — then we rowed off to they
main where we took in fresh water and a few
Cabage trees — and then put out to Sea —
the^{natives}here is quite naked of a Copper Colour
Shock hair — they have Cannoos made of bark

7

and to get out of their reach as fast as we
Could—and what to Do we Could not tell
But on Consulting with each other it was
Determined for to Row up they harbour which
accordingly we Rowed up they harbour 9 or 10
Miles till we made a little white Sandy Isl^d[435]
in they Middle of they harbour—which land^d
upon and hawld up our Boat and Repair her
Bottom with what Little matariels we had
whilst our Stay of 2 Days we had no Interup^on
from they Natives—then we rowed of to they
main[436] where we took in fresh water and a few
Cabage trees—and then put out to Sea—
they ^natives here is quiet naked of a Copper Colour
Shock hair—they have Cannoos made of bark

there we proceed:d they Northard, having a Stead
Breez from they S:W. But that night they
wend they Changed and Drove us Quite out of sight
of Land,— which we hauld our wind having a sort
of Sails in they Boat accordingly they next Day
we Made Close into they Land But they Surf oun
So very hard we C:not attempt to land but
kept along shore but Making no harbour or
Creek for near three weeks we were much Dis
tress:d for water and Wood — accordly perceiving
they surf to abate two of our men Swam on shore
thinking to get Some water But being afraid
of they natives which they see in numbers
they return:d — without any, But a little wood
which threw into they water which we took

[169–186]

8

then we proceedd they Northard, having a leadg
Brees from they S:W—But that night437 they wind
 ₍they Changed and Drove us Quite out of sight
of Land—which we hawld our wind having a set
of Sails in they Boat accordingly they next Day438
we Made Close into they land But they Surf rung
so very hard we Cd not attempt to land but
kept along shore but Making no harbour or
Creek for nere three weeks we were much Distressd
for water and wood—accordly perceving
they Surf to abate Two of our Men Swam on shor
thinking to get some Water439 But being afraid
of they natives which they see in numbers
they returnd without any, But a little wood
which threw into they water which we took
           up
                              We

We put over on the other Side of the Bay
expecting to meet with a Convenient Harbour
we found a little River which with great
Difficulty we got up our Boat being very leaky
at that Time that it was with great difficulty
we could keep her above Water — wen we
Landed & hauled her up putting some Soap
in the Seams which Answered very well
— at this Place we coud get no Shell Fish or
Fish of any kind in this Bay here we stopped
two Days & two Nights — then we left this
Place & went down the Bay about 20 Miles
expecting to meet with a Harbor to get some
Refreshment but coud see none nor the End
of the Bay the Wind being favourable we Tack'd
about & put to sea the Land here seemd to be
much the same as at Botany Bay ——

9

We put over on the other side of the Bay
    pec
  excepting to meet with a Convenient Harbour
we found a little River which with great
difficulty we got up our Boat being very leaky
at that Time that it was with great difficulty
we Could keep her above Water—were we
Landed & hauled her up putting some Soap
in the Seams which Answered very well
—at this Place we Cou'd get no Shell Fish or
Fish of any kind in this Bay here we stopped
two Days & two Nights—then we left this Bay
Place[440] & went down the Bay about 20 Miles
expecting to meet with a Harbor to get some
Refreshment—but cou'd see none nor the End
of the Bay the Wind being favourable we Tack'd
about & put to sea the Land here seem'd to be
                                        accordingly
much the same as at Botany Bay   up

accordingly we up grapling so stood to the
Northward but our Boat being very Deep we
were Oblidged to trow all our Cloothing over
board they Better to lighten our Boat as the
Sea Breaking over us Quite Eayse ——
that Night we ran into an Open Bay & Could
see no Place to Land at the Surf running that
we were Afraid of Staving our Boat to
Pieces. We Came to a Grapling in that Bay
the same Night about 2 oClock in the
Morn? our Grapling Broke & we were drove
in the Middle of the Surf expecting every Moment
that our Boat wou'd be Staved to Pieces &
every Soul Perish but as God wou'd have we
Got our Boat save on Shore without any
Loss or Damage excepting one Oar we Hauld
our Boat up & there remaind two Days & 2 Nights

10

accordingly we up grappling so stood to they
Northward but our Boat being very Deep we
were Oblidged to trow all our Cloathing over
Board they Better to lighten our Boat as they
Sea Breaking over us Quite Rapid——
that Night we Ran into an Open Bay[441] & Could
see no Place to Land at the Surf Running that
we were Afraid of Staving our Boat to
Pieces—We Came to a Grapling in that Bay
the same Night about 2 oClock in the
Morn^g[442] our Grapling Broke & we were drove
in the Middle of the ^Surf Expecting every Moment
that our Boat wou'd be Staved to Pieces &
every Soul Perish but as God wou'd have we
Got our Boat save on Shore without any
Loss or Damage excepting one Oar we Hauld
our Boat up & there Remain two days & 2 Nights[443]

                                                                               there

there we Kindled a Fire with great Difficulty every thing that we had being very Wet — we Got Plenty of Shell Fish there & Fresh Water the Natives Came down in great Numbers we Discharged a Musquet over their Heads & they dispersed immediately & we saw no more of them we put our things in the Boat & with great Difficulty we Got out to Sea for 2 or 3 Days we had very Bad Weather our Boat Shipping many heavy Seas, so that One Man was always Employed in Bailing out the Water to keep her up — the next Place we made was White Bay being in Latt.d 27=00. we Ran down that Bay 2 or 3 Leagues before we Cou.d see a convenient Place to Land the Surf Running very High we saw two Women & 2 Children with a Fire brand

11

there we Kindled a Fire with great Difficulty
every thing that we had being very Wet—we
Got Plenty of Shell Fish there & Fresh Water
the Natives Came down in great Numbers we
Discharged a Musquet over their Heads & they
dispersed immediately & we saw no more of them
we put our things in the Boat & with great
Difficulty we Got out to Sea for 2 or 3 Days
we had very Bad Weather our Boat Shipping
many heavy Seas, so that One Man was always
Employed in Bailing out the Water to keep her
up—the next Place we made was White Bay[444]
being in Latt^d 27^d:00 we ran down that Bay
2 or 3 Leagues before we Cou'd see a convenient
Place to Land the Surf Running very High
we saw two Women & 2 Children with a Fire
                                                              brand

Brand in their Hands¹² at this Place we Landed the two Women being Frightened Ran away but we made Signs that we wanted a Light which they Gave us Crying at the same Time in their Way we took our things out of the Boat & put them in two Hutts which was there — the next Morn.ᵍ about 11 oClock a great Number of the Natives Came towards us — as soon as we saw we went to meet them & Fired a Musquet over their Heads as soon as they Heard the Report they Ran into the Woods & we saw no more of them the Natives there is Quite Naked — there we Stopped two Days & two Nights, the Surf Running so very High that we were in great Danger of Staving y.ᵉ Boat

12

Brand in their Hands at this Place we Landed
the two Women being Frightened Ran
away but we made Signs that we wanted
a Light which they Gave us Crying at the
same Time in their Way we took our things
out of the Boat & put them in two Huts
which was there—the next Morn^g about 11 oClock[445]
a great Number of the Natives Came towards
us—as soon as we saw we went to meet them
& Fired a Musquet over their Heads as soon as
they Heard the Report they Ran into the Woods
& we saw no more of them the Natives[446] there
is Quite Naked—there we Stopped two days
& two Nights;[447] the Surf Running so very High
that we were in great Danger of Staving ye Boat

              that

that Night we were drove out to Sea by a heavy Gale of Wind & Current, expecting every Moment to go to the Bottom next Morn.g saw no Land the Sea running Mountains high we were Under a Close reeft Mainsail & kept so untill Night & then came too under a Droge all the Night with her Head to the Sea thinking every Moment to be the Last the Sea Coming in so heavy upon us every now & then that two Hands was Obliged to keep Bailing out & it rained very hard all that Night the next Morn.g we took our Droge in but Could see no Land but Hawling towards the Land to make it as soon as possible the Gale of Wind Still Continuing we kept on under a Close reeft Main=sail but coud make no Land all that Day I will Leave you to Consider what Distress we must be in the Woman & the two little Babies was in a bad Condition

13

that Night[448] we ˄drove out to Sea by a heavy Gale
of Wind & Current, expecting every Moment to go to
the Bottom next Morn^g[449] saw no Land the Sea
running Mountains high we were Under a Close
Reeft Mainsail[450] & kept so untill Night[451] & then
came too under a Droge[452] all the Night with her
Head to the sea thinking every Moment to be
the Last the sea Coming in so heavy upon us every
now & then that two Hands was Obliged to keep
Bailing out & it Rained very hard all that Night
the next Morn^g[453] we took our Droge in but Could see
no Land but Hawling towards the Land to make
it as soon as possible the Gale of Wind still
Continuing we kept on under a Close Reeft Mainsail
but cou'd make no Land all that Day—I will
Leave you to Consider what distress we must be in
the Woman & the two little Babies was in a bad
                                                  Condition

(insertion above "we": were)

Condition every thing being so Wet that we Could by no Means light a Fire we had nothing to Eat except a little raw rice at Night we Came too under a Droge as we did the Night before the next Morn.g we took in our Droge & kept to the North.wd on purpose to make the Land about 8 oClock we made Land which proved to be a little Island about 30 Leagues from the Main the Surf running so very High we were rather fearful of going in for fear of Staving our Boat but we Concluded amongst Ourselves that we might as well Venture in there as to keep out to Sea seeing no Probability that if we kept out to Sea that we should every Soul Perish — All round this Island there was nothing but reefs but a little sandy Beach which we got in safe without much Damage & hauld our Boat up out

14

Condition every thing being so Wet that we Cou'd by no Means light a Fire we had nothing to Eat except a little Raw Rice at Night[454] we Came too under a Droge as we did the Night before the next Morn^g[455] we took in our Droge & kept to the North^wd on purpose to make the Land about 8 oClock we made Land which proved to be a little Island about 30 Leagues from the Main[456] the Surf Running so very High we were rather fearful of going in for fear of Staving our Boat but we Concluded amongst Ourselves that we might as well Venture in there as to keep out to Sea seeing no Probability that if we kept out to Sea that we shou'd every Soul Perish—All Round this Island there was nothing but Reefs but a little sandy Beach which we got in safe without much Damage & haul'd our Boat up out

15

of the ^(ways of the) Surf we got all our things out of the Boat
then we Went to get a Fire which with great
Difficulty we got a Fire which being almost
Starving we put on a little Rice for to Cook when
we went to this Island we had but one Gallon of
fresh Water for there was not a Drop of fresh
Water to be had on this Island the Island was
about one Mile in Circumference after the Tide
fell we went to Look for some Shell fish but
found a great Quantity of very fine Large Tur
-tles which was left upon the Reef which ^(we) turned
five of them & hawled them upon the Beach
this Reef Runs about a Mile & half out in the Sea
& Intirely Dry when low Water we took & killed
One of the Turtles & had a Noble Meal this Night
it rain'd very Hard when we Spread our Mainsail
& filled our ^(two) Breakers full of Water ——

15

  ways of the
of the ^ Surf we got all our things out of the Boat
then we Went to get a Fire which with great
Difficulty we got a Fire which being almost
Starving we put on a little Rice for to Cook when
we went to this Island we had but one Gallon of
fresh Water for there was not a drop of fresh
Water to be had on this Island the Island was
about one Mile in Circumference after the Tide
fell we went to Look for some Shell Fish but
found a great Quantity of very fine Large Turtles[457]
           we
which was left upon the Reef which ^ turned
five of them & hawled them upon the Beach
this Reef Runs about a Mile & half out in the Sea
& Intirely Dry when low Water we took & killed
One of the Turtles & had a Noble Meal this Night[458]
it rain'd very Hard when we Spread our Mainsail
    two
& filled our ^ Breakers[459] full of Water—

               We

We staid on this Island six Days during that Time
we Killed twelve Turtles & some of it we Sook &
Dry'd over the Fire to take to Sea with us
It seemed to us that there had never been any Natives
on this Island there is a kind of Fruit grows like
unto a Bell pepper which seemed to Taste very well
there was a great Quantity of Fowls which stayed
at Night in Holes in the ground we Could not think
of taking any live Turtles with us because our
Boat would not admit of it we Paid the Seams
of our Boat all over with Soap before we put
to Sea at the End of the Six Days we Launched
our Boat & put to Sea at 8 oClock in the Morn.^t
& Steered to the Northward; this Island was in
Lat: 26:27 we made the main Land in the
Evening we passed a great Number of Small
Islands which we put into a great many of them
exceeding

[169–194]

16

We staid on this Island six days during that Time
we Killed twelve Turtles & some of it we Took &
Dry'd over the Fire to take to Sea with us
It seemed to us that there had never been any Natives
on this Island there is a kind of Fruit grows like
unto a Bell pepper which seemed to Taste very well[460]
there was a great Quantity of Fowls which stayed
at Night in Holes in the ground[461] we Could not think
of taking any live Turtles with us because our
Boat wou'd not admit of it we Paid the Seams
of our Boat[462] all over with Soap before we put
to Sea at the End of the Six Days we Launched
our Boat & put to sea at 8 oClock in the Morn^g[463]
& Steered to the Northward: this Island was in
Lat: 26^d : 27^m we made the main Land in the
Evening we passed a great Number of Small
Islands[464] which we put into a great many of them

                                                expecting

expecting to find some Turtle but never found
any in any of the Islands we put into Afterwards
we found a great Quantity of Shell Fish but
none of them very fit to Eat but being very Hungred
we were Glad to Eat them & Thank God for it if it
had not been for the Shell Fish & the little Turtle that
we had we must have Starved very seldom put into
any Place but found plenty of Fresh Water but nothing
we could find bit to Eat when we Came to the Gulf of
Carpentara which is in Latt: 10:11 we ran down
the Gulf Nine or Ten Miles we saw several small
Islands on which we saw several of the Natives in
two Canoes landing on One of the small Islands
we steered down towards them as soon as they
saw us they sent their two Canoes round to the
Back of the Island with one Man in each of them
when we Came down to them they seemed to stand

17

[169–195]

expecting to find some Turtle but never found
any in any of the Islands we put into Afterwards
we found a great Quantity of Shell Fish but
none of them ^very^ fit to Eat but being very Hungred
we were Glad to Eat them & Thank God for it if it
had not been for the Shell Fish & the little Turtle that
we had we must have Starved very seldom put into
any Place but found plenty of Fresh Water but nothing
We could find ^fit^ to Eat when we Came to the Gulf of
Carpentaria which is in Latt: $10^d : 11^m$ we Ran down
the Gulf Nine or Ten Miles we saw Several small
Islands on which we saw several of the Natives in
two Canoes landing on One of the small Islands[465]
we steered down towards them as soon as they
saw us they sent their two Canoes[466] Round to the
Back of the Island with one Man in each of them
when we Came down to them they seemed to stand
in

in a posture of Defence against us we fired a Musquet over them and immediately they began firing their Bows & Arrows at us we immediately hoisted up our Sails & rowed away from them but as God woud have it none of their Arrows came into the Boat but Dropped along Side we Could not get Hold of any of them but they seemed to be about Eighteen Inches long the Natives seemed to be very Stout & fat & Blacker they were in other Parts we seen before there was One which we took to be the Chief with some Shells Around his Shoulders we rowed down a little farther down the Gulf & landed upon the Main for to get some Water we found plenty of fresh Water we saw a small Town of Huts about 20 of them just by were the fresh Water was there was none of the Inhabitants in their Huts or about them that we Could see their Huts was large enough for Six or seven

18

in a posture of Defence against us we fired a Musquet
over them and immediately they began Firing their
Bows & Arrows at us we immediately hoisted up our
Sails & Rowed away from them but as God wou'd
have it none of their Arrows ~~reached~~ Came into the the Boat
but dropped along side we Could not get Hold
of any of them but they seemed to be about Eighteen
Inches long the Natives seemed to be very Stout & fat
& Blacker they were in other Parts we seen before
there was One which we took to be the Chief with some
Shells Around his Shoulders we Rowed down a little
farther down the Gulf & landed upon the Main
for to get some Water we found plenty of fresh
Water we saw a small Town of Huts about 20 of
them just by were the fresh Water was there was
none of the Inhabitants in their Huts or about them
that we Could see their Huts was large enough for Six or
seven

17

of them to Stand upright in they were made of Bark
& Covered Over with Grass we filled our 2 Breakers
with fresh Water & Came on Board of our Boat
again for we were Afraid of Staying on Shore for
fear of the Natives we went three or four Miles
from the Shore & Dropt our Killock & there Stopped
all Night the next Morn.^g we was Determined to Go
to the same Place to recruit our Water but as we were
making to the Shore we saw two very large Canoes
coming towards us we did not know what to do
for we were Afraid to meet them there seemed to us
to be 30 or 40 Men in each Canoe they had Sails
in their Canoes seemed to made of Matting one of
their Canoes was a Head of the others a little Way
Stopt untill the other Came up & then she Hoisted
her Sails & made after us as soon as we saw that
we tack'd about with Salt Water we had Determined to

19

seven
of them to Stand upright in they were made of Bark
& Covered Over with Grass we filled our 2 Breakers
with fresh Water & Came on Board of our Boat
again for we were Afraid of Staying on Shore for
fear of the Natives we went three or four Miles
from the Shore & Dropt our Killock[467] & there Stopped
all Night the next Morn^g we was determined to Go
to the same Place to Recruit our Water but as we were
making to the Shore we saw two very large Canoes
coming towards us we did not know what to do
for we were Afraid to meet them there seemed to us
to be 30 or 40 Men in each Canoe they had Sails
in their Canoes seemed to made of Matting one of
their Canoes was a Head of the others a little Way
Stopt untill the other Came up & then she Hoisted
her Sails & made after us as soon as we saw that
we Tack'd about with ^what Water we had—Determined
to

Thos. Chapman No. 11 George
Street Foster Lane
Cheapside —

N.B Lett me now by
the bearer if you had
a pair of Wheels of
Richhold of Melford
I paid him half what
that came to the 31st
of March 1791. which
was £10.11 — —

Thos Chapman[468] N° 11 George
Street Foster Lane
Cheapside.[469]
N.B Lett me now by
the bearer if you had
a pair of Wheels of
Richhold of Melford[470]
I paid him half what
that came to the 31st
of March 1791 which was £1 0^s 11^d

20

to Cross the Gulf which was about five Hundred Miles
Across which as God woud have it we But then them
they followed us untill we Lost sight of them.
we having but little fresh Water & no Wood to make
a Fire with but in four Days & a half we made
the other Side of the Gulf we put on Shore to look
for some fresh Water but Coud find none at that
Place but we kept along Shore untill the Even.g
we saw a little small river which we made to
& Got plenty of Fresh Water we put of to Sea
the same Night we saw no more Land untill
we Came into the Lattitude of North End
of the Island we hauled up to make the Land to
get some fresh Water but saw no Land but a
heavy Swell running which had liked to have
Swallowed us up then we Concluded as the best Way
to Shape our Course for the Island of Timor with what
little Water we had which we made it in 36 Hours after we

20

to Cross the Gulf[471] which was about five Hundred Miles
Across[472] which as God wou'd have it we Out Run them
they followed us untill we Lost sight of them
we having but little fresh Water & no Wood to make
a Fire with but in four days & a half we made
the other side of the Gulf we put on Shore[473] to look
for some fresh Water but Cou'd find none at that
Place but we kept along Shore untill the Even^g
we saw a little small River which we made to
& Got plenty of Fresh Water we put of to Sea[474]
the same Night we saw no more Land untill
we Came into ~~No~~ the Lattitude of North End
of the Island[475] we hawled up to make the Land to
get some fresh Water but saw no Land but a
heavy Swell Running which had liked to have
swallowed us up then we Concluded as the best Way
to Shape our Course for the Island of Timor with what
little Water we had which we made it in 36 Hours after we

[169–198ᵛ]

Mr Jackson[476] No. 10 Bishop head
head Court[477]

which we run along the Island of Timor till we came to the Dutch Settlement where we went on Shore to the Governor house where he behaved extremely well to us filled our Bellies & Cloathed Double with every that was wore on the Island which we rem'd every happy at our work for two Months till W'm Bryant had words with his wife went and Informed against himself wife & children and all of us which we was immediately taken Prisoners and was put into the Castle we were strictly Examined after been Examined we was allowed to Go out of the Castle 2 at a Time for one Day on the Next Day 2 more & Sow. Continued till Captain Edwards who had been on search of the Bounty Pirates which had taken some of the Pirates at Otaheite which he lost the Pandora frigate betwixt New Guinea & New Holland which he made Island of Timor in the Pinnace Two yawls and his Long boat & 120 hands what was saved

which

21

Which we run a long the Island of Timor Till we came to
the Dutch Settlement[478] where we went on Shore to the Governor
house[479] where he behaved extremely well to us filld our
Bellies & Cloathed Double with every that was wore on the
Island which we rem^d very happy at our work for two
Months till Wm Bryant had words with his wife
went and Informed against himself wife & Children
and all of us which we was immediately taken
Prisoners and was put into the Castle[480] we were strictly
Examined after been Examined we was allowed to
Go out of the Castle 2 at a time for one Day
and the Next Day 2 more & So we Continued till
Captain Edwards[481] who had been on search of the
Bounty Pirates which had taken some of the
Pirates at Otaheite[482] which he lost the Pandour[483]
frigate betwixt New Guinea & New Holland[484]
which he made Island of Timor in the Pinnace[485]
Two yawls[486] and his Long boat & 120 hands which
was saved[487]

                                                           which

which Captain Edwards Came to us to know what we were which we told him we was Convicts and had made our Escape from Botany Bay which he told us we was his prisoners and put us on board the Vam bang Dutch Companys Ship & put us Both Legs in Irons Called the ~~bilbos~~ bilboes which we was Conveyed to Bretava which we was taken aut of the Vam bang & put on board a Dutch Guardship in Irons again there we lost the Child 6 Days after the father of the Child was taken Bad & Died which was both buried at Bretava 6 weeks after we was put on 3 Different Ships bound to the Cape of Good hope which we was Both on tho before we reach'd the Cape when we Came there the Gorgon man of war which had brought the marines from Botany Bay which we was put on board of Gorgon which we was known well by all the marine officers which

22

[169–200]

which Captain Edwards Came to us to know what
we were which we told him we was Convicts and
had made our Escape from Botany Bay which
he told us we was his prisoners and put us on board
the Yam bang[488] Dutch Companys Ship & put us
Both Legs in Irons Called the ~~biloes~~ bilboes[489]
which we was Conveyed to bretava[490] which we
was taken out of the Yam bang & put on board
a Dutch Guardship in Irons again there we
Lost the Child[491] 6 Days after the father of the
Child was taken Bad & Died[492] which was both
buried at Bretava 6 weeks after we was put
on 3 Different Ships bound to the Cape of
Good hope[493] which we was 3 Months before we
Reachd the Cape when we Came there the Gorgon[494]
man of war which had brought the marines
from Botany Bay which we was put on board
of Gorgon which we was known well by all the
marine officers[495]

which

which was all glad that we had not perished
at sea which was brought home to England
in the Gorgon we was Brought a Shore
at Purfleet and from there Conveyed by the
Constables to Bowst office London and was
taken before Justice Bond and was fully committed
to Newgate 1 W:m Moatton Navigator
of the Boat Died James Cox Died Sam:l
Sam:l Burd Died W:m Bryant Died
A Boy of 12 months old Died
A Little Girl 3 y:rs and a Quarter old Died
the mother of the 2 Children Mary Brian
alive Jame Martin alive W:m Allen alive
John Broom alive Nath:l Lilley alive

23

which was all Glad that we had not perished
   we were
at sea ~~which was~~ brought home to England
in the Gorgon we was Brought a shore
at Purfleet and from there Conveyed by the
Constables to Bow st office London and was
taken before Justice Bond[496] and was fully committed
to Newgate. Wm Moatton Navigatotor[497]
of the Boat Died James Cox[498] Died ~~Saml~~
Saml Burd[499] Died Wm Bryant[500] Died
A Boy of 12 months old[501] Died
A little Girl 3 y^{rs} and a Quarter old[502] Died
the mother of the 2 Children Mary Brion[503]
alive James Martin[504] alive Wm Allen[505] alive
John Broom[506] alive Nathl Lilly[507] alive

Fair copy of *Memorandoms* by James Martin

Memorandoms by James Martin.

I James Martin being Convicted at the City of Exeter in the County of Devonshire being found guilty of Stealing lb ½ of old Lead & L[b] ½ of old Iron the Property of Lord Courtney of Powderham Castle near Exeter — Received Sentence to be Transported to Botany Bay for 7 Years — Returned from the Bar to Exeter Goal and there remained 2 months. from thence sent on Board the Dunkirk there remained 10 months from thence put on board the Charlotte Transport then bound to Botany Bay — March 12th 1787. Sailed round to Spithead there remained to the 13 of May — then sailed in Company with 10 sail for Botany Bay under the Command of Governor Philips. Made the Peek of Tenereef 5th of June, there remained 7 days, then sailed for the Island of Rio de Janeira, being 8 Weeks on our Passage remained there 1 Month, then sailed for the Cape of Good Hope being 8 Weeks and 3 days on our passage, then sailed for Botany Bay being 10 Weeks on our passage. — Came to Anchor in Port Jackson — sent on shore in two days — the Convicts being sent on shore began to work on Governments account on being landed we were Encamped and formed into squads of six in a tent — after being Encamped some of us were sent to clear the Ground others to build Huts — I remained on the Island from January 1788 till March 1791 — on the 28th of March I made my Escape in Company with 7 Men, one Woman and two Children in an open six oared Boat, having of provisions on board one hundred Weight of flower, one Cwt. of Rice, 14 lb. of Pork, and about

Memorandoms by James Martin.

   I James Martin being Convicted at the City of Exeter in the County of Devonshire being found guilty of Stealing 16^{lb} ½ of old Lead & 4^{lb} ½ of old Iron[407] the Property of Lord Courtney[408] Powderham Castle near Exeter[409]—Received Sentence to be Transported to Botany Bay[410] for 7 Years—Returned from the Bar to Exeter Goal and there remained 2 Months—from thence sent on Board the Dunkirk[411] there remained 10 Months from thence put on board the Charlotte Transport[412] then bound to Botany Bay—March 12th: 1787.[413] Sailed round to Spithead there remained to the 13 of May—then sailed in Company with 10 Sail[414] for Botany Bay under the Command of Governor Philips.[415] Made the Peek of Tenereef 5th of June,[416] there remained 7 days, then sailed for the Island of Rio de Janeira,[417] being 8 Weeks on our Passage remained there 1 Month, then sailed for the Cape of Good Hope being 8 Weeks and 3 days on our passage,[418] then sailed for Botany Bay being 10 Weeks on our passage.[419]—Came to Anchor in Port Jackson—sent on shore in two days—the Convicts being sent on shore began to work on Government's account—[420] on being landed we were Encamped and formed into squads of size in a tent—after being Encamped some of us were sent to clear the Ground others to build Huts[421]—I remained on the Island[422] from January 1788 till March 1791—on the 28th of March I made my Escape in Company with 7 Men, one Woman and two Children in an open six oared Boat, having of provisons on board one hundred Weight[423] of flower, one Cwt. of Rice, 14lb. of Pork, and

                                                about

about 8 gallons of water; having a Compass Quadrant & Chart After Sailing 2 days we reached a little Creek, about 2 Degrees to the Northward of Port Jackson, there we found a quantity of fine burning Coal, we remained there 2 Nights & 1 day and found a great many Cabbage trees some of which we cut down and procured the Cabbage. The Natives came down to whom we gave some Cloaths and other articles, and they went away very well satisfied. The Land appeared much better than at Sidney Cove, here we got a great many fishes which were very refreshing to us — After our Stay of two Nights and one day we continued our Voyage to the Northward after two days sail we made a very fine harbour seeming to run up the Country for many Miles and very commodious for the Anchorage of Shipping; here we found plenty of fresh water, we hauled our boat ashore to repair her bottom with some Bees wax and Rosin which we had a small quantity of. But on the same Night we were drove off by the Natives, which meant to destroy us, we launched our boat and rode off in the stream quite out of reach of them. That being Sunday, Monday we were off in the Stream we rowed lower down, thinking to land some miles below — on Monday morning we attempted to land, and we found a place convenient for to repair our boat, we accordingly put some of our things part being ashore when the Natives came in great numbers armed with Spears and Shields &c. we found ourselves in parts, one party of us made towards them to pacify them by signes, but they took not the least notice accordingly we fired a Musket thinking to affright them but they paid no attention to it — on perceiving them

rush

about 8 gallons of water; having a Compass Quadrant & Chart.[424]
After Sailing 2 days we reached a little Creek,[425] about 2 Degrees
to the Northward of Port Jackson,[426] there we found a quantity
of fine burning Coal, we remained there 2 Nights & 1 day
and found a great many Cabbage trees some of which we
cut down and procured the Cabbage.[427] The Natives came
down to whom we gave some Cloaths and other articles, and
they went away very well satisfied.[428] The Land appeared much
better than at Sidney Cove, here we got a great many fishes
which were very refreshing to us—After our Stay of two Nights
and one day we continued our Voyage to the Northward[429] after
two days sail[430] we made a very fine harbour seeming to run
up the Country for many Miles and very commodious for
the Anchorage of Shipping;[431] here we found plenty of fresh
water, we hawled our boat a shore to repair her bottom with
some Bees-wax and Resin which we had a small quantity
of. But on the same Night we were drove off by the Natives,[432]
which meant to destroy us, we launched our boat and rode
off in the stream quite out of reach of them. That being
Sunday,[433] Monday[434] we were off in the Stream we rowed lower
down, thinking to land some Miles below—on Monday
morning we attempted to land, and we found a place convenient
for to repair our boat, we accordingly put some of
our things part being ashore when the Natives came in
great numbers armed with Spears and Shields & c. we form'd
ourselves in parts, one party of us made towards them to
pacify them by signes, but they took not the least notice accordingly
we fired a Musket thinking to affright them
but they paid no attention to it—on perceiving them
                                                              rush

rush forwards we were forced to take to our boat and get out of their reach as fast as we could, and what to do we could not tell, but consulting together we were determined to row up the harbour which accordingly we did 9 or 10 Miles till we made a little white sandy Island in the middle of the harbour which we landed upon and hawled up our boat and repaired her bottom with what materials we had, during our stay of 2 days we had no interruption from the Natives; then we rowed off to the main where we took in fresh water and a few cabbage trees and then put out to sea — the natives here are quite naked, of a copper colour, short hair, they have canoes made of bark — then we proceeded to the northward, having a leading breze from the S.W — but that night the wind changed and drove us out of sight of land — when we hawled our wind having a set of sails in the boat accordingly the next day we made close into land, but the Surf running very hard we could not attempt to land but kept along shore. but making no harbour or creek for near 3 Weeks we were very much distressed for water & wood; but perceiving the Surf to abate two of our men swam ashore to get some water, but being afraid of the Natives which they saw in numbers they returned without any but a little wood which they threw into the water and we took up —
We put over on the other side of the bay expecting to meet with a convenient harbour we found a little river which with great difficulty we got up our boat being very leaky at that time that is was with great diffuulty we could keep her above Water — were we landed & hawled her up putting some soap in the Seams which answered very well — at this place we could get no fish of any kind here we stopped two days and two nights then we left this place and went farther down the bay about 20 miles expecting to meet with a harbour to get some Refreshment but could not

see

rush forwards we were forced to take to our boat and get out of their
reach as fast as we could, and what to do we could not tell, but consulting
together we were determined to row up the harbour which accordingly
we did 9 or 10 Miles till we made a little white sandy Island in the
middle of the harbour[435] which we landed upon and hawled up our boat
and repaired her bottom with what materials we had: during our
stay of 2 days we had no interruption from the Natives; then we rowed
off to the main[436] where we took in fresh water and a few Cabbage trees
and then put out to sea—the natives here are quite naked, of a copper
colour shock hair, they have Canoes made of bark—then we proceeded
to the northward, having a leading breze from the S:W—but that
night[437] the wind changed and drove us out of sight of land—when
we hawled our wind having a set of Sails in the boat accordingly the
next day[438] we made close into land, but the Surf running very hard
we could not attempt to land but kept along Shore but making
no harbour or creek for near 3 Weeks we were very much distressed
for water & wood: but perceiving the Surf to abate two of our men
swam ashore to get some water,[439] but being afraid of the Natives
which they saw in numbers they returned without any but a
little wood which they threw into the water and we took it up—
We put over on the other side of the bay expecting to meet with
a convenient harbour we found a littler river which with great difficulty
we got up our boat being very leaky at that time that is was
with great difficulty we could keep her above Water—were we
landed & hawled her up putting some Soap in the Seams which
answered very well—at this place we could get no fish of any
kind here we stopped two days and two nights then we left this
place[440] and went ~~farther~~ down the bay about 20 miles expecting
to meet with a harbour to get some Refreshment but could not

see

see any nor the end of the bay the wind being favourable we tacked about and put to Sea the land here seemed to be much the same as at Botany Bay. Acordingly we up Grapling and stood to the Northward but our boat being very deep we were obleiged to throw all our Cloathing overboard the better to lighten our boat as the Sea broke over us quite rapid.— that night we ran into an open Bay but could see no place to land as the Surf ran so that we were afraid of staving our boat to pieces — we came to a Grapling in the bay the same night but about 2 oClock in the morning our Grapling broke and we were drove in the middle of the Surf expecting every moment that our boat would be staved to pieces and every Soul perish but as God would have it we got our boat safe on shore without any loss or damage excepting an oar we hauled our boat up and there remained 2 days & 2 Nights there we kindled a fire with great difficulty every thing being very wet, we got plenty of Shell fish & fresh water the natives came down in great numbers we discharg'd a Musket over their heads, they dispersed immediately and we saw no more of them we put our things in the boat and with great difficulty we put out to Sea for 2 or 3 days we had very bad weather our boat shipping many heavy Seas, so that one man was always employed in bailing out the water to keep her up — the next place we made was White Bay being in Latitutde 27.00 we run down that bay 2 or 3 leagues before we could see a convenient place to land the Surf running very high we saw two Women & two Children with a fire brand in their hand at this place we landed the two women being frightened ran away but we made Signs that we wanted a light which they gave us expiring at the same time in their way we took our things out of the boat and put them in two huts which was there the next morning about 11 oClock a great number of the natives came towards us as soon as we saw them we went to meet them and fired a musket

over

see any nor the end of the bay the wind being favourable we tacked
about and put to Sea the land here seemed to be much the same as
at Botany Bay. Accordingly we up Grapling and stood to the Northward
but our boat being very deep we were obliged to throw all our
Cloathing overboard the better to lighten our boat as the Sea broke
over us quite rapid—that night we ran into an open Bay[441] but
could see no place to land as the Surf ran so that we were afraid of staving
our boat to pieces—we came to a Grapling in the bay the same
night, but about 2 oClock in the morning[442] our Grapling broke and
we were drove in the middle of the Surf expecting every moment
that our boat would be staved to pieces and every Soul perish but as
God would have it we got our boat safe on shore without any loss or
damage excepting an oar we hawled our boat up and there remained
2 days & 2 Nights[443]—there we kindled a fire with great
difficulty every thing being very wet, we got plenty of Shell fish &
fresh water the natives came down in great numbers we discharg'd
a Musket over their heads, they dispersed immediately and we
saw no more of them we put our things in the boat and with
great difficulty we put out to Sea for 2 or 3 days we had very bad
weather our boat shipping many heavy Seas, so that one man
was always employed in bailing out the water to keep her up—the
next place we made was White Bay[444] being in Latitude 27^d. 00 we
ran down that bay 2 or 3 Leagues before we could see a convenient
place to land the Surf running very high we saw two Women &
two Children with a fire brand in their hand at this place we
landed the two women being frightened ran away but we made
Signs that we wanted a light which they gave us crying at the
same time in their way we took our things out of the boat and
put them in two huts which was there—the next morning about
11 oClock[445] a great number of the Natives came towards us as soon
as we saw them we went to meet them and fired a musket

over

over their heads as soon as they heard the report they ran into the woods and we saw no more of them, the natives are quite naked there we stopped 2 days & 2 nights, the Surf running so very high that we were in great danger of staving the boat; that night we were drove out to Sea by a heavy gale of wind & current expecting every moment to go to the bottom next morning saw no land the Sea running mountains high we were under a close reeft mainsail and kept so untill night then came to under a droge all the night with her head to the Sea thinking every moment to be the last the Sea coming in so heavy upon us every now and then that two hands were obliged to keep bailing out it rained very hard all that night the next morning we took our droge in but could not see any land but hawling towards the land to make it as soon as possible the Gale of wind still continuing we keep on under a close reeft mainsail but could not make land all that day — I will leave you to consider what distress we must be in the Woman and the two little babies were in a bad condition every thing being so wet that we could by no means light a fire we had nothing to eat except a little raw Rice at night we came to under a droge as we did the night before the next morning we took in our droge and kept to the northward on purpose to make the land about 8 o'clock we made the land which proved to be a small Island about 30 Leagues from the main the Surf running so very high we were rather fearful of going in for fear of staving our boat but we concluded amongst ourselves that we might as well venture in there as to keep out to Sea seeing no probability but that if we kept out to Sea we should every Soul perish — All round this Island there was nothing but reefs and a

little

over their heads as soon as they heard the report they ran into the woods
and we saw no more of them, the natives[446] are quite naked there we stopped
2 days & 2 nights,[447] the Surf running so very high that we were in great
danger of staving the boat; that night[448] we were drove out to Sea by a
heavy gale of wind & current expecting every moment to go to the
bottom next morning[449] saw no land the Sea running mountains high
we were under close reeft Mainsail[450] and kept so untill night[451] then
came to under a droge[452] all the night with her head to the Sea thinking
every moment to be the last the Sea coming in so heavy upon
us every now and then that two hands were obliged to keep bailing
out it rained very hard all that night the next morning[453]
we took our droge in but could not see any land but hawling towards
the land to make it as soon as possible the Gale of wind
still continuing we keep on under a close reeft Mainsail but
could not make land all that day—I will leave you to consider
what distress we must be in the Woman and the two little babies
were in a bad Condition every thing being so wet that we could
by no means light a fire we had nothing to eat except a little
raw Rice at night[454] we came to under a droge as we did the
night before the next morning[455] we took in our droge and
kept to the northward on purpose to make the land about
8 oClock we made ~~the~~ land which proved to be a small
Island about 30 Leagues from the main[456] the Surf running
so very high we were rather fearful of going in for fear of staving
our boat but we concluded amongst ourselves that we might as
well venture in there as to keep out to Sea seeing no probability
but that if we kept out to Sea we should every Soul perish—
All round this Island there was nothing but reefs and a

little

little sandy beach which we got in safe without much damage and hawled our boat up out of ~~out~~ of the way of the surf and got all our things out of the boat then we went to make a fire which with great difficulty we did & being almost starving we put on a little rice to cook when we landed on this Island we had but one Gallon of fresh water for there was not a drop to be had on this Island the Island was about 1 mile in Circumference after the tide fell we went to look for some shell fish but found a great quantity of very fine large Turtles which ~~were~~ left upon the reef, we turned 5 of them and hawled them upon the beach this reef runs about a mile and a half out in the Sea & is entirely dry when low water we killed one of the Turtles and had a noble meal that night it rained very hard when we spread our mainsail & filled our two Breakers full of water. We staid on the Island 6 days during that time we killed 12 Turtles and some of them we took and dried over the Fire to take to Sea with us. It seemed to us that there had never been any natives on this Island there was a kind of fruit which grew like a bell pepper and tasted very well there was a great quantity of fowls which stayed at night in holes in the ground we could not think of taking any live Turtles with us because our boat would not admit of it we paid the seams of our boat all over with soap before we put to Sea at the end of the 6 days we launched our boat & put to sea at 8 O'Clock in the morning and steered to the northward; this Island was in Latitude 26°-27" we made the main land in the Evening. we passed a great number of small Islands and put into a great many of them expecting to find some Turtles but never found any in any of the Islands we put into afterwards we found a great quantity of shellfish but none of them very fit to eat but being

very

little sandy beach which we got in safe without much damage and
hawled our boat up out of ~~out of~~ the way of the surf and got all our
things out of the boat then we went to make a fire which with great
difficulty we did & being almost starving we put on a little rice to
cook when we landed on this Island we had but one Gallon of fresh
water for there was not a drop to be had on this Island the Island
was about 1 mile in Circumference after the tide fell we went to look
for some shell fish but found a great quantity of very fine large
Turtles[457] which ~~was~~ were left upon the reef, we turned 5 of them and
hawled them upon the beach this reef runs about a mile and a
half out in the Sea & is entirely dry when low water we killed
one of the Turtles and had a noble meal that night[458] it rained
very hard when we spread our mainsail & filled our two
Breakers[459] full of water. We staid on the Island 6 days during
that time we killed 12 Turtles and some of them we took
and dried over the Fire to take to Sea with us—It seemed
to us that there had never been any natives on this Island
there was a kind of fruit which grew like a bell pepper and
tasted very well[460] there was a great quantity of fowls which
stayed at night in holes in the ground[461] we could not think
of taking any live Turtles with us because our boat would not
admit of it we paid the Seams[462] of our boat all over with Soap
before we put to Sea at the end of the 6 days we launched our
boat & put to Sea at 8 oClock in the morning[463] and Steered to

the northward; this Island was in Latitude $26^d : 27^m$ we made
the main land in the Evening, we passed a great number
of small Islands[464] and put into a great many of them expecting
to find some Turtles but never found any in any
of the Islands we put into afterwards we found a great
quantity of shellfish but none of them very fit to eat but being

very

very hungry we were glad to eat them & thank God for it for if it had not been for the Shell fish and the little Turtle which we had we must have Starved: we very seldom put into any place but found plenty of fresh water but we could not find any thing fit to eat when we came to the Gulph of Carpentara which is in latitude 10:11 we ran down the Gulph 9 or 10 Miles & saw several small Islands in which were several of the Natives in 2 Canoes landing upon one of the Islands we steered down towards them as soon as they saw us they sent their 2 Canoes round to the back of the Island with 1 man in each when we came down to them they seemed to stand in a posture of defence against us we fired a Musket over them & immediately they began firing their Bows and Arrows at us we immediately hoisted up our Sails and rowed away from them but as God would have it none of their arrows came into the Boat but dropped along side we could not get hold of any of them but they seemed to be about 10" Inches long the Natives seemed to be very stout and fat and blacker than ~~them~~ three we saw in other parts; there was one which we took to be the chief with some shells round his Shoulders we rowed a little farther down the Gulph & landed upon the Main for to get some water we found plenty and saw a small Row of huts about 20 just by were the fresh water was there were not any of the inhabitants in their huts or about them as we could see their huts were large enough for 6 or 7 of them to stand upright in they were made of bark & covered over with Grass we filled our

two

[169–204a^r]

very hungry we were glad to eat them & thank God for it for if it
had not been for the Shell fish and the little Turtle which we had
we must have Starved: we very seldom put into any place but found
plenty of fresh water but we could not find any thing fit to eat
when we came to the Gulph of Carpentara which is in latitude
10^d : 11^m we ran down the Gulph 9 or 10 Miles & saw several small
Islands⁴⁶⁵ on which were several of the Natives in 2 Canoes⁴⁶⁶ landing
upon one of the Islands we steered down towards them
as soon as they saw us they sent their 2 Canoes Round to the
back of the Island with 1 man in each when we came down
to them they seemed to stand in a posture of defence against
us we fired a Musket over them & immediately they began
firing their Bows and Arrows at us we immediately hoisted
up our Sails and rowed away from them but as God would
have it none of their arrows came into the Boat but dropped
along side we could not get hold of any of them but they
seemed to be about 18 Inches long the Natives seemed to be
                                       those
very stout and fat and blacker than ~~them~~ we saw in other
parts; there was one which we took to be the chief with some
shells round his Shoulders we rowed a little farther down the
Gulph & landed upon the Main ~~for~~ to get some water we found
plenty and saw a small Row of huts about 20 just by were
the fresh water was there were not any of the inhabitants in
their huts or about them as we could see their huts were
large enough for 6 or 7 of them to stand upright in they
were made of bark & covered over with Grass we filled our

                                 two

breakers with fresh water and came aboard of our boat again for we were afraid of staying ashore for fear of the Natives, we went 3 or 4 miles from the shore and dropt our Killock and stopped there all night the next morning we were determined to go to the same place to recruit our water but as we were making towards the shore we saw two very large Canoes coming towards us we did not know what to do for we were afraid to meet them there seemed to be about 30 or 40 men in each Canoe they had sails seemed to be made of Matting one of the Canoes was a head of the other a little way it stopt till the other came up and then she hoisted her Sails and made after us as soon as we saw that we tacked about with what water we had determined to cross the Gulph which was about 500 Miles but as God would have it we out run them they followed us till we lost sight of them, having but little fresh water and no wood to make a fire with, but in four days and a half we made the other side of the Gulph we put on shore to look for some fresh water but could not find any at that place we kept along shore till the evening, we saw a small river which we made to and got plenty of fresh water, we put off to sea the same night & saw no more land till we came into latitude of North End of the Island we hawled up to make the land to get some fresh water but saw nothing but a heavy swell which had liked to have swallowed us up then we conceived the best way to shape our course would be for the Island of Timor with what little water we had which we made in 36 Hours we ran along the Island of Timor till we came to the Dutch

Settlements

breakers with fresh water came aboard of our boat again
for we were afraid of staying ashore for fear of the Natives, we
went 3 or 4 miles from the shore and dropt our Killock[467] and
stopped there all night the next morning we were determined
to go to the same place to recruit our water but as we were making
towards the shore we saw two very large Canoes coming towards
us we did not know what to do for we were afraid to meet them
there seemed to be about 30 or 40 men in each Canoe they had
sails seemed to be made of Matting one of the Canoes was a
head of the other a little way it stopt till the other came up
and then she hoisted her Sails and made after us as soon as
we saw that we tacked about with what water we had determined
to cross the Gulph[471] which was about 500 Miles[472] but as
God would have it we out run them they followed us till
we lost sight of them, having but little fresh water and no
wood to make a fire with, but in four days and a half we
made the other side of the Gulph we put on shore[473] to look for
some fresh water but could not find any at that place we kept
along shore till the evening, we saw a small river which we
made to and got plenty of fresh water; we put off to sea[474] the same
night & saw no more land till we came into Latitude of
North End of the Island[475] we hawled up to make the land to
get some fresh water but saw nothing but a heavy swell which
had liked to have swallowed us up then we concluded the best
way to shape our course would be for the Island of Timor with
what little water we had which we made in 36 Hours we
ran along the Island of Timor till we came to the Dutch
                                                    Settlements

Settlements where we went ashore to the Governor's house who behaved extremely well to us filled our bellies and Cloathed us double with every thing that was worn on the Island where we remained very happy for two Months till W.m Bryant had words with his Wife who went and informed against himself, wife, Children and all of us; we were immediately taken prisoners and put in the Castle and strictly examined afterwards we were allowed to go out of the Castle 2 at a time for 1 day and the next day 2 more & so we continued till Captain Edwards who had been in search of the Bounty Pirates who had taken some of the Pirates at Otaheite where he lost the Pandora Frigate between New Guinea and new Holland, he made the Island of Timor in the Pinnace two yawls and his long Boat & 120 hands which were saved; which Captain Edwards came to us to know who we were we told him we were Convicts and had made our escape from Botany Bay he told us we were his Prisoners & he put us on board the Rambang Dutch Companys Ship and put both our Legs in irons called the Bilboes in which we was conveyed to Bretava Batavia where we were taken out of the Rambang and put on board a Dutch Guard Ship in irons again there we lost the Child, 6 days after the Father of the child was taken bad & died they were both buried at Bretava 6 Weeks after we were put in 3 different Ships bound to the Cape of Good Hope we were 3 Months before we reached the Cape when we came there the Gorgon Man of War which had brought the Marines from Botany Bay which we were put on board of and we were known well by all the Marine officers. We were all glad that we had not perished at Sea we were brought to England in the Gorgon

and

Settlements[478] where we went ashore to the Governors house who[479] behaved
extremely well to us filled our bellies and Cloathed us double with
every thing that was worn on the Island where we remained
very happy for two Months till Wm Bryant had words with
his Wife who went and informed against himself, wife, Children
and all of us; we were immediately taken prisoners and put
in the Castle[480] and strictly examined afterwards we were allowed
to go out of the Castle 2 at a time for 1 day and the next day
2 more & so we continued till Captain Edwards[481] who had been in
search of the Bounty Pirates who had taken some of the Pirates
at Otaheite[482] when he lost the Pandora[483] Frigate between New Guinea
and new Holland,[484] he made the Island of Timor in the
Pinnace[485] two Yawls[486] and his Long Boat & 120 hands[487] which were
saved: which Captain Edwards came to us to know who we
were we told him we were Convicts and had made our escape
from Botany Bay he told us we were his Prisoners & he put
us on board the Rambang[488] Dutch Companys Ship and put both
our legs in irons called the Bilboes[489] in which we was conveyed to
Batavia   were
Bretava[490] where we ~~was~~ taken out of the Rambang and put on board
a Dutch Guard Ship in irons again there we lost the Child,[491] 6
days after the Father of the child was taken bad & died[492] they were
both buried at Bretava 6 Weeks after we were put in 3 different
Ships bound to the Cape of Good Hope[493] we were 3 Months before
we reached the Cape when we came there the Gorgon Man
of War[494] which had brought the Marines from Botany Bay
                        we were
which we were put on board of and ~~was~~ known well by all
the Marine officers.[495] We were all glad that we had not
perished at Sea we were brought to England in the Gorgon

and

set ashore at Purfleet from thence conveyed by the Constables to Bow Street Office London, and taken before Justice Bond & was fully committed to Newgate.

 W.m Sloatton Navigator of the Boat
 James Cox
 Samuel Burd
 W.m Bryant
 a Boy of 12 Months old
 and a little Girl 3 years and a quarter old died
 The mother of the 2 Children Mary Bryant
 James Martin
 W.m Allen
 John Broom
 and Nathaniel Lilly alive

set ashore at Purfleet from thence conveyed by the Constables to
Bow Street Office London; and taken before Justice Bond[496] & ~~was~~ were
fully committed to Newgate.

        Wm Moatton[497] Navigator of the Boat
        James Cox[498]
        Samuel Burd[499]
        Wm Bryant[500]
        A Boy of 12 Months old[501]
        and a little Girl 3 years and a quarter old died[502]
        The Mother of the 2 Children Mary Bryant[503]
        James Martin[504]
        Wm Allen[505]
        John Broom[506]
        and Nathaniel Lilly[507] alive

Notes

Introduction

1. Brian Elliott. 1966. 'Antipodes: An Essay in Attitudes', *Australian Letters*, vol.vii, p.51.
2. Arthur Phillip (1738–1814), naval officer and Governor of New South Wales 1788–92. Phillip was born in London, the second child of Jacob and Elizabeth Phillip. He entered the Royal Navy at the age of nine and by February 1760 had reached the rank of fourth lieutenant. He and Margaret Denison (1722–92) married in July 1763, but separated six years later. Phillip was on half-pay from July 1771 to January 1775 when he enlisted in the Portuguese navy, before returning to England and rejoining the Royal Navy in 1778. He was appointed captain in 1782. He married Isabella Whitehead (1751–1823) in May 1794 and returned to active service in March 1796. By the time of his death Phillip had been promoted to admiral of the blue.
3. Governor Phillip to Lord Sydney, 15 May 1788, *HRA*, vol.i, p.18.
4. The order founding the colony of New South Wales was officially promulgated on 7 February 1788.
5. The administrative history of the First Fleet and its voyage is told in Alan Frost. 2012. *The First Fleet: The Real Story*. Collingwood, Vic.: Black Inc. For the voyage see pp.159–78.
6. Grace Karskens. 2009. *The Colony: A History of Early Sydney*. Crows Nest, NSW: Allen and Unwin. 32–60, esp. p.49. See also Inga Clendinnen. 2005. *Dancing With Strangers*. Edinburgh: Canongate.
7. For a list of the known First Fleet accounts see the comprehensive Wikipedia page at https://en.wikipedia.org/wiki/Journals_of_the_First_Fleet. The Mitchell and Dixson Library collections at the State Library of New South Wales hold nine manuscript journals of the First Fleet, digital facsimiles of which are available from http://www2.sl.nsw.gov.au/archive/discover_collections/history_nation/terra_australis/journals/index.html.
8. Jeremy Bentham (1748–1832), philosopher and reformer.
9. The Bentham Papers are arranged into 176 archival boxes and consist of approximately 60,000 manuscript folios. For an outline of their contents see Alexander Taylor Milne. 1962. *Catalogue of the Manuscripts of Jeremy Bentham in the Library of University College, London*, second edition. London: Athlone Press; *The Bentham Papers Database*, http://www.benthampapers.ucl.ac.uk/. The British Library holds, approximately, a further 12,500 folios of Bentham manuscripts.
10. James Martin (b.c.1757–63), convicted as 'James Martyn', though the former spelling is used here throughout for consistency.
11. ASSI 23/8, TNA.
12. See Mollie Gillen. 1993. *The Founders of Australia: a Biographical Dictionary of the First Fleet*. Sydney: Library of Australian History. 238–9; Marlies K. Danziger and Frank Brady, eds. 1989. *Boswell the Great Biographer, 1789–1795* (Yale Edition of the Private Papers of James Boswell, vol.xiii). London: Yale University Press and William Heinemann. 218. For Martin's convict indent see NRS 12188 4/4003, p.316, SRNSW.
13. See Governor Phillip to Lord Grenville, 5 November 1791, enclosure no.4, 'Description of Convicts who have absconded from Sydney', CO 201/6/88, TNA.
14. Mary Broad (bap.1765), known as Mary Bryant from 1789. Broad's surname is sometimes spelled 'Braund' in the records and she was convicted under that name. The

former spelling is used here throughout for consistency. For her convict indent see NRS 12188 4/4003, p.43, SRNSW.

15 Catherine Prior (c.1765–93), who was convicted under the name of Catherine Fryer, served on the *Dunkirk* hulk and was transported to New South Wales by the *Charlotte*. Her son, probably with John Arscott (b.c.1767), was baptised John Matthew in Sydney on 10 February 1788. The child lived for little more than a month and was buried on 18 March. Arscott was sentenced to death at Cornwall Assizes at Bodmin on 18 March 1783 on two counts of theft, a sentence which was commuted to seven years' transportation. He was subsequently detained in the *Dunkirk* hulk and though Arscott was initially embarked on the *Charlotte* for New South Wales he was transferred to the *Scarborough* before the First Fleet sailed. Fryer and Arscott married on 8 December 1792 and departed New South Wales together in April 1793 aboard the *Shah Hormuzear*, which sailed in company with the *Chesterfield*. The couple became separated in July 1793 when Arscott went ashore at Tate Island – now Kioa Island in Fiji – with a party in search of fresh water. Arscott and two others were the only survivors of an attack by the island's people, but were presumed dead and left behind by the departing ships. Arscott and his companions escaped and he reached Batavia on 10 October 1794, only to learn that his wife had died aboard the *Shah Hormuzear* two days before it made port in September 1793. See Gillen, *Founders of Australia*, pp.293 and 12–13.

16 Mary Hayden (b.c.1765), known as Mary Shepherd in New South Wales, was detained in the *Dunkirk* hulk before being transported to New South Wales by the *Charlotte*. She was sent to Norfolk Island in the *Sirius* in March 1790, where she twice received 50 lashes: in June 1791 for being drunk and rowdy in camp, and in October for falsely invoking the name of Major Robert Ross (1740–94) to allow a private to go to Queenborough. In June 1794 Shepherd was living with the former marine John Howell (b.c.1759), and they left Norfolk Island for Sydney in November that year. They married in Sydney on 30 June 1795. Howell subsequently joined the New South Wales Corps, and it appears that the couple left the colony together in 1810. See Gillen, *Founders of Australia*, pp.327 and 180.

17 ASSI 23/8, TNA.

18 Charlotte Spence Bryant (1787–92), who was presumably named after the ship on which she was born.

19 See Gillen, *Founders of Australia*, pp.47–8, and John Cobley. 1970. *The Crimes of the First Fleet Convicts*. Sydney: Angus and Robertson. 36.

20 CO 201/6/88, TNA; HO 26/1, p.106, TNA.

21 William Bryant (b.c.1758–61, died 1791). He may have been the William Briant baptised on 27 January 1760 in Saint Hilary (the son of Francis and Ann) or the William Bryant baptised on 23 March 1761 (the son of John, the mother's name not being recorded). See Ancestry.com, *England, Select Births and Christenings, 1538–1975* [database online], Provo, Utah. For his convict indent see NRS 12188 4/4003, p.53, SRNSW and for his physical description see CO 201/6/88, TNA.

22 For Bryant's crime see ASSI 23/8 and HO 13/2 pp.35–6, TNA; Gillen, *Founders of Australia*, p.57 and Cobley, *Crimes of the First Fleet Convicts*, p.41. Some modern authors suggest that Bryant was transported for smuggling and/or resisting officers of the revenue, but all of the available primary records state that he was transported for forgery. See Basil Thomson, 1915. 'Introduction' in *Voyage of H.M.S. Pandora, Despatched to Arrest the Mutineers of the Bounty in the South Seas, 1790–91, Being the Narratives of Captain Edward Edwards, R.N., the Commander, and George Hamilton, the Surgeon*. London: Francis Edwards. 24; Geoffrey Rawson. 1938. *The Strange Case of Mary Bryant*. London: Robert Hale. 21n; Charles H. Currey. 1963. *The Transportation, Escape and Pardoning of Mary Bryant*. Sydney: Angus and Robertson. 2.

23 4 Geo. I c. 11 § 1.

24 Alan Frost notes that 'Contrary to popular belief', from 1776 to the sailing of the First Fleet in 1787, the authorities did not 'pack criminal remorselessly into the hulks'. He found that from 1776 to 1780 the number of prisoners confined in the hulks reached a maximum of around 510, 'then declined steadily, reaching a low point of about 180 in 1783–84'. At this point transportation was 're-instated as the fundamental punishment for felonies' and the number of people convicted 'increased markedly'; as a result, 'even with a large expansion, the hulks system was unable to cope with these numbers'. See Alan Frost. 2012. *Botany Bay: The Real Story*. Collingwood, Vic.: Black Inc. 55–80, esp. 79.

25   See Hamish Maxwell-Stewart. 2010. 'Convict Transportation from Britain and Ireland, 1615–1870', *History Compass* vol.xi, pp.1224–7; A. Roger Ekirch. 1987. *Bound for America: The Transportation of British Convicts to the Colonies, 1718–1775*. Oxford: Clarendon Press; Emma Christopher. 2011. *A Merciless Place: the Lost Story of Britain's Convict Disaster in Africa*. Oxford: Oxford University Press.
26   James Cox (b.c.1759–65, d.1791), also known as James Rolt or Rott. For his convict indents see NRS 12188 4/4003, p.102, SRNSW. Cox is sometimes mistakenly referred to in the literature as 'Banbury Jack'. However, this was the alias of a different man named John Matthew Cox (c.1754–1808), who was sentenced to death at the Old Bailey on 7 July 1784 with John Pontie (b.c.1759) for stealing 13 yards of thread lace from a haberdashery on King Street, Little Tower Hill, London. 'Banbury Jack' was transported to New South Wales in the *Scarborough*, and in New South Wales he was known as John Massy Cox. In November 1791 he was sent to Norfolk Island, where he remained until 1808 when he embarked upon the *Queen* for Van Diemen's Land. He was buried in Hobart Town under the name of John Massa Cox. Presumably the cause of the mistaken identity was the coincidence that both Coxes were transported for stealing thread lace. See Gillen, *Founders of Australia*, pp.84–5. For examples of the error see Judith Cook. 1999. *To Brave Every Danger: The Epic Life of Mary Bryant of Fowey*. Truran Books. 69; Carolly Erickson. 2005. *The Girl from Botany Bay*. Hoboken, NJ: John Wiley & Sons. 99–100. For the trial of 'Banbury Jack' see *OBP*, 7 July 1784, trial of John Pontie and John Matthew Cox (t17840707-32).
27   See Gillen, *Founders of Australia*, p.84, and *OBP*, 11 September 1782, trial of James Cox (t17820911-14).
28   Christopher, *A Merciless Place*, p.255.
29   Frederick North (1732–92), second Earl of Guilford, Chancellor of the Exchequer 1767–82, Prime Minister of Great Britain 1770–82, Home Secretary 1783.
30   The *Swift* reached Baltimore in early 1784. Local opinion ran high against both the landing of convicts and Moore and Salmon's deception (who both suffered significant financial losses as a result of the endeavour). See Christopher, *A Merciless Place*, pp.255–8, Ekirch, *Bound for America*, pp.233–5 and Gillen, *Founders of Australia*, p.434.
31   Christopher, *A Merciless Place*, pp.258–63 and 268–72; Ekirch, *Bound for America*, p.235; and Gillen, *Founders of Australia*, p.435. When the *Mercury* finally reached America no port would admit it to land its convict cargo; instead the prisoners were sent to Honduras. The *Swift* and the *Mercury* both made their initial departures from England under the same master, a Captain Pamp.
32   John Heath (1736–1816), lawyer and Judge of the Common Pleas 1780–1816, a position to which he succeeded Sir William Blackstone (1723–80).
33   8 Geo. III c. 15.
34   At £20 per head for 66 people the *Helena*'s crew would have shared £1320 between them (approximately £83,000 in today's money).
35   *The Western Flying Post or Sherborne and Yeovil Mercury*, 31 May 1784, p.3. See also Gillen, *Founders of Australia*, p.435.
36   Gillen, *Founders of Australia*, p.84.
37   CO 201/6/88, TNA.
38   Samuel Bird (c.1763/4–92), also known as John Simms. For his convict indent see NRS 12188 4/4003, p.39, SRNSW.
39   James Bird (b.c.1748) was, like Samuel Bird, transported to New South Wales by the *Alexander*. James was punished for theft during the voyage and in the colony he was sentenced to 25 lashes on 13 April 1789 for refusing to obey the coxswain of a boat, though the flogging was remitted. On 20 July 1789 he was ordered to receive 100 lashes for trafficking with fish intended for the colony's hospital. He married Mary Desmond (d.c.1792) on 29 December 1790. Desmond had arrived in the colony in the Second Fleet earlier that year aboard the *Neptune*, having been convicted with Mary Butler (c.1773–1812) and sentenced to seven years' transportation at the Old Bailey on 9 September 1789 for stealing nine pecks of French beans from Covent Garden market. She may have been the Mary Dimond who was buried at Parramatta on 4 April 1792. See Gillen, *Founders of Australia*, p.35; Michael Flynn. 1993. *The Second Fleet: Britain's grim Convict Armada of 1790*. Sydney: Library of Australian History. 244 and 186–7; *OBP*, 9 September 1789, trial of Mary Desmond and Mary Butler (t17890909-14).

40 See Gillen, *Founders of Australia*, p.35, and CO 201/6/88, TNA.
41 'Numerical List of the Library Books at Norfolk Island, 1852', Mfm G6611, 143a–b: National Library of Australia.
42 Edward Cormick (d.1788), referred to by David Collins and known in the colony as Corbet, was convicted on two counts at Hertford on 2 March 1786. The first was of stealing 'one Scarlet cloth Cardinal', the second of stealing a sack and five pecks of wheat. Cormick's wife Ann was also tried on the first charge, but was found not guilty. Cormick was detained on the *Ceres* hulk, and was subsequently embarked on the *Alexander* for New South Wales on 6 January 1787 under a sentence of seven years' transportation. See Gillen, *Founders of Australia*, p.83.
43 David Collins (1756–1810), deputy Judge-Advocate of New South Wales 1788–97 and Lieutenant-Governor of Van Diemen's Land 1803–10.
44 David Collins, 1798 and 1802, [1975]. *An Account of the English Colony in New South Wales*, 2 vols, vol.i. Sydney: A. H. & A. W. Reed PTY. 25–6 and 541n; Gillen, *Founders of Australia*, p.83.
45 John 'Black' Caesar (c.1763–96) was convicted at the Kent Assizes on 13 March 1786 and sentenced to transportation for life for stealing £12 from a dwelling house. He was transported to New South Wales by the *Alexander* in the First Fleet. Lieutenant William Bradley (1757–1833), naval officer, believed that Caesar was from Madagascar. However, Cassandra Pybus argues that Caesar – 'the most ubiquitous male name for chattel in English slave societies' – was one of the runaway slaves who fought for the loyalists during the American Revolutionary Wars and who were evacuated to Nova Scotia, the West Indies and Britain after the British surrender in 1783. See Cassandra Pybus. 2006. *Black Founders: the Unknown Story of Australia's First Black Settlers*. Sydney: UNSW Press. 46–7; Chris Cunneen and Mollie Gillen. 'Caesar, John Black (1763–1796)', *ADB*, http://adb.anu.edu.au/biography/caesar-john-black-12829.
46 John Hunter (1737–1821), naval officer and Governor of New South Wales 1795–1800.
47 Governor Hunter to the Duke of Portland, 15 February 1798, *HRA*, vol.i, pp.128–31.
48 John Wilson (c.1768–1800), known in the colony as Bun-bo-e. Wilson was convicted at Wigan on 10 October 1785 of stealing nine yards of velveret cloth and was sentenced to seven years' transportation; he arrived in New South Wales in the First Fleet by the *Alexander*. When his sentence expired Wilson took to the bush and lived, for years, at several intervals, along the Hawkesbury river among the Dharug people, who named him Bun-bo-e. He was declared an outlaw on 13 May 1797 for being at large, and for advising and assisting in Aboriginal attacks upon settlers' farms. Though the notice of outlawry gave him a fortnight to surrender, Wilson did not return to Sydney until November. Governor Hunter pardoned him as he wished to make use of his knowledge of the country and, as David Collins put it, if he was punished and sent to hard labour then Wilson would 'quickly rejoin his late companions'. On a second expedition in March 1798 Wilson became the first European to identify a route to land to the south-west of Sydney which avoided having to cross the Blue Mountains. See A. H. Chisholm. 'Wilson, John (?–1800)', *ADB*, http://adb.anu.edu.au/biography/wilson-john-2803; Collins, *Account*, vol.ii, p.43; and John Maynard and Victoria Haskins. 2016. *Living with the Locals: Early Europeans' Experience of Indigenous Life*. Canberra: National Library of Australia. 9–25.
49 Governor Hunter to the Duke of Portland, 15 February 1798, *HRA*, vol.ii, pp.128–31; David Levell, 2008. *Tour to Hell: Convict Australia's Great Escape Myths*. St Lucia: University of Queensland Press. 50–5, 64–72. See also Alan Atkinson. 1997. *The Europeans in Australia—A History, Volume One: The Beginning*. Oxford: Oxford University Press. 248–50. In this work Atkinson suggests that the drawn compass may have been indicative of membership a secret fraternity rather than an example of ignorance.
50 Levell, *Tour to Hell*, p.74.
51 *Sydney Gazette*, 30 October 1830, pp.2–3. The *Gazette* was founded in 1803 as an official government publication, but ceased to be censored by the colonial government in October 1824.
52 David Burn (c.1799–1875), colonist, actor and playwright.
53 See David Burn. 'Journal of a Voyage from London to Hobart in the barque *Calcutta*, 31 July–22 Nov. 1841, and journal, 1 Aug. 1844–19 Feb. 1845', p.255, CY 846, SLNSW. For absconding from the supposedly inescapable Norfolk Island penal station see Timothy Causer. 2010. '"Only a place fit for angels and eagles": the Norfolk Island penal settlement, 1825–1855'. London: PhD thesis, University of London. 210–29.
54 Karskens, *The Colony*, p.282.
55 James Cook (1728–1779), naval officer, navigator and cartographer.

56 William Bligh (1754–1817), naval officer and Governor of New South Wales 1806–8. On 26 January 1808 Bligh was overthrown and arrested by the military during what is commonly referred to as the 'Rum Rebellion'.
57 Fletcher Christian (1764–1793?), sailor and mutineer.
58 See Alan Frost. 'Bligh, William (1754–1817)', *ODNB*, http://www.oxforddnb.com/view/article/2650?docPos=6.
59 Watkin Tench (bap.1758, d.1833), military officer and author of *A Complete Account of the Settlement at Port Jackson, in New South Wales*. 1793. London: G. Nicol and J. Sewell. 108. Also contained and more widely available in Watkin Tench, 1996. *1798: Comprising A Narrative of the Expedition to Botany Bay and A Complete Account of the Settlement at Port Jackson*. Tim Flannery, ed. Melbourne: The Text Publishing Company.
60 The First Fleet has been characterised as being organised in a haphazard manner by the government, but Alan Frost notes that there 'may have been a selection of male convicts according to skills'. See Frost, *First Fleet*, p.70. For an analysis of the skills of convicts transported to New South Wales between 1817 and 1840 see *Convict Workers: Reinterpreting Australia's Past*. 1988. Stephen Nicholas and Peter M. Shergold, eds. Cambridge: Cambridge University Press. 62–84.
61 Collins, *Account*, vol.i, p.44
62 Collins, *Account*, vol.i, p.85.
63 Augustus Alt (1731–1815), soldier, Surveyor-General of New South Wales 1788–1801. Alt first requested to be relieved as Surveyor-General in 1791, but was not officially invalided from the service until 1801. See Bernard T. Dowd. 'Alt, Augustus Theodore (1731–1815)', *ADB*, http://adb.anu.edu.au/biography/alt-augustus-theodore-1702.
64 Collins, *Account*, vol.i, p.45.
65 Joseph Paget (b.c.1760) was convicted of an unknown offence at the Devon Assizes at Exeter on 10 January 1786 and sentenced to transportation for seven years. He was originally due to be transported to New South Wales by the *Charlotte*, but was transferred to the *Scarborough* prior to the First Fleet setting sail. In New South Wales Paget was employed in William Bryant's fishing boat until February 1789. In March 1790 he was sent to Norfolk Island in the *Sirius*, and by July the following year he had a lot at Queenborough and was self-sufficient. According to Gillen, he may have been the Joseph Pagett mustered on the *Supply* at Port Jackson on 29 October 1795 as an able seaman from Yorkshire. The same man was mustered on the *Buffalo* on 1 August 1799, again at Port Jackson, and later deserted at Portsmouth on 12 January 1802. See Gillen, *Founders of Australia*, p.272.
66 John White (c.1756–1832), naval surgeon and naturalist.
67 Currey, *Mary Bryant*, pp.4–5.
68 Collins, *Account*, vol.i, p.48–9. On 18 March 1789 a broken key was found in one of the locks of the public storehouse. Private Joseph Hunt turned King's Evidence and revealed that he and Askew, Baker, Brown, Dukes, Jones and Hines had acquired a key with which they freely entered and robbed the store, doing so only when one of the others was on sentry duty and could provide cover. The six men were tried and convicted on 25 and 26 March at the court of criminal judicature. According to fellow Private John Easty (fl.1786–93), soldier and diarist, the condemned stated on the gallows that Hunt 'was the ocation of all their Deaths' and had been the originator of the conspiracy. Hunt was given a free pardon. See John Easty. 1965. *Memorandum of the Transactions of a Voyage from England to Botany Bay, 1787–1793 – A First Fleet Journal*. Sydney: Trustees of the Public Library of New South Wales in Association with Angus and Robertson. 110–1. The original of Easty's journal is: 'Pr Jno Easty A Memarandom of the Transa[ctions] of a Vy Voiage from England to Botany Bay in the Scarborough Transport Captn Marshall Commander kept by me your humble Servan[t] John Easty marine wich began 1787', DLSPENCER 374, ML, SLNSW.
69 Collins, *Account*, vol.i, p.45.
70 Grace Karskens. 2005. '"This Spirit of Emigration": the Nature and Meanings of Escape in Early New South Wales', *Journal of Australian Colonial History*, vol.vii, pp.11–2. Similarly Ian Duffield rejected the fallacy that convict piracy was random and chaotic. See Ian Duffield. 2013. 'Cutting Out and Taking Liberties: Australia's Convict Pirates, 1720–1829', *International Review of Social History*, vol.lviii, pp.197–8.
71 Collins, *Account*, vol.i, p.112–3.
72 John Turwood or Tarwood (b.c.1761) was convicted at the Old Bailey on 19 July 1786, together with James Gall and Daniel Chambers, of the violent highway robbery of Thomas

Holmes and John Ellis in Green Park, Knightsbridge. The case was prosecuted by the renowned lawyer William Garrow (1760–1840). One of the men – probably Gall – levelled a pistol at Holmes, and snapped it at him twice when he fought back. The weapon misfired, and Holmes was beaten by the men and robbed of a silver watch valued at 40 shillings, a steel chain valued at sixpence, a seal, a hat and some cash. Gall confessed his guilt, but claimed Turwood and Chambers were innocent and had nothing to do with the robbery. All three men were sentenced to hang, but Turwood and Chambers were reprieved on condition of being transported for life. See *OBP*, 19 July 1786, trial of James Gall, Daniel Chambers and John Turwood (t17860719-28); Flynn, *Second Fleet*, pp.582–3.
73 For the crime of George Lee (b.c.1769) and George Connoway (c.1770–1808), who were convicted together, see p.14.
74 John Watson (b.c.1766) was sentenced to seven years' transportation at the Old Bailey on 23 May 1787 for stealing seven cloth coats valued at £3, four cloth waistcoats valued at 10 shillings, three pairs of breeches valued at 19 shillings, six pairs of stockings valued at six shillings, a cotton counterpane valued at 2 shillings and four shirts valued at 10 shillings, belonging to Anthony Burt. Watson stole the goods from a chest aboard a ship at Wapping. See *OBP*, 23 May 1787, trial of John Watson (t17870523-79); Flynn, *Second Fleet*, pp.598–9.
75 Joseph Sutton (d.1795) was, according to Michael Flynn, probably the man convicted, under the name of Suttle, at the Surrey Assizes at Guildford on 14 July 1788. He was found guilty of stealing £3 of property from Dennis Cotterell and sentenced to seven years' transportation. See Flynn, *Second Fleet*, p.559.
76 Collins, *Account*, vol.i, pp.112–3.
77 William Broughton (1762–1821), naval officer and surveyor.
78 Collins, *Account*, vol.i, pp.356–7, and Maynard and Hoskins, *Living with the Locals*, pp.5–6.
79 *OBP*, 30 August 1786, trial of George Lee, Alexander Seaton and George Connoway (t17860830-16).
80 See Collins, *Account*, vol.i, p.107, and Governor Phillip to Under Secretary Nepean, 23 August 1790, *HRA*, vol.i, p.207.
81 See Flynn, *Second Fleet*, pp.583, and Governor Hunter to Duke of Portland, 10 January 1798, *HRA*, vol.ii, p.115.
82 Cook, *To Brave Every Danger*, p.147.
83 Collins, *Account*, vol.i, p.128.
84 *Evening Mail*, 29 June–2 July 1792, p.3. See also *London Chronicle*, 30 June–3 July 1792, p.2, and *Diary or Woodfall's Register*, 2 July 1792, p.3.
85 Collins, *Account*, vol.i, p.88.
86 Collins, *Account*, vol.i, pp.89–90.
87 Collins, *Account*, vol.i, p.90.
88 See Right Hon. W. W. Grenville to Governor Phillip, 19 June 1789, *HRA*, vol.i, pp.120–1; M. D. Nash, ed. 1989. *The Last Voyage of the Guardian, Lieutenant Riou, Commander, 1789–1791*. Cape of Good Hope: The Van Riebeeck Society.
89 Governor Phillip to Under Secretary Nepean, 16 June 1790, *HRA*, vol.i, p.178; Bateson, Charles. 1985. *The Convict Ships, 1787–1868*. Glasgow: Brown, Son & Ferguson. second edition. 120–3.
90 An estimated 939 male and 78 female convicts were embarked upon the three ships, of whom 256 male and 11 female convicts died on the voyage. See Bateson, *Convict Ships*, p.127, and Governor Phillip to Right Hon. W. W. Grenville, 13 July 1790, *HRA*, vol.i, pp.188–9.
91 Collins, *Account*, vol.i, p.99.
92 Richard Johnson (c.1753–1827), Church of England Minister and chaplain to the colony of New South Wales 1788–1800.
93 Rev. R. Johnson to Mr Thornton, c.July 1790, *HRNSW*, vol.ii, pp.386–9.
94 Donald Trail (c.1745–1814), sailor and master of slave and convict ships. Trail was probably born in Orkney and served in the Royal Navy during the American Revolutionary Wars. Around 1787 he was the master of the *Recovery*, a slave ship owned by Camden, Calvert and King, which ran between London, West Africa and America. See Flynn, *Second Fleet*, pp.576–8.
95 Emma Christopher, 2007. '"The Slave Trade is Merciful Compared to [This]": Slave Traders, Convict Transportation and the Abolitionists' in *Many Middle Passages: Forced Migration and the Making of the Modern World*. Emma Christopher, Cassandra Pybus and Marcus Rediker, eds. London: University of California Press. 109–28.
96 Governor Phillip to Right Hon. W. W. Grenville, 13 and 17 July 1790, *HRA* vol.i, pp.188 and 197.

97 William Ellerington (nd.).
98 Thomas Evans (nd.), lawyer. See Bateson, *Convict Ships*, p.130, and Under-Secretary King to Governor Phillip, 10 January 1792, *HRA*, vol.i, p.334.
99 Probably Jane Elley (nd.), convicted at the Old Bailey on 28 October 1789 of stealing 10 yards of muslin from a draper at Holborn Bridge. She was sentenced to seven years' transportation and transported to New South Wales by the *Neptune*. Elley was pregnant at the time of her transportation – her husband, William, remained in England – but there is no record of her child either being born or having survived the voyage. She was sent to Norfolk Island in August 1790, where she lived with Alexander Dollis (who arrived in New South Wales as a convict on the *Admiral Barrington* in 1791). They married and had four children by the time they left Norfolk Island in the *Dart* for Sydney in September 1803. The family appears to have set out for Britain shortly after arriving in New South Wales. See Flynn, *Second Fleet*, p.262; *OBP*, 28 October 1789, trial of Jane Elley (t17891028-72).
100 For an account of the trial see Christopher, '"The Slave Trade is Merciful Compared to [This]"', pp.116–20.
101 Flynn, *Second Fleet*, p.578.
102 Emanuel Bryant (1790–1).
103 Collins, *Account*, vol.i, p.131. This government order has not been located.
104 William Allen (b.c.1737–46). See Flynn, *Second Fleet*, pp.130–1; *The World* (London), 2 July 1792, p.3. For Allen's convict indents see NRS 12188 4/4003, p.34, SRNSW.
105 John Moutray (1722/3–85), naval officer.
106 It has not been possible to identify 'Captain Marotter'.
107 *Boswell the Great Biographer, 1789–1795*, p.218. Thomas Graves (1725–1802), naval officer and colonial administrator, Governor of Newfoundland 1761–4, first Baron Graves from 1794.
108 See J. D. Davies. 'Moutray, John, of Roscobie (1722/3–1785)', *ODNB*, http://www.oxforddnb.com/view/article/19449. £1,500,000 in today's money would be approximately £94,000,000.
109 See 'Graves, Thomas (1725–1802)', *ODNB*, http://www.oxforddnb.com/view/article/11319.
110 ASSI 33/7 p.213, TNA.
111 James Campbell (c.1740–95), military officer. See Flynn, *Second Fleet*, pp.130–1.
112 CO 201/6/88, TNA. Contemporary medical dictionaries typically define a 'rupture' as a hernia of some kind, and it seems likely that Allen was marked with some kind of swelling. See, for example, Robert Hooper, 1799. *A Compendious Medical Dictionary. Containing an Explanation of the Terms in Anatomy, Physiology, Surgery, Materia Medica, Chemistry, and Practice of Physic. Collected from the Most Approved Authors*. London: Murray and Highley.
113 Samuel Broom (b.c.1742–4), also known as John Butcher. Confusingly he is referred to as 'John Broom' on page 23 of the *Memorandoms* (UC clxix. 201). For Broom's convict indents see NRS 12188 4/4003, p.40, SRNSW.
114 ASSI 2/25, TNA.
115 Flynn, *Second Fleet*, pp.175–6, and HO 26/56, p.7, TNA.
116 CO 201/6/88, TNA.
117 Nathaniel Lillie (b.c.1753–1763), whose surname is sometimes spelt 'Lilly' or 'Lilley' in the records. 'Lillie' is used here throughout for consistency. For his convict indents see NRS 12188 4/4003, p.282, SRNSW.
118 See Flynn, *Second Fleet*, pp.403–4; the *Norfolk Chronicle*, 19 March 1788, p.4; and HO 47/7, p.263, TNA. Flynn notes that a man by the name of Nathaniel Lillie had been due to stand trial at the Suffolk Assizes of March 1783 for highway robbery, but appears to have been discharged from custody before the case got to court.
119 CO 201/6/88, TNA.
120 William Morton (b.c.1759–63, d.1792); his surname is sometimes spelled 'Moreton' in the records, but the former spelling is used here throughout for consistency. For his convict indents see NRS 12188 4/4003, p.332, SRNSW.
121 UC clxix. 201. See also Collins, vol.i, p.130; James Scott. 1963. *Remarks on a Passage to Botany Bay, 1787–1792: A First Fleet Journal*. Sydney: The Trustees of the Public Library of New South Wales in Association with Angus and Robertson. 62. The original manuscript of Scott's journal is: 'Remarks on a passage to Botnay [sic] Bay 1787 [13 May 1787–20 May 1792]', Safe/DLMSQ 42, ML, SLNSW
122 Flynn, *Second Fleet*, pp.440–1.
123 CO 201/6/88, TNA.
124 Collins, *Account*, vol.i, p.130, and Scott, *Remarks*, p.62.

125 Collins, *Account*, vol.i, p.130.
126 See *Convict Workers*, Nicholas and Shergold, eds, p.81.
127 Collins, *Account*, vol.i, p.126. Judith Cook found it 'surprising' that William Bryant included the four Second Fleeters in his crew and speculated that they 'secured their passage through blackmail'. Cook based this assumption on a misquotation of the sentence cited above from Collins's *Account*, which misses out the word 'five'. Cook claims that William Bryant's 'tongue had run away with him again' and that those he was overheard talking to were his First Fleet colleagues. However, Samuel Bird, Mary Bryant, James Cox and James Martin were only four in number. Moreover, given that the escape took place within a few weeks of this report, it seems highly likely that the Second Fleeters would have been recruited to the conspiracy some time before. See Cook, *To Brave Every Danger*, p.147.
128 Collins, *Account*, vol.i, pp.126–7.
129 Bennelong (c.1764–1813). See Keith Vincent Smith. 'Woollarawarre Bennelong', *Dictionary of Sydney*, http://dictionaryofsydney.org/entry/woollarawarre_bennelong.
130 Carangarang (b.c.1771, d.c.1837). See Keith Vincent Smith. 'Carangarang', *Dictionary of Sydney*, http://dictionaryofsydney.org/entry/carangarang.
131 Collins, *Account*, vol.i, p.127.
132 Cook states: 'It is said that Bennelong played a vital role at this point, and willingly helped his white friend get away', and that Bennelong 'or one of his tribe' brought the fishing boat to shore and held it fast while the escapees boarded. Cook does not state by whom 'It is said'. See *To Brave Every Danger*, p.152.
133 Cook, *To Brave Every Danger*, pp.143–4. These assertions are repeated in Judith Cook. 'Bryant [née Broad], Mary (b.1765)', *ODNB*, http://www.oxforddnb.com/view/article/65443, accessed 20 January 2017.
134 Collins, *Account*, vol.i, p.128.
135 *Waaksamheyd* is Dutch for 'vigilance' or 'watchfulness'. I am grateful to Katy Roscoe for the translation.
136 Private James Scott of the Marines suggests that Bryant was going out to fish on the night of 28 March, but 'he has thought. propper to. put. to Sea in order to make his escape'. See Scott, *Remarks*, p.62.
137 Also known as Smith or Smyth.
138 Collins, *Account*, vol.i, p.129–30. Judith Cook fictionalised the negotiations between the Bryants and Smith for the goods, suggesting not only that did they rely upon Mary Bryant's feminine wiles – 'There is no doubt Smith found Mary attractive and he may well have harboured hopes that the relationship could be put on a more intimate footing' – but claiming that there were 'suggestions that Mary "sold herself" in exchange for Smith's assistance'. Cook advanced no evidence for these claims and nor did she state who made these unfounded 'suggestions'. See Cook, *To Brave Every Danger*, pp.146–8.
139 See Easty, *Memorandum*, pp.126–7.
140 UC clxix. 180 (original) and 202ʳ (fair copy). See the *London Evening Mail*, 29 June–2 July 1792, p.3; *London Chronicle*, 30 June–3 July 1792, p.2.
141 *The World*, 2 July 1792, p.3.
142 Easty, *Memorandum*, p.127.
143 Collins, *Account*, vol.i, p.130.
144 Sarah Young (nd.) was convicted, with Mary Arbin, at the Old Bailey on 11 July 1787 of stealing nine yards of check muslin, valued at 30 shillings, from John Fisher's drapery in London's West End. Her death sentence was commuted to transportation for seven years and on 7 May 1789 she was embarked upon the *Lady Juliana* for New South Wales. A few weeks later, on 12 September 1787, Young's husband, William Bramsley (b.c.1752), also known as Bransley, was himself convicted, with Charles Stokes, George Nadam and William Lamb of theft at the Old Bailey; he was sentenced to transportation for seven years. On 25 August 1789 Bramsley addressed a petition to the Home Secretary, asking to be sent to New South Wales by the next ship so he could be reunited with his 'lawful and affectionate wife'. Though Bramsley's request was acceded to, and he was transported by the *Surprize*, the affection between husband and wife did not appear to last, given Young's relationship with James Cox. After Cox absconded, Young appears to have lived briefly with Lieutenant Richard Bowen (1761–97), the naval agent to the Third Fleet, during his time in the colony. See Flynn, *Second Fleet*, pp.635–6, and 171, and *OBP*, 11 July 1787, trial of Mary Arbin and Sarah Young (t17870711-39), and 12 September 1787, trial of Charles Stokes, William Bramsley, George Nadan and William Lamb (t17870912-114).

145 Collins, *Account*, vol.i, p.129.
146 UC clxix. 182 (original) and 202ᵛ (fair copy).
147 UC clxix. 182 (original) and 202ᵛ (fair copy).
148 Warwick Hirst. 2003. *Great Convict Escapes in Colonial Australia*. Sydney: Kangaroo Press. Revised edition. 13.
149 Timotheus Wanjon (nd.), Governor of Kupang 1789–97. Wanjon assumed the role after the death of the incumbent – and his father-in-law – William Adriaan van Este (d.1789), who had been governor since 1777. Wanjon left Kupang in the wake of the town's destruction by the British in 1797. See Hans Hägerdal. 2012. *Lords of the Land, Lords of the Sea: Conflict and adaptation in early colonial Timor, 1600–1800*. Leiden: KITLV Press. 426.
150 William Bligh. 1792/3. 'A Log of the proceedings of His Majesty's Ship Providence on a Second Voyage to the South Sea under the command of Captain William Bligh, to carry the Breadfruit Plant from the Society Islands to the West Indies, written by himself, vol.2, 20 July 1792 [to] 6 Sep 1793', Safe/A564/2, p.150, ML, SLNSW.
151 Steven Farram. 2007. 'Jacobus Arnoldus Hazaart and the British interregnum in Netherlands Timor, 1812–1816', *Journal of the Humanities and Social Sciences of Southeast Asia and Oceania*, vol.clxiii, p.470.
152 Bligh, 'Log', p.151.
153 Bligh, 'Log', p.151.
154 George Tobin (1768–1838), naval officer and artist.
155 George Tobin, 1797. 'Journal on HMS *Providence* 1791–1793, written in 1797, with additions to 1831', Safe 1/406 (A 562), pp.287–8. The journal was published as Roy Schreiber, ed. 2007. *Captain Bligh's Second Chance: An Eyewitness Account of His Return to the South Seas by Lt. George Tobin*. London: Chatham Publishing. I am grateful to Craig Gordon for bringing Tobin's writings to my attention.
156 UC clxix. 183 (original) and 202ᵛ (fair copy).
157 Hirst, *Convict Escapes*, p.13.
158 UC clxix. 183 (original and 202ᵛ (fair copy).
159 UC clxix. 184 (original) and 202ᵛ (fair copy).
160 UC clxix. 184–5 (original) and 203ʳ¹ (fair copy).
161 UC clxix. 185 (original) and 203ʳ¹ (fair copy).
162 UC clxix. 186 (original) and 203ʳ¹ (fair copy).
163 UC clxix. 187 (original) and 203ʳ¹ (fair copy).
164 UC clxix. 188 (original) and 203ᵛ¹ (fair copy).
165 UC clxix. 189 (original) and 203ᵛ¹ (fair copy).
166 UC clxix. 189 (original) and 203ᵛ¹ (fair copy), and Hirst, *Convict Escapes*, p.15.
167 UC clxix. 189–90 (original) and 203ᵛ¹ (fair copy).
168 UC clxix. 190 (original) and 203ᵛ¹ and 203ʳ² (fair copy).
169 UC clxix. 191–2 (original) and 203ʳ² (fair copy).
170 UC clxix. 192–4 (original) and 203ʳ² and 203ᵛ² (fair copy), and Hirst, *Convict Escapes*, p.16.
171 UC clxix. 195 (original) and 204aʳ (fair copy).
172 UC clxix. 195–6 (original) and 204aʳ (fair copy).
173 UC clxix. 196–7 (original) and 204aʳ and 204aᵛ (fair copy).
174 UC clxix. 197ʳ and 198ʳ (original) and 204aᵛ (fair copy).
175 Bligh, 'Log', p.151.
176 Bligh, 'Log', pp.149–51.
177 UC clxix. 199 (original) and 204bʳ (fair copy).
178 UC clxix. 199 (original) and 204bʳ (fair copy), and *Evening Mail*, 29 June–2 July 1792, p.3.
179 UC clxix. 199 (original) and 204bʳ (fair copy).
180 Collins, *Account*, vol.i, p.131, and Erickson, *The Girl from Botany Bay*, pp.145–7.
181 Cook, *To Brave Every Danger*, p.177.
182 Atkinson, *Europeans in Australia*, p.130.
183 Tobin, 'Journal', p.288.
184 Bligh, 'Log', p.149.
185 Collins, *Account*, vol.i, p.182.
186 Tench, *Complete Account*, p.108–9n.
187 Cook, *To Brave Every Danger*, pp.176–7; Jonathan King. 2004. *Mary Bryant: Her Life and Escape from Botany Bay*. Pymble, NSW: Simon and Schuster. 216–21. Cook, without any evidence, states that William Bryant's 'Achilles' heel' was alcohol. She invents a scenario in which,

after arguing with his wife, he 'took himself off to a bar, got drunk and ... bragged about the amazing escape he had masterminded, about how they had stolen the Governor's own boat and how his brilliant seamanship had brought them safely into Kupang. From what is known of him, it would have been quite in character'. In fact we know next to nothing about William Bryant's character.

188 Edward Edwards (1742–1815), naval officer. Edwards entered the Royal Navy as a lieutenant in 1759 and served on a number of ships (including as commanding officer of HMS *Carcass* and HMS *Hornet*) until March 1784, when he was placed on half-pay. In August 1790 Edwards received command of the frigate HMS *Pandora* and a commission to pursue the mutineers who had seized HMS *Bounty* in 1789. He was court-martialled in England on 17 September 1792 over the loss of the *Pandora*, but he and his fellow officers were exonerated. Edwards was promoted to vice-admiral in 1809.

189 Peter Gesner. 1998. 'George Hamilton's Account of HMS *Pandora*: The Last Voyage, the Discovery, the Significance' in George Hamilton, *A Voyage Round the World, in His Majesty's Frigate Pandora, Performed under the Direction of Captain Edwards, in the years, 1790, 1791, and 1792. With the DISCOVERIES made in the South-Sea; and the many Distresses experienced by the Crew from Ship-wreck and Famine, in a Voyage of Eleven Hundred Miles in open Boats, between Endeavour Straits and the Island of Timor* [1793]. Sydney: Hordern House. 13–26. As Gesner notes, three of the *Bounty* mutineers were released from '*Pandora*'s Box' to help pump the stricken *Pandora*, but when the ship was abandoned and began to sink the remaining 11 were still confined to the Box. All would have drowned had William Moulter, the bosun's mate, not released them (p.20).

190 George Hamilton (d.1796?), naval surgeon. Hamilton served during the American Revolutionary Wars and was on half-pay from 1786 until August 1790, when he embarked upon the *Pandora*. After returning to Britain in June 1792 he subsequently served in the Mediterranean aboard the *Lowestoft* from December 1792. Hamilton was discharged in March 1794 after losing his left arm following a battle with French forces off Corsica. He was declared unfit for service two months later and was recommended for superannuation. As Peter Gesner suggests, Hamilton likely died during 1796 as he no longer appears in naval superannuation records after December of that year. See Gesner, 'George Hamilton's Account', pp.25–6.

191 Hamilton, *Voyage*, p.143.

192 For examples of this error see Cook, *To Brave Every Danger*, p.176; Erickson, *The Girl from Botany Bay*, p.147; King, *Mary Bryant*, p.216–22.

193 UC clxix. 199 (original) and 204b^r (fair copy).

194 UC clxix. 200 (original) and 204b^r (fair copy), and Admiralty Secretary Philip Stephens to Governor Arthur Phillip, 21 July 1792, enclosure, 'A List of Convicts, Deserters from Port Jackson, delivered to Captain Edward Edwards, 5 October 1791', *HRA*, vol.i, p.369.

195 The *Verenigde Oostindische Compagnie*, or United East Indian Company.

196 Gesner, 'George Hamilton's Account', pp.21–2.

197 UC clxix. 200 (original) and 204b^r (fair copy), and Hamilton, *Voyage*, pp.149–50.

198 James Cook. *Captain Cook's Journal During His First Voyage Round the World Made in H. M. Bark [sic] Endeavour, 1768–71*. W. J. L. Wharton, ed. 1893. London: Elliot Stock. 364.

199 Hamilton, *Voyage*, p.156–7.

200 See Admiralty Secretary Philip Stephens to Governor Arthur Phillip, 21 July 1792, enclosure, 'A List of Convicts, Deserters from Port Jackson, delivered to Captain Edward Edwards, 5 October 1791', *HRA*, vol.i, p.369.

201 UC clxix. 200 (original) and 204b^r (fair copy).

202 See Admiralty Secretary Philip Stephens to Governor Arthur Phillip, 21 July 1792, enclosure, 'A List of Convicts, Deserters from Port Jackson, delivered to Captain Edward Edwards, 5 October 1791', *HRA*, vol.i, p.369.

203 Edward Edwards to Philip Stephens, 19 March 1792 in *Voyage of H.M.S. Pandora*, pp.83–4.

204 Hamilton, *Voyage*, p.158.

205 See Admiralty Secretary Philip Stephens to Governor Arthur Phillip, 21 July 1792, enclosure, 'A List of Convicts, Deserters from Port Jackson, delivered to Captain Edward Edwards, 5 October 1791', *HRA*, vol.i, p.369; Hamilton, *Voyage*, p.158. Private James Scott, when aboard HMS *Gorgon* on the journey to Britain, had evidently heard the version of events given by Hamilton when he wrote that Cox 'Made his escape from A Duch Ship At. timor'. See Scott, *Remarks*, p.77. 'Honroost' refers to Onrust Island, or Pulau Kapal – one of a chain of islands off the north of Batavia (Jakarta), which housed a VOC shipyard.

206 UC clxix. 201 (original) and 204b^v (fair copy).
207 See Admiralty Secretary Philip Stephens to Governor Arthur Phillip, 21 July 1792, enclosure, 'A List of Convicts, Deserters from Port Jackson, delivered to Captain Edward Edwards, 5 October 1791', *HRA*, vol.i, p.369.
208 UC clxix. 200–1 (original) and 204b^r (fair copy). The *Gorgon*'s captain was John Parker (c.1749–94), who died of yellow fever off Martinique in August 1794. In 1795 his widow Mary Ann (1765/6–1848), in order to raise money to support her children, published by subscription an account of the ship's voyage from England to New South Wales and back again. Despite the proceeds raised from sales of the book, her pension and the support of Literary Fund committee members, she lost her house and was confined to debtors' prison in 1804. Mary Ann Parker's account of New South Wales was the first by a woman to be published and is of enormous historical importance. She made no mention of the surviving escapees. See Mary Ann Parker. 1795. *A Voyage Round the World in the Gorgon Man of War: Captain John Parker. Performed and Written by His Widow; For the Advantage of a Numerous Family*. London: John Nichols; Deirdre Coleman. 'Parker, Mary Ann (1765/6–1848)', *ODNB*, http://www.oxforddnb.com/view/article/45859.
209 Tench, *Complete Account*, pp.108–9n. Tench could only have been referring to James Martin here: the other escapees transported to New South Wales by the *Charlotte* – William Bryant and James Cox – were dead (or, in the case of Cox, missing presumed dead).
210 Ralph Clark (1762–94), military officer and diarist. See *The Journal and Letters of Lt. Ralph Clark, 1787–1792*. Paul G. Findlon and R. J. Ryan, eds. Sydney: Australian Documents Library in Association with the Library of Australian History. The original of Clark's journal is: 'Ralph Clark—Journal Kept on the Friendship during voyage to Botany Bay and Norfolk Island; and on the Gorgon returning to England, 9 March 1787–31 December 1787, 1 January 1788–10 March 1788, 15 February 1790–2 January 1791, 25 January 1791–17 June 1792', Safe 1/27a, ML, SLNSW.
211 Clark, *Journal and Letters*, p.234. The death of Charlotte Bryant is also noted in Scott, *Remarks*, p.82.
212 UC clxix. 201 (original) and 204b^v (fair copy).
213 Nicholas Bond (1743–1807), magistrate at Bow Street from 1785.
214 *The Times*, 1 July 1792, p.3, and the *Evening Mail*, 29 June–2 July 1793, p.3.
215 *London Chronicle*, 30 June–3 July 1792, p.2.
216 See HO 26/1, p.106, TNA and HO 26/6, pp. 7–8, TNA; *London Chronicle*, 7–10 July 1792, p.27.
217 *London Chronicle*, 7–10 July 1792, p.27.
218 James Boswell (1740–95), ninth Laird of Auchinleck from 1782, best known for his *Life of Samuel Johnson* (1791).
219 Henry Dundas (1742–1811), first Viscount Melville from 1802, Treasurer of the Navy 1782–3, 1784–1800, Home Secretary 1791–4, Secretary of War 1794–1801, Keeper of the Privy Seal of Scotland 1800–11, First Lord of the Admiralty 1804–5.
220 Boswell to Dundas, 16 August 1792, GEN MSS 89, L 475 BRBML.
221 Evan Nepean (1752–1822), first baronet from 1802, politician and colonial governor, Under-Secretary of State for the Home Department 1782, 1782–94, Under-Secretary of State for War 1794–5, First Secretary to the Admiralty 1795–1804, Chief Secretary for Ireland 1804–5, Governor of Bombay 1812–9.
222 Journal entry for 14 November 1792 in *Boswell the Great Biographer*, p.198.
223 During September 1797 the *Cumberland* – 'the largest and best boat in the colony belonging to government', according to Collins – was seized on its voyage carrying stores from Sydney to the Hawkesbury river farms. The group of convict pirates included George Lee and John Turwood (see pp.13–14 above). In the following month a boat was stolen by convicts at Parramatta and they sailed unobserved out of Port Jackson. Armed boats were sent out after both groups of escapees, but they successfully got away. See Governor Hunter to Duke of Portland, 10 January 1798, *HRA*, vol.ii, p.115.
224 Collins, *Account*, vol.ii, p.38.
225 Easty, *Memorandum*, pp.137–8.
226 'Pardon for Mary Bryant, alias Broad', HO 26/56, p.57, TNA.
227 *St. James's Chronicle or the British Evening Post*, 14 May 1793, p.4.
228 See, for example: *Northampton Mercury*, 18 May 1793, p.2; *Reading Mercury*, 20 May 1793, p.2; *Bath Chronicle and Weekly Gazette*, 23 May 1793, p.1; *Derby Mercury*, 23 May 1793, p.1.

229 *Dublin Chronicle*, 4 June 1793, p.118.
230 Boswell to Elizabeth Puckey, 14 August 1793, GEN MSS 89, L 1088, BRBML.
231 Journal entry for 18 August 1793, *Boswell the Great Biographer*, p.226.
232 Journal entry for 25 August 1793, *Boswell the Great Biographer*, p.229. Dolly Broad was then working as a cook for a Mr Morgan in Charlotte Street, Bedford Square, work which Boswell thought 'was much too hard for her, a young and slender girl. I resolved to exert myself to get her a place more fit for her'.
233 Journal entry for 12 October 1793, *Boswell the Great Biographer*, p.241–2.
234 William Johnson Temple (bap.1739, d.1796), Church of England clergyman, essayist and one of Boswell's closest friends since they studied together at the University of Edinburgh.
235 Temple to Boswell, 18 July 1793, GEN MSS 89, C 2938, BRBML.
236 Edward Thurlow (1731–1806), politician and lawyer, Baron Thurlow from 1778, Solicitor General 1770–1, Attorney General 1771–8, Lord Chancellor 1778–92.
237 Journal entry for 24 December 1793, *Boswell the Great Biographer*, p.271.
238 John Baron (d.1816), clergyman. Baron was told by a Henry Harvey that, ever since Mary Bryant had returned to Fowey, '(as far as I can learn) she has behaved herself soberly & prudently'. In October 1794 Boswell's brother reported that he had sent £5 to Reverend Baron, as per his request. See Baron to James Boswell, 1 May 1794, GEN MSS 89, C 100 and Thomas David Boswell to James Boswell, 23 October 1794, GEN MSS 89, C 528, both BRBML.
239 The notice of the dividend is given in the *London Chronicle*, 19–22 March 1791, p.275.
240 Edward Puckey to James Boswell, 16 February 1794, GEN MSS 89, C 2328, BRBML.
241 James Boswell to Edward Puckey, 6 May 1794, GEN MSS 89, L 1088, BRBML.
242 Edward Puckey to James Boswell, 16 February 1794, GEN MSS 89, C 2328, BRBML.
243 James Boswell to Edward Puckey, 6 May 1794, GEN MSS 89, L 1088, BRBML.
244 William Parsons (d.1828), member of the Della Cruscan circle of sentimental poets.
245 'Heroic Epistle from Mary Broad in Cornwall to James Boswell, Esq., in London' quoted in Frank Brady. 1984. *James Boswell: The Later Years, 1769–1795*. New York: McGraw-Hill Book Company. 465–6.
246 Brady, *Boswell: The Later Years*, pp.96–105.
247 As the editors of Boswell's papers point out, 'At the top of the right-hand margin Boswell later added in parentheses: "This I afterwards found not be true as to Lilley. See certificate of his conviction."' As we have seen, Lillie was transported for a burglary. See 'Draft of a Petition for the Botany Bay Prisoners—14 May 1793', *Boswell the Great Biographer*, p.217.
248 'Draft of a Petition for the Botany Bay Prisoners—14 May 1793' in *Boswell the Great Biographer*, pp.217–8.
249 Lady Jane Hope (1766–1829) was the second wife of Henry Dundas, whom she married on 2 April 1793. Dundas and his first wife Elizabeth Rannie (1751–1843) divorced in 1778 on grounds of Elizabeth's adultery. See Michael Fry. 'Henry Dundas, first Viscount Melville (1742–1811), *ODNB*, http://www.oxforddnb.com/view/article/8250?docPos=1.
250 Boswell to Jane Dundas, 14 May 1793, GEN MSS 89, L 480, BRBML. Boswell attempted to charm Lady Jane, noting that though he had 'seen you but once ... I have seen you constantly in my minds eye and had I been as fortunate as my College Companion Harry Dundas you should have had the choice of two secretaries of State'.
251 Jane Dundas to Boswell, 1793 (undated note), GEN MSS 89, C 1153, BRBML.
252 *Boswell the Great Biographer*, p.221.
253 Journal entry for 19 August 1793, *Boswell the Great Biographer*, pp.226–7.
254 Boswell to Evan Nepean, 13 September 1793 in *Letters of James Boswell*, 1924. Chauncey Brewster Tinker, ed. Oxford: Clarendon Press, vol.ii. 456–7. Original emphasis.
255 Joseph White (nd.), assistant solicitor to the Treasury 1781–94, Treasury Solicitor 1794–1806.
256 White to Nepean, 1 November 1793, HO 48/3, TNA. Original emphasis.
257 Journal entry for 3 November 1793, *Boswell the Great Biographer,* pp.247–8.
258 Frederick A. Pottle. 1938. *Boswell and the Girl from Botany Bay*. London: William Heinemann. 28.
259 Cook, *To Brave Every Danger*, pp.235–6.
260 King, *Mary Bryant*, pp.277–81.
261 Erickson, *The Girl from Botany Bay*, p.196.
262 J. P. Griffin. 2008. 'Changing Life Expectancy Throughout History', *Journal of the Royal Society of Medicine*, vol.ci. 577.
263 HO 26/12, p. 11, TNA; *OBP*, September 1806, trial of Mary Broad (t18060917-112).

264 HO 107/15/4, p.20, TNA.
265 *Boswell the Great Biographer*, p.217.
266 *The World*, 2 July 1792, p.3, and *Boswell the Great Biographer*, pp.217–8.
267 *The World*, 2 July 1793, p.3.
268 *Boswell the Great Biographer*, p.218.
269 John Butcher to Henry Dundas, 23 January 1793, CO 201/8/123, TNA.
270 See Thomson, 'Introduction' to *Voyage of H.M.S. Pandora*, p.24; Currey, *Mary Bryant*, p.44; Rawson, *Strange Case*, pp.280–1; Hughes, *The Fatal Shore*, p.208; Cook, *To Brave Every Danger*, p.240; Gerald Hausman and Loretta Hausman. 2003. *The True Story of Mary Bryant: Escape from Botany Bay*. New York: Orchard Books. 218; Erickson, *The Girl from Botany Bay*, p.212n.
271 Thomas Keneally. 2006. *The Commonwealth of Thieves*, London: Chatto and Windus, p.410, and King, *Mary Bryant*, p.278.
272 Louis Becke (George Louis Becke) and Walter Jeffery. 1896. *A First Fleet Family: A Hitherto Unpublished Narrative of Certain Remarkable Adventures Compiled from the Papers of Sergeant William Dew of the Marines*. London: T. Fisher Unwin. 253–4.
273 *Boswell the Great Biographer*, p.218, and CO 201/6/88, TNA.
274 Bateson, *Convict Ships*, p.147.
275 Eliza Stewart (b.c.1801).
276 See the *Biographical Database of Australia*, http://www.bda-online.org.au, person IDs B#15001017401 and B#10015368401; *Findmypast*, http://www.findmypast.co.uk/; Bateson, *Convict Ships*, pp.145–7. For the 1822 New South Wales musters see *General Muster and Land and Stock Muster of New South Wales, 1822*. Carol J. Baxter, ed. 1988. Sydney: ABGR Project in Association with the Society of Australian Genealogists. 69 and 541. I am very grateful to Babette Smith for providing me with this information from the 1822 muster. For the 1828 census see HO 10/21 p.181, TNA.
277 *Boswell the Great Biographer*, p.218; *The World*, 2 July 1792, p.3. Nathaniel Lillie and Deborah Jones married on 29 March 1784 in Sudbury. Two of the Lillies' children have been identified: William (b.1785) and Nathaniel junior (b.1788), both of whom were born in the Saint Gregory parish of Sudbury, Suffolk. William spent ten unhappy years at the Philanthropic Society's reform school in London from January 1793. In January 1796 he was blinded in one eye in an accident while working as a shoemaker's apprentice, and he later ran away from the school at least twice. See *findmypast.co.uk*, 'England—Marriages, 1538–1973, Transcription'; *Ancestry.com*, 'England, Select Births and Christenings, 1538–1975' [database online], Provo, Utah; Flynn, *Second Fleet*, pp.403–4.
278 HO 27/9, pp.581–2, TNA; *The Suffolk Chronicle; or Weekly General Advertiser & County Express*, 14 August 1813, p.4 and 21 August 1813, p.4; *Bury and Norwich Post*, 22 September 1813, p.2.
279 HO 9/8 pp.78–9, TNA.
280 *Boswell the Great Biographer*, p.218.
281 See 'Botany Bay: Leaves from Botany Bay used as Tea', GEN MSS 89, P 27, BRBML. In 1991 some of these tea leaves were donated to the Mitchell Library, State Library of New South Wales. See http://archival-classic.sl.nsw.gov.au/item/itemDetailPaged.aspx?itemID=455934 Judith Cook and Carolly Erickson assume that the tea was given to Boswell by Mary Bryant, citing *The Private Papers and Journal of James Boswell, 1789–1794*. 1934, vol.18. Geoffrey Scott and Frederick A. Pottle, eds. United States of America: Privately Printed. 203–4. However, this source does not say from whom Boswell received the tea leaves; they could have been given to him by any of the survivors. See Erickson, *The Girl From Botany Bay*, p.192, and Cook, *To Brave Every Danger*, p.232.
282 Bowring, vol.iv, p.193.
283 John Thomas Bigge (1780–1843), judicial commissioner, Chief Justice of Trinidad 1813–18. Bigge toured New South Wales and Van Diemen's Land, gathering evidence for his reports, from September 1819 until February 1821. See John Ritchie. 1970. *Punishment and Profit: The Reports of Commissioner John Bigge on the Colonies of New South Wales and Van Diemen's Land, 1822–1823; their Origins, Nature, and Significance*. Melbourne: Heinemann.
284 *Commons Sessional Papers* (1823), vol.xxxiii, p.79.
285 *Commons Sessional Papers* (1823), vol.xxxiii, p.79.
286 Duffield, 'Cutting Out and Taking Liberties', pp.212–3.
287 Charlotte Badger (bap.1778) was convicted at the Worcester Assizes on 11 July 1796 of breaking and entering the house of Benjamin Wright in Bromsgrove, and stealing four guineas and

a Queen Anne half-crown. Her death sentence was commuted to seven years' transportation, and she arrived in New South Wales aboard the *Earl Cornwallis* in June 1801. See Duffield. 2005. '"Haul away the anchor girls": Charlotte Badger, tall stories and the pirates of the "bad ship *Venus*"', *Journal of Australian Colonial History*, vol.vii, pp.39–42.
288 Catherine Hagerty (d.c.1806?) arrived in New South Wales in the *Kitty* in November 1792. Her offence is unknown.
289 For an analysis of the seizure of the *Venus* see Duffield, '"Haul away the anchor girls"', pp.35–64.
290 Hamish Maxwell-Stewart. 2001. 'Seven Tales for a Man with Seven Sides' in *Chain Letters: Narrating Convict Lives*. Lucy Frost and Hamish Maxwell-Stewart, eds. Melbourne: Melbourne University Press. 64–76.
291 Clare Anderson. 2009. 'Discourses of exclusion and the "convict stain" in the Indian Ocean, c. 1800–1850' in *The Limits of British Colonial Control in South Asia: Spaces of disorder in the Indian Ocean region*. Ashwini Tambe and Harald Fischer-Tiné, eds. Abingdon: Routledge. 105–20, esp. p.106. See also Clare Anderson. 2001. 'Multiple Border Crossings: "Convicts and Other Persons Escaped from Botany Bay and residing in Calcutta"', *Journal of Australian Colonial History*, vol.iii, no.2, pp.1–22. For other discussions of convict escape see *Escape: Essays on Convict Australia*, a special issue of the *Journal of Australian Colonial History*. 2005. David Andrew Roberts, ed., vol.vii; *Mutiny and Maritime Radicalism in the Age of Revolution: A Global Survey*, a special issue of the *International Review of Social History*, 2013. Clare Anderson, Niklas Frykman, Lex Heerma van Voss and Marcus Rediker, eds, vol.lviii.
292 Henry George Grey (1802–94), known as Viscount Howick 1807–45, third Earl Grey 1845, Secretary at War 1835–49, Secretary of State for War and the Colonies 1846–52.
293 Earl Grey to Lieutenant-Governor William Denison, 22 December 1848, *Commons Sessional Papers* (1849), vol.xliii (Command Paper no.1121), p.278.
294 See Erin Ihde. 2008. 'Pirates of the Pacific: The Convict Seizure of the *Wellington*', *The Great Circle*, vol.xxx. 3–17.
295 Borrit (b.c.1815) was originally sentenced to 15 years' transportation at the Old Bailey on 8 July 1839 after he, John Stapleton, Cornelius Strong and Robert Wiseman burgled a shop at St Paul's, London. After escaping from Norfolk Island and returning to Britain he was convicted at Liverpool on 5 August 1844 of returning from transportation; he was sentenced to transportation for life and sent straight back to Norfolk Island by the *Hyderabad*, which arrived at the island on 20 February 1845. In April 1847 Borrit was transferred to Van Diemen's Land, but absconded from the colony in 1849. He returned to Britain again and was convicted of returning from transportation for a second time at the Old Bailey on 2 February 1852. This time Borrit was sentenced to be imprisoned for six months and then transported for life. Borrit was first sent to Pentonville and, on 30 June 1853, was recorded as being confined on a hulk at Portsmouth. He does not appear to have been sent to Australia for a third time, as in February 1856 John Jones *alias* George Parker *alias* James Punt Borrit, John Munro *alias* Wilson and George Richardson were arrested and committed for trial for burgling the house of a Mr Faulkner and stealing goods valued up to £30. See *OBP*, 8 July 1839, trial of James Punt Borrit, John Stapleton, Cornelius Strong and Robert Wiseman (t18390708-2057) and 2 February 1852, trial of James Punt Borrit (t18520202-275); CON 33/1/86, 19809, TAHO; *The Times*, 11 February 1856, p.11; HO 24/16, TNA, prisoner no. 23544, TNA; HO 8/116, p.130, TNA. Borrit's life story is told, edited by the Reverend Henry John Hatch, as 'James Thrayle: A Story Founded on Fact' in James Harris, Henry John Hatch and James Foster Turner Wiseman. 1870. *The Paglesham Oyster: containing tales of fact, fiction and romance*. Rochford: publisher unknown.
296 William Vine (b.c.1812) was convicted at the Old Bailey on 16 September 1839 of stealing a quadrant, a jacket and a coat from his master, Daniel Brown, captain of the *Lion* which was lying at West India Dock in London. Vine had been employed by Brown as chief mate of the vessel, which was about to sail to the West Indies. He was sentenced to ten years' transportation. See *OBP*, 16 September 1839, trial of William Vine (t18390916-2491).
297 John Day (b.c.1818) was sentenced to ten years' transportation at the Old Bailey on 20 August 1838 for breaking and entering the dwelling house of Alexander Robinson in Hammersmith, London and burgling it of over £30 worth of goods. See *OBP*, 20 August 1838, trial of John Day (t18380820-1830).

298 William Pedder (b.c.1819) was sentenced to 15 years' transportation for burglary at the Lancaster Assizes of 23 March 1839. See HO 27/58, p.88, TNA.
299 For poetry see 'The Escape of Mary Bryant' in Dullaghan, Frank. 2014. *The Same Roads Back*. Blaenau Ffestiniog: Gwynedd Cinnamon Press. 54.
300 Melodramatic re-tellings of the Mary Bryant story appeared reasonably regularly in Australian newspapers during the early-to-mid twentieth century. See, for example: 'Epic Drama of Escape: Convict Girl's 3,000 Miles Voyage to Kupang', *The Mercury* (Hobart) Weekend Magazine, 2 April 1938, p.8; Clem Lack, 'Escape from Sydney Cove', parts 1 and 2, *Sunday Mail* (Brisbane) Magazine, 16 and 23 June 1940, pp.3 and 7; 'The Love of Mary Bryant', *The Mail* (Adelaide) Sunday Magazine, 21 July 1951, pp.4–5; 'The Adventures of Mary Bryant', *Brisbane Telegraph*, 18 July 1953, p.11. On 25 March 1947 the Sydney radio station 2UW broadcast *The Australian Story*, a play about William and Mary Bryant. See *The Sun* (Sydney), 25 March 1947, p.6.
301 Duffield, 'Cutting Out and Taking Liberties', p.207.
302 Becke and Jeffery, *A First Fleet Family*, pp.v–vi. Becke and Jeffery collaborated on five other works including a novel about the *Bounty* mutiny, *The Mutineer: A Romance of Pitcairn Island* (London: T. Fisher Unwin, 1898).
303 William Dew (nd.).
304 Gillen, *Founders of Australia*, p.104.
305 Contemporary reviews made clear that *A First Fleet Family* was a novel. See, for example, *The Brisbane Courier*, 15 February 1897, p.6 and *The Australasian* (Melbourne), 18 July 1896, p.41.
306 Rawson, *Strange Case*, pp.1–22, 151–3 and 281–2; Becke and Jeffery, *A First Fleet Family*, pp.30–6, 221–2 and p. 257. Rawson's book reproduces a facsimile, between pages 88 and 89, of Mary Bryant's transportation order (ASSI 24/26, TNA). He quotes from it as though it states that she was convicted at an assizes at the 'Castle of Winchester', when the document clearly reads 'Castle of Exeter'. See also Basil Thomson, 'Introduction', *Voyage of H.M.S. Pandora*, pp.23–4. In describing the gallant officer who was Mary Bryant's salvation, Becke and Jeffery may have relied upon the unreliable report in the *Dublin Chronicle* of 4 June 1793, p.118. It claimed a 'gentleman of high rank in the army' heard of her story in the newspapers and visited her in Newgate. 'The next day he returned, and told the old gentleman who keeps the prison, that he had procured her pardon, which he shewed him, at the same time requesting that she should not be apprized of the circumstance. The next day he returned with his carriage, and took the poor woman, who almost expired with the excess of gratitude.'
307 Rawson, *Strange Case*, p.259.
308 Though billed as 'the true story', this work of fiction is told from Mary Bryant's first-person perspective.
309 For the American edition, see Frederick A. Pottle. 1937. *Boswell and the Girl from Botany Bay*. New York: Viking.
310 Hirst, *Great Convict Escapes*, pp.6–26.
311 See, for example, Erickson, *The Girl from Botany Bay*, pp.135–40 and p.142. In the latter example, while at Kupang, Erickson suggests that 'To find herself surrounded by warmth and solicitude, after so many years of coldness and punitive deprivation, must have made Mary's tears flow daily'.
312 Cook, *To Brave Every Danger*, pp.27 and 159–60.
313 Cook, *To Brave Every Danger*, pp.40–1, 85 and 165.
314 UC clxix. 191–2 (original) and 203a[r] (fair copy).
315 *The Annual Register, or a View of the History, Politics, and Literature, For the Year 1792: Part II. Chronicle, State Papers, Characters, &c*. 1798. London: F. and C. Rivington. 28–30, esp. p.30.
316 Erickson, *The Girl from Botany Bay*, p.219.
317 King, *Mary Bryant*, p.vii.
318 King, *Mary Bryant*, p.74.
319 Anthony S. Veitch. 1980. *Spindrift: the Mary Bryant Story: a Colonial Saga*. London: Angus and Robertson; Lesley Pearse. 2003. *Remember Me*. Leicester: Charnwood; John B. Durand. 2005. *The Odyssey of Mary B*. Elkhorn, WI: Puzzlebox Press, 2005; Jo Anne Rey,. 2005. *The Sarsaparilla Souvenir*. United States of America: XLibris Corporation; Laurie Sheehan. 2006. *Mary Bryant, The Convict Girl: the real story . . .* Kinloss: Librario.

320 Timberlake Wertenbaker, 1988. *Our Country's Good*. London: Methuen. For the Australian production of *Boswell for the Defence* see the *Canberra Times*, 14 January 1991, p.14.
321 See the *Australian Womens' Weekly*, 15 October 1980, p.33.
322 See Susan Lever. 2008. 'Masculinity, Guilt and the Moral Failures of the Body: Nick Enright's Screenplays' in *Nick Enright: An Actor's Playwright*. Anne Pender and Susan Lever, eds. New York: Rodopi. 53.
323 K. S. Inglis. 2006. *This is the ABC: The Australian Broadcasting Commission, 1932–1983*. Melbourne: Black Inc. 205. The previous three serials were: *Stormy Petrel* (1960) by Rienits, about William Bligh as Governor of New South Wales from 1806 to 1808; *The Outcasts* (1961), again by Rienits, which took as its subject New South Wales under Lachlan Macquarie (1762–1824), Governor from 1810 to 1821; and *The Patriots* (1962) by Phillip Grenville Mann, set during the 1820s. I am grateful to the staff at the Australian Broadcasting Corporation Library Sales for confirming that all four serials are held in the ABC archive.
324 Nan Musgrove, 'Who's the boss of your TV?', *Australian Women's Weekly*, 4 September 1963, p.11.
325 *The Incredible Journey of Mary Bryant* (2005), dir. Peter Andrikis.
326 Kate Matthews, 'Curator's Notes: *The Incredible Journey of Mary Bryant*', *Australian Screen*, http://aso.gov.au/titles/tv/incredible-journey-mary-bryant/notes/.
327 Jacqueline Z. Wilson. 2008. *Prison: Cultural Memory and Dark Tourism*. New York: Peter Lang. 206–7.
328 Thomas Watling (b.1762) was charged on 27 November 1788 in Dumfries with forging Bank of Scotland guinea notes, a capital offence. He denied the charge but, rather than run the risk of being convicted and executed, took the option open to defendants in the Scottish courts of requesting to be transported, duly receiving a sentence of 14 years. Watling arrived in New South Wales aboard the *Pitt* on 7 October 1792, and received a pardon on 5 April 1797. He lived in Calcutta from 1801 to 1803 before returning to Scotland, where on 10 January in Edinburgh 1806 he was tried for forgery, but the charge was not proven. He is supposed to have died, in poverty, in London at an unknown date, though a Thomas Watling born in 1762 was buried at St Mary's parish in Battersea on 14 July 1836. See Rex Rienits, 'Watling, Thomas (b. 1762), *ADB*, http://adb.anu.edu.au/biography/watling-thomas-2776, and *Ancestry.com*, 'England, Select Births and Christenings, 1538–1975' [online database], Provo, Utah.
329 Cook, *To Brave Every Danger*, p.240.
330 Thomas Brownlow Forde (c.1744–1814), Ordinary of Newgate 1798–1814.
331 See Bentham to Forde, 24 December 1802 and Forde to Bentham, 25 December 1802, 27 December 1802, 8 January 1803 and 12 May 1803. 1988. *The Correspondence of Jeremy Bentham (CW)*, vol.vii. J. Dinwiddy, ed. Oxford: Clarendon Press. 171–2, 173–4, 176–7 and 181–5.
332 Jeremy Bentham, 1812. *Panopticon versus New South Wales; or, The Panopticon Penitentiary System and the Penal Colonization System Compared, Containing 1. Two Letters to Lord Pelham. 2. Plea for the Constitution, anno 1803, printed, now first published*. London: R. Baldwin. Reproduced in Bowring, vol.iv, pp.173–284.
333 Bowring, vol. iv, p.193.
334 Samuel Bentham (1757–1831), naval engineer and inventor.
335 Prince Grigory Aleksandrovich Potemkin (1739–91), Russian nobleman and military leader.
336 See Ian. R. Christie,. 1993. *The Benthams in Russia, 1780–1791*. Oxford: Berg; Philip Steadman. 2012. 'Samuel Bentham's Panopticon', *Journal of Bentham Studies*, vol.xiv, http://discovery.ucl.ac.uk/1353164/; and Roger Morriss, 2015. *Science, Utility and Maritime Power: Samuel Bentham in Russia, 1779–91*. Farnham: Ashgate. 176–9.
337 Bentham to Charles Brown, 18/29 December 1786, *The Correspondence of Jeremy Bentham (CW)*, vol.iii, 1971. Ian R. Christie, ed. London: Athlone Press. 502.
338 For an account of the panopticon scheme see Janet Semple, 1993. *Bentham's Prison: A Study of the Panopticon Penitentiary*. Oxford: Oxford University Press.
339 Bowring, vol.iv, p.39.
340 For the original 'Panopticon Letters' (written in 1786) and the more elaborate 'postscripts' (written in 1790 and 1791) see Bowring, vol.iv, pp.37–66, and 67–172.
341 Michel Foucault, 1991. *Discipline and Punish: The Birth of the Prison*. Alan Sheridan, ed. and trans. London: Penguin. First published in 1975 as *Surveiller et punir: Naissance de la prison*.

342 Anne Brunon-Ernst, 2013. *Beyond Foucault: New Perspectives on Bentham's Panopticon*. Abingdon: Routledge. 2–3.
343 34 Geo. III c. 84.
344 George Spencer (1758–1834), second Earl Spencer from 1783, First Lord of the Admiralty 1794–1801, Home Secretary 1806–7.
345 Robert Grosvenor (1767–1845), Viscount Belgrave 1784–1802, Earl Grosvenor 1802–31 and first Marquess of Westminster from 1831.
346 See Philip Schofield, 2009. *Bentham: A Guide for the Perplexed*. New York: Continuum. 12–3. For Bentham's theory of 'sinister interest' see Schofield, 2006. *Utility and Democracy: The Political Thought of Jeremy Bentham*. Oxford: Oxford University Press. 109–36.
347 See Semple, *Bentham's Prison*, especially pp.111–281.
348 UC cxx. 466.
349 John Bowring (1792–1872), politician and translator, Governor of Hong Kong 1854–9.
350 *Bowring*, vol.x, p.250.
351 Charles Long (1760–1838), first Baron Farnborough from 1826, Junior Secretary to the Treasury 1791–1801, Lord of the Treasury 1804–6, Chief Secretary for Ireland 1805–6, Paymaster-General of the Forces 1807–26.
352 Bentham to William Wilberforce, unsent latter dated 24/25 May 1799. *The Correspondence of Jeremy Bentham (CW)*, vol.vi. 1984, John R. Dinwiddy, ed. Oxford: Clarendon Press, 1984. 151–2n.
353 Semple, *Bentham's Prison*, p.219.
354 Reginald Pole Carew (1753–1835), politician.
355 Bentham to Carew, 25 May 1799, *Correspondence (CW)*, vol.vi, pp.151–2.
356 Bunbury to Bentham, 15 June 1803, *Correspondence (CW)*, vol.vii, p.240.
357 William Pitt (1759–1806), known as Pitt the Younger, leader of the administration as First Lord of the Treasury and Chancellor of the Exchequer 1783–1801, 1804–6.
358 Henry Addington (1757–1844), first Viscount Sidmouth 1805, Prime Minister of the United Kingdom 1801–4, Chancellor of the Exchequer 1801–4, Home Secretary 1812–22.
359 William Henry Cavendish Cavendish-Bentinck (1738–1809), third Duke of Portland 1762, Prime Minister of Great Britain 1783, Home Secretary 1794–1801, Lord President of the Council 1801–5, Minister without Portfolio 1805–6 and Prime Minister of the United Kingdom 1807–9.
360 See UC cxvi. 439. For an outline of the various sections of the 'Picture' see UC cxxi. 14, and L. J. Hume. 1973. 'Bentham's panopticon: An administrative history—I', *(Australian) Historical Studies*, vol.xv, p. 721. For a more general discussion of the 'Picture' see Semple, *Bentham's Prison*, pp.218–53.
361 Jeremy Bentham. 1802. 'Panopticon versus New South Wales, &c. In a Letter to the Right Honourable The Lord Pelham, &c. &c. &c. and Second Letter to Lord Pelham, &c. &c. &c.' London: unknown printer; 'A Plea for the Constitution' 1803. London: Mawman, Poultry and Hatchard. Reprinted in Bowring, vol.iv. 173–248 and 249–85.
362 Bentham to Bunbury, 6 May 1791, *Correspondence (CW)*, vol.iv, p.278.
363 Treasury Minute, 13 August 1800, *Commons Sessional Papers* (1801), vol.cxviii, pp.79–80, reproduced in *Correspondence (CW)*, vol.vi, p.352n.
364 Patrick Colquhoun (1745–1820), statistician and magistrate. Bentham's work with Colquhoun on a preventive police force is the subject of a forthcoming volume of *The Collected Works of Jeremy Bentham*, edited by Michael Quinn.
365 'Twenty-Eighth Report from the Select Committee on Finance: Police, including Convict Establishments', *Commons Sessional Papers* (1798), vol.cxii, pp.1–214.
366 Bentham sent the 'Letters to Lord Pelham' to Collins, and they met and dined together in early 1803 on at least three occasions. He also gave him a copy of 'A Plea for the Constitution' prior to Collins' setting sail again for the Antipodes in April 1803. See Collins to Bentham, 11 January 1803; Bentham to Collins, 27 January 1803; Jeremy Bentham to Samuel Bentham, 22 February 1803; Bentham to Collins, 5 April 1803, *Correspondence (CW)*, vol.vii, pp.188, 194, 205 and 220–3.
367 Sir Thomas Charles Bunbury (1740–1821), sixth baronet, horse-racing administrator and MP for Suffolk 1761–1812.

368 Thomas Pelham (1756–1826), second earl of Chichester 1805–1826, Chief Secretary for Ireland 1783–4 and 1795–8, Home Secretary 1801–3, Postmaster-General 1807–26. See Bunbury to Bentham, 13 August 1802, *Correspondence* (*CW*), vol.vii, pp.77–8.
369 Bentham to Bunbury, 11 August 1802, *Correspondence* (*CW*), vol.vii, pp.76–7.
370 Bunbury to Bentham, 20 August 1802, *Correspondence* (*CW*), vol.vii, pp.79–80.
371 William Wilberforce (1759–1833), politician and abolitionist.
372 Charles Abbot (1757–1829), first Baron Colchester, politician and lawyer, Speaker of the House of Commons 1802–17. Abbot's mother, Sarah Abbot née Farr (d.1809), married Jeremiah Bentham (1712–92) after the death of his first wife, Alicia Bentham née Whitehorne (d.1759).
373 Sir John William Anderson (c.1736–1813), MP for London 1793–1806; French Laurence (1757–1809), literary executor of Edmund Burke, regius professor of civil law at Oxford and MP for Peterborough 1796–1809; and William Eden (1744–1814), first Baron Auckland from 1789, politician, diplomat and penal reformer. See respectively Bentham to Wilberforce, 27 August 1802; Bentham to Abbot, 30 December 1802; Bentham to Anderson, 18 December 1802; Bentham to Laurence, 18 December 1802; and Baron Auckland to Bentham, 26 December 1802, *Correspondence* (*CW*), vol.vii, pp.91–2, 178–9, 163–4, 164–5 and 174.
374 Samuel Romilly (1757–1818), legal reformer and politician. See Jeremy Bentham to Étienne Dumont, *Correspondence* (*CW*), vol.vii, p.96.
375 Jeremy Bentham to Samuel Bentham, c.21 August 1802, *Correspondence* (*CW*), vol.vii, pp.89–90.
376 Messrs Brooke and Clarke to Jeremy Bentham, 24 February 1803, *Correspondence* (*CW*), vol. vii, p.206.
377 Bunbury to Bentham, 6 June 1803, *Correspondence* (*CW*), vol.vii, p.236.
378 For example, see Keneally, *The Commonwealth of Thieves*, pp.452–3.; Robert Hughes. 1987. *The Fatal Shore: A History of the Transportation of Convicts to Australia 1787–1868*. London: Collins Harvill. 122–3; J. B. Hirst, 1983. *Convict Society and Its Enemies*. Sydney: Allen and Unwin. 12.
379 Cesare Beccaria, Marchese Di Beccaria-Bonensa (1738–94), jurist, philosopher and politician; author of *Dei delitti e delle penne* (1764), first translated into English as *On Crimes and Punishments* in 1767.
380 Jeremy Bentham, 1996. *An Introduction to the Principles of Morals and Legislation* (*CW*). J. H. Burns and H. L. A. Hart, eds, with a new introduction by Frederick Rosen. Oxford: Oxford University Press. 158.
381 Bowring, vol.iv, p.186.
382 Bentham considered 'the most important end of all' in punishment was 'Example'. See Bentham, *An Introduction to the Principles of Morals and Legislation* (*CW*), p.159n.
383 Bowring, vol.iv, p.211.
384 See, for example, the discussion in R. V. Jackson, 1993. 'Theory and Evidence: Bentham, Collins, and the New South Wales Penal Settlement', *Australian Journal of Politics & History*, vol.xxxix, pp.318–29.
385 UC cxvi. 110.
386 John Gascoigne with Patricia Curthoys, 2002. *The Enlightenment and European Australia*. Cambridge: Cambridge University Press. 129.
387 Henry Grey Bennett (1777–1836), MP for Shrewsbury 1811–26, *Letter to Viscount Sidmouth*, 1819. London: J. Ridgway.
388 Richard Whately (1787–1863), Archbishop of Dublin 1831–63. 1832. *Thoughts on Secondary Punishments, in a Letter to Earl Grey*. London: B. Fellows.
389 John Hirst, 1995. 'The Australian Experience' in *The Oxford History of the Prison: The Practice of Punishment in Western Society*. Norval Morris and David J. Rothman, eds. Oxford: Oxford University Press. 256.
390 Sir William Molesworth (1810–55), eighth Baronet from 1823, Secretary of State for the Colonies 1855.
391 John Ritchie, 1976. 'Towards Ending an Unclean Thing: The Molesworth Committee and the Abolition of Transportation to New South Wales, 1837–40', *Australian Historical Studies*, vol. xvii, p.153.
392 For the reports and evidence of the Committee see *Commons Sessional Papers* (1837), vol.xix and *Commons Sessional Papers* (1837–8), vol.xxii.

393 For Molesworth's attitude towards evidence see Norma Townsend, 1977. 'The Molesworth Enquiry: Does the Report Fit the Evidence', *Journal of Australian Studies*, vol.i, pp.33–51.
394 Jeremy Bentham to Samuel Bentham, *c*.21 August 1802, *Correspondence* (*CW*), vol.vii, p.90.
395 Transportation continued to Van Diemen's Land until 1853 and Western Australia received male convicts from 1850 to 1868.
396 *Memorandoms by James Martin*. Charles Blount, ed., 1937. Cambridge: Rampant Lions Press. This was the fifth book published by Rampant Lions Press. See *The Rampant Lions Press: A Narrative Catalogue*, compiled by Sebastian Carter. 2013. New Castle, Delaware: Oak Knoll Press. 14–15.
397 *Memorandoms*, ed. Blount, p.xi.
398 See Charles Blount, 'Bentham, Dumont and Mirabeau, an Historical Revision', 1952. *University of Birmingham Historical Journal*, vol.iii, pp.53–167. Pierre Étienne Louis Dumont (1759–1829), Genevan political writer who produced five recensions of Bentham's works between 1802 and 1829, and Honoré Gabriel Riqueti, Comte de Mirabeau (1749–91), French statesman.
399 See Nathaniel Lucas (1764–1818). Morton Herman, *ADB*, http://adb.anu.edu.au/biography/lucas-nathaniel-2380.
400 *Escape from Botany Bay 1791, Being 'Memorandoms' by James Martin*. 1991. Victor Crittenden, ed. Canberra: Mulini Press.
401 Peter Clayton, 2015. 'Victor Crittenden 1925–2014', *Australian Academic and Research Libraries*, vol.xlvi, pp.56–7.
402 *The Memorandoms of James Martin*. 2014. Tim Causer, ed. London: UCL Bentham Project.
403 Milne, *Catalogue of the Manuscripts of Jeremy Bentham*, p.57.
404 *Memorandoms*, ed. Blount, p.4.
405 See *Boswell the Great Biographer*, p.242.
406 *Memorandoms*, ed. Blount, p.16.

Memorandoms by James Martin

407 Martin was convicted at the Cornwall Assizes of 20 March 1786. See ASSI 23/8, TNA.
408 William Courtenay (1742–88), second Viscount Courtenay and eighth Earl of Devon from 1762. He married Frances Clack (*c*. 1740–82) on 16 May 1762 and the couple had 11 children.
409 Powderham Castle, the ancestral home of the Earls of Devon.
410 Botany Bay, part of the country of the Eora people. The British first landed at Botany Bay on 29 April 1790, during then-Lieutenant James Cook's first Pacific voyage. It was partly owing to Cook's favourable reports of the land that would become New South Wales that the British government decided to found a penal colony there.
411 HMS *Dunkirk* was completed in 1755. It was fitted out to receive convicts at Plymouth in June and July 1785 and operated as a hulk until 1792, when it was sold. See Rif Winfield, *British Warships in the Age of Sail, 1714–1792: design, construction, careers and fates*. Barnsley: Seaforth, 2007, p.130.
412 The *Charlotte* convict transport, master Thomas Gilbert and surgeon John White. According to Alan Frost, 86 male and 20 female convicts were embarked upon the *Charlotte* for the voyage to New South Wales, while according to Charles Bateson there were 88 male and 20 female convicts on board at the time of sailing. See Frost, *First Fleet*, p.125; Bateson, *The Convict Ships*, p.100. The *Charlotte* departed from Port Jackson on 8 May 1788 for Canton, under contract with the East India Company. It returned to England in June 1789, where it was sold to the merchants Bond & Company. The *Charlotte* was sold to a Quebec-based merchant in 1810 and was lost off the coast of Newfoundland in November 1818. Four prisoners died on the voyage to Sydney: William Brown, Edward Chanin, John Clark and Ishmael Coleman. See Michaela Ann Cameron, 'Charlotte', *The Dictionary of Sydney*, http://dictionaryofsydney.org/entry/charlotte.
413 According to the records James Martin, along with Mary Broad, William Bryant and James Cox, was discharged from the *Dunkirk* to the *Charlotte* on 11 March 1787. See Gillen, *Founders of Australia*, respectively pp. 238–9, 47–8, 57 and 84.
414 The First Fleet departed from Portsmouth on 13 May 1787. It was comprised of six convict transports, two Royal Navy warships and three store ships. The convict ships were the

Alexander, the *Charlotte*, the *Friendship*, the *Lady Penrhyn*, the *Prince of Wales* and the *Scarborough*; the Royal Navy escorts were HMS *Sirius* and HMS *Supply*; and the store ships were the *Golden Grove*, the *Fishburn* and the *Borrowdale*. Aboard the First Fleet were approximately 210 officers and marines (some with their families) and between 750 and 775 convicts. See Frost, *First Fleet*, pp.64–73 and 125 for the numbers embarked, and pp.159–78 for an account of the voyage; this includes a challenge to the previously accepted wisdom, described on pp.1–13, that the Fleet was badly prepared and equipped.

415 Arthur Phillip (1738–1814). For a biography see n.2.
416 The First Fleet sighted the Peak of Tenerife on 2 June 1787 and reached Santa Cruz the following day – not on 5 June as stated in the *Memorandoms*. The Fleet set sail again on 10 June. See Frost, *First Fleet*, p.167.
417 The First Fleet reached Rio de Janeiro in early August 1787 and set sail again on 4 September. See Frost, *First Fleet*, pp.168–70.
418 The First Fleet sighted Cape Town on 13 October 1787 and set sail again on 11 November. See Frost, *First Fleet*, pp.170–4.
419 Though the First Fleet reached Botany Bay on 18 January 1788, Governor Arthur Phillip decided to relocate the settlement to Sydney Cove in Port Jackson. Nevertheless, 'Botany Bay' remained an – often pejorative – synonym for New South Wales for decades to come.
420 The convicts began to be disembarked at Port Jackson on 27 January 1788. See Collins, *Account*, vol.i, p.5.
421 David Collins described the apparent confusion when the troops and convicts were disembarked in January 1788, which he thought 'will not be wondered at, when it is considered that every man stepped from the boat literally into a wood'. He writes of how various parties were employed: 'some in clearing ground for the different encampments; others in pitching tents, or bringing up such stores as were more immediately wanted … As the woods were opened and the ground cleared, the various encampments were extended, and all wore the appearance of regularity'. See Collins, *Account*, vol.i, p.5.
422 'Island' presumably refers to the Australian continent.
423 A hundredweight is equivalent to 100 lbs (45.36 kg).
424 The compass, quadrant and chart were acquired by William Bryant from Detmer Smit, master of the Dutch snow *Waaksamheyd* (p.22).
425 The escapees reached this creek on or around 30 March 1791. Warwick Hirst suggests that this place was Glenrock Lagoon, south of present-day Newcastle on Australia's eastern coast. See Hirst, *Great Convict Escapes*, p.13.
426 Degrees of latitude are approximately 69 miles (111 km) apart, so 'Fortunate Creek', according to the *Memorandoms*, was located approximately 138 miles (222 km) north of Port Jackson.
427 Probably the fruit of the cabbage-tree palm (*Livistona Australis*), which grows widely along the coasts of New South Wales and Queensland.
428 If this was indeed Glenrock Lagoon (see above, n.425), then these may have been the people generally referred to as Awabakal in the literature.
429 On or around 1 April 1791.
430 On or around 3 April 1791.
431 Warwick Hirst suggests, from Martin's description, that this was Port Stephens. See Hirst, *Great Convict Escapes*, p.12.
432 If this was Port Stephens, then these may have been members of the Worimi people.
433 Probably Sunday 3 April 1791.
434 Probably Monday 4 April 1791.
435 From the description – and assuming that this was Port Stephens, and that the escapees rowed up to 10 nautical miles down the harbour – then this little island could have been any one of Boandabah, One Tree Island, Shag Island, Bushy Island, Dowadee Island or Snapper Island. Each of these islands have sandy beaches and all could reasonably be said to be 'in the middle' of Port Stephens.
436 On or around 6 April 1791.
437 On or around the night of 6 April 1791.
438 On or around 7 April 1791.
439 If the escapees were at sea for almost three weeks, then this attempt to find fresh water took place on or around 28 April 1791.

440 It has not been possible to identify this place, though the escapees left it on or around 30 April 1791.
441 It has not been possible to identify this 'Open Bay', though the escapees ran into it on or around 30 April 1791.
442 The morning of on or around 1 May 1791.
443 The escapees left this place on or around 3 May 1791.
444 The escapees reached 'White Bay' on or around 6 May 1791. Hirst suggests that this place was Moreton Bay. See Hirst, *Great Convict Escapes*, p.15.
445 On or around 7 May 1791.
446 If this was Moreton Bay these people may have belonged to the Yuggera, Waka Waka or Gubbi Gubbi peoples.
447 Departing on or around 9 May 1791.
448 On or around 9 May 1791.
449 On or around 10 May 1791.
450 That is, rolling the sail in on itself to reduce its area, a safety precaution during heavy weather.
451 On or around 10 May 1791.
452 A storm drogue – a device attached to the stern of a boat to slow it down and keep it upright during heavy weather.
453 On or around 11 May 1791.
454 On or around 11 May 1791.
455 On or around 12 May 1791.
456 Hirst suggests that this was Lady Elliot Island, which from the description and the presence of the turtles seems likely to be correct. See *Great Convict Escapes*, p.16.
457 Probably Green Sea Turtles (*Chelonia Mydas*), which can grow up to 1.5 metres in length and have nesting grounds in and around the north-eastern and northern coasts of Australia.
458 On or around 12 May 1791.
459 A small keg or cask.
460 It is not clear to which fruit this refers. It cannot be the fruit of the elliptic yellowwood (*Ochrosia elliptica*), which has a waxy skin similar to a red pepper but is poisonous to humans.
461 Probably wedge-tailed shearwaters, commonly known as muttonbirds.
462 This was to cover or seal the seams of the boat.
463 On or around 18 May 1791. After this point in the narrative, it becomes impossible to gauge the passage of time.
464 These islands were probably in the vicinity of the Great Barrier Reef and the north Queensland coastline, but owing to the imprecise description it is impossible to tell.
465 As there are no small islands 'nine or ten miles' down the western side of Cape York, this presumably refers to the islands at the Cape's tip, such as Badu, Moa, Muralug (Prince of Wales Island) or Waiben (Thursday Island).
466 These people were probably Torres Strait Islanders, the indigenous peoples of the Torres Strait Islands.
467 A small anchor.
468 It has not been possible to identify this Thomas Chapman.
469 Probably present-day Foster Lane, which runs from Cheapside to the south, and Gresham Street to the north. Newgate Gaol used to stand less than half a mile from Foster Street.
470 According to the 1851 Census of the United Kingdom, a Peter Richold, a Coach Maker by trade, lived at 18 Hall Street, Long Melford, Suffolk. He was then aged 73, so would have only been 13 in 1791. However, it is possible that his father or other relative may have passed on the trade to him and that he, Peter's ancestor, might have been the 'Richhold' mentioned in this note. Peter Richold lived in 1851 with his wife Mary (aged 59), daughter Hannah (24) and four sons: Thomas (28), also a coach maker; William (26), a 'Cocoa nut Manufacturer'; Patrick (22), a smith; and Samuel (19), a painter. See HO 107/1789, fo.427, TNA.
471 The Gulf of Carpentaria.
472 The Gulf is 366 miles (590 km) wide at its mouth.
473 Given that the escapees had just crossed the Gulf of Carpentaria, it seems likely that they landed somewhere on the northern shore of Arnhem Land, now one of the five regions of the Northern Territory of Australia.

474 The *Memorandoms* suggests that the escapees searched for fresh water in the vicinity of the eastern coast of Cape Arnhem. As most of the rivers there are salt water, they may have had to travel inland and upriver to find fresh water, perhaps at Trial Bay or Cape Bradshaw. Given the imprecise description it is, however, impossible to tell. I am grateful to one of my anonymous referees for information on the geography of Arnhem Land.
475 Presumably meaning somewhere in the vicinity of the top of Cape Arnhem.
476 It has not been possible to identify this Mr Jackson.
477 This was probably Bishop's Head Court, a small alleyway running from off the west side of Gray's Inn Road until its junction at the south with High Holborn. It is unclear whether or not it was part of the Gray's Inn Estate and no trace of the street now remains. See 'Bishop's Head Court', *UCL Bloomsbury Project*, http://www.ucl.ac.uk/bloomsbury-project/streets/bishops_head_court.htm.
478 Kupang, an important Dutch East India Company (VOC) trading post on the western coast of the island of Timor, was first officially occupied by the Dutch in 1653. On 10 June 1797 Kupang was surrendered to the British, but fighting broke out and the invading force set fire to the town and destroyed the Dutch fort. Kupang, and other parts of the Netherlands Indies, changed hands between Britain and the Netherlands several times in the early nineteenth century. West Timor became part of the independent Republic of Indonesia in 1949. See Farram, 'British interregnum in Netherlands Timor', pp.455–75.
479 Timotheus Wanjon (nd.). For a biography see n.149.
480 Presumably the Dutch fort at Kupang.
481 Edward Edwards (1742–1815), naval officer. For a biography see n.188.
482 Tahiti.
483 HMS *Pandora*.
484 The Australian continent was known to Europeans as 'New Holland' from the mid-1640s, after its naming by the Dutch navigator Abel Janszoon Tasman (1603–59) in December 1642. After the British had established New South Wales in 1788, 'New Holland' was generally used to refer to the western part of the continent. The term did not fall into disuse in Europe until about the mid-nineteenth century.
485 A generic term for a ship's boat, usually masted.
486 A ship's boat, resembling a pinnace but usually smaller.
487 Only 99 people survived the wrecking of the *Pandora*. See Gesner, 'George Hamilton's Account', p.21.
488 The VOC ship *Rembang*, chartered by Captain Edwards to take the survivors of the wrecking of the *Pandora*, the captured *Bounty* mutineers and the Bryant party to Batavia.
489 A type of leg-iron. Shackles were attached to both of the prisoner's legs, with a locked rod running through the shackles to prevent much in the way of movement.
490 Batavia, present-day Jakarta, formerly the centre of the VOC's commercial activities in the East Indies. After the bankrupt VOC was dissolved in 1800, Batavia became the capital of the Dutch East Indies until 1942, when it fell to the Japanese during the Second World War. Jakarta was proclaimed the capital of the independent Republic of Indonesia in December 1949.
491 Emanuel Bryant (1790–1).
492 William Bryant. See p.4 and n.21.
493 Namely the VOC ships *Vreedenberg*, *Horssen* and *Hoornwey*.
494 HMS *Gorgon*, master John Parker (c.1749–94), arrived in Sydney on 21 September 1791 with the Third Fleet. The *Gorgon* left Port Jackson for England on 18 December 1791, taking the remainder of the Marine detachment which had travelled to New South Wales in the First Fleet. On 11 March 1792 the ship reached Cape Town, where it took on board Edwards' party, before leaving in April and arriving at Portsmouth on 18 June 1792. See Governor Phillip to Lord Grenville, 5 November 1791, and Governor Phillip to the Right Hon. Henry Dundas, 19 March 1792, *HRA*, vol.i, pp.273 and 337, and Mary-Ann Parker, *Voyage Around the World*, p.127.
495 Among the Marine officers aboard the *Gorgon* were Captain Watkin Tench, Lieutenant Ralph Clark, Sergeant James Scott and their irascible commanding officer, Major Robert Ross.
496 Nicholas Bond. For a biography see p.36 and n.213.
497 William Morton. See p.19 and n.120.

498 James Cox. See pp.5–7 and n.26.
499 Samuel Bird. See p.7 and n.38.
500 William Bryant. See p.4 and n.21.
501 Emanuel Bryant. See p.17 and n.102.
502 Charlotte Spence Bryant. It is erroneously stated in the *Memorandoms* that Charlotte was three and-a-quarter years old when she died; as she was born on 8 September 1787, she was in fact aged four years and seven months. See p.4 and n.18.
503 Mary Bryant. See pp.3–4 and n.14.
504 James Martin. See pp.2–3 and n.10.
505 William Allen. See pp.17–18 and n.104.
506 Samuel Broom *alias* John Butcher. See pp.18–19 and n.113.
507 Nathaniel Lillie. See p.19 and n.117.

Bibliography

Archival Sources

Beinecke Rare Book and Manuscript Library, Yale University

GEN MSS 89: The Boswell Collection. (Digital facsimiles of these manuscripts are available at http://brbl-dl.library.yale.edu/vufind/Record/3441591.)

The National Archives of the United Kingdom

ASSI 2: Assizes – Oxford Circuit, Crown Minute Books.
ASSI 23: Assizes – Western Circuit, Gaol Books.
ASSI 33: Assizes – Norfolk Circuit, Gaol Books.
CO 201: Colonial Office and Predecessors: New South Wales Original Correspondence.
HO 8: Home Office – Convict Hulks, Convict Prisons and Criminal Lunatic Asylums, Quarterly Returns of Prisoners.
HO 9: Home Office – Convict Prison Hulks: Registers and Letter Books.
HO 10: Home Office – Settlers and Convicts, New South Wales and Tasmania: Records.
HO 13: Home Office – Criminal Entry Books 1782–1871.
HO 26: Home Office – Criminal Registers, Middlesex.
HO 24: Home Office: Prison Registers and Statistical Returns 1838–75.
HO 27: Home Office – Criminal Registers, England and Wales.
HO 47: Home Office – Judges' Reports on Criminals 1784–1830.
HO 107: Home Office – Census Returns.

National Library of Australia

'Numerical List of the Library Books at Norfolk Island, 1852', Mfm G6611.

State Library of New South Wales

Bligh, William, 'A Log of the proceedings of His Majesty's Ship Providence on a Second Voyage to the South Sea under the command of Captain William Bligh, to carry the Breadfruit Plant from the Society Islands to the West Indies, written by himself, vol. 2, 20 July 1792 [to] 6 Sep 1793', Safe/A564/2. (Digital facsimile at http://archival.sl.nsw.gov.au/Details/archive/110368665.)

Burn, David, 'Journal of a Voyage from London to Hobart in the barque *Calcutta*, 31 July–22 Nov. 1841, and journal, 1 Aug. 1844–19 Feb. 1845', CY 846.
Clark, Ralph, 'Journal Kept on the Friendship during voyage to Botany Bay and Norfolk Island; and on the Gorgon returning to England, 9 March 1787–31 December 1787, 1 January 1788–10 March 1788, 15 February 1790–2 January 1791, 25 January 1791–17 June 1792, Safe 1/27a. (Digital facsimile at http://archival.sl.nsw.gov.au/Details/archive/110316465.)
Easty, John, 'P.t Jn° Easty A Memorandum of the Transa[ctions] of a V̶y̶ Voiage from England to Botany Bay in the Scarborough Transport Capt.n Marshall Commander kept by me your humble Servan[t] John Easty marine wich began 1787', DLSPENCER 374. (Digital facsimile at http://archival.sl.nsw.gov.au/Details/archive/110316472.)
Scott, James, 'Remarks on a passage to Botnay [sic] Bay 1787 [13 May 1787–20 May 1792]', Safe/DLMSQ 42. (Digital facsimile at http://archival.sl.nsw.gov.au/Details/archive/110316480.)
Tobin, George, 'Journal on HMS *Providence* 1791–1793, written in 1797, with additions to 1831', Safe 1/406 (A 562). (Digital facsimile at http://archival.sl.nsw.gov.au/Details/archive/110328115.)

State Records Authority of New South Wales

NRS 12188: Convict Indents 1788–1842.

Tasmanian Archive and Heritage Office

CON 18: Description Lists of Male Convicts, 1828–53.
CON 31: Conduct Registers of Male Convicts Arriving in the Period of the Assignment System, 1803–43.
CON 33: Conduct Registers of Male Convicts Arriving in the Period of the Probation System, 1840–53.

University College London Library Special Collections

Bentham Papers.

Newspapers and periodicals

Australian Women's Weekly.
Brisbane Telegraph.
Bury and Norwich Post.
Canberra Times.
Diary or Woodfall's Register.
The Dublin Chronicle.
Evening Mail.
The London Chronicle.
The Mail (Adelaide).
The Mercury (Hobart).
The Suffolk Chronicle; or Weekly General Advertise & County Express.
The Sun (Sydney).
The Sunday Mail (Brisbane).
The Times.
The Western Flying Post or Sherborne and Yeovil Mercury.
The World.

Parliamentary publications

Commons Sessional Papers (1798), vol.cxii.
Commons Sessional Papers (1801), vol.cxviii.
Commons Sessional Papers (1823), vol.xxxiii.
Commons Sessional Papers (1837), vol.xix.
Commons Sessional Papers (1837–8), vol.xxii.
Commons Sessional Papers (1849), vol.xliii (Command Paper no.1121).

Published primary sources

The Annual Register, or a View of the History, Politics, and Literature, For the Year 1792: Part II. Chronicle, State Papers, Characters, &c. 1798. London: F. and C. Rivington.
Baxter, Carol J., ed. 1988. *General Muster and Land and Stock Muster of New South Wales, 1822.* Sydney: ABGR Project in Association with the Society of Australian Genealogists.
Bennett, Henry Grey. 1819. *Letter to Viscount Sidmouth.* London: J. Ridgway.
Bentham, Jeremy. 1843. *The Works of Jeremy Bentham*, published under the superintendence of John Bowring, 11 vols. Edinburgh: William Tait.
Bentham, Jeremy. 1802. *Panopticon versus New South Wales, &c. In a Letter to the Right Honourable The Lord Pelham, &c. &c. &c.*, and *Second Letter to Lord Pelham, &c. &c. &c. In Continuation of the Comparative View of the System of Penal Colonization System in New South Wales, and the Home Penitentiary System, Prescribed by two Acts of Parliament of the Years 1794 & 1799.* London: unknown printer,.
Bentham, Jeremy. 1803. *A Plea for the Constitution: Shewing the Enormities Committed to the Oppression of British Subjects, Innocent as Well as Guilty, in Breach of Magna Charta, The Petition of Right, The Habeas Corpus Act, And the Bill of Rights; As Likewise of the Several Transportation Acts; in and by the Design, Foundation and Government of the Penal Colony of New South Wales: Including an Inquiry into the Right of the Crown to Legislate Without Parliament in Trinidad, and Other British Colonies.* London: Mawman, Poultry; and Hatchard.
Bentham, Jeremy. 1812. *Panopticon versus New South Wales; or, The Panopticon Penitentiary System and the Penal Colonization System Compared, Containing 1. Two Letters to Lord Pelham. 2. Plea for the Constitution, anno 1803, printed, now first published.* London: R. Baldwin.
Bentham, Jeremy, [1789], 1996. *An Introduction to the Principles of Morals and Legislation (CW).* J. H. Burns and H. L. A. Hart, eds, with a new introduction by Frederick Rosen. Oxford: Oxford University Press.
Blount, Charles, ed. 1937. *Memorandoms by James Martin.* Cambridge: Rampant Lions Press.
Christie, Ian R., ed. 1971. *The Correspondence of Jeremy Bentham (CW)*, vol.iii. London: Athlone Press.
Collins, David. 1975. *An Account of the English Colony in New South Wales*, 2 vols [1798 and 1802]. Brian Fletcher, ed. Sydney: A. H. & A. W. Reed PTY.
Crittenden, Victor, ed. 1991. *Escape from Botany Bay 1791, Being 'Memorandoms' by James Martin.* Canberra: Mulini Press.
Danziger, Marlies K. and Brady, Frank, eds. 1989. *Boswell the Great Biographer, 1789–1795* (Yale Edition of the Private Papers of James Boswell, vol.xiii. London: Yale University Press and William Heinemann.
Dinwiddy, John R., ed. 1984. *The Correspondence of Jeremy Bentham (CW)*, vol.vi. Oxford: Clarendon Press.
Dinwiddy, John R., ed. 1988. *The Correspondence of Jeremy Bentham (CW)*, vol.vii. Oxford: Oxford University Press.
Easty, John. 1965. *Memorandum of the Transactions of a Voyage from England to Botany Bay, 1787–1793 – A First Fleet Journal.* Sydney: Trustees of the Public Library of New South Wales in Association with Angus and Robertson.
Findlon, Paul G. and Ryan, R. J., eds. 1981. *The Journal and Letters of Lt. Ralph Clark, 1787–1792.* Sydney: Australian Documents Library in Association with the Library of Australian History.

Hamilton, George, 1988. *A Voyage Round the World, in His Majesty's Frigate Pandora, Performed under the Direction of Captain Edwards, in the years, 1790, 1791, and 1792. With the DISCOVERIES made in the South-Sea; and the many Distresses experienced by the Crew from Ship-wreck and Famine, in a Voyage of Eleven Hundred Miles in open Boats, between Endeavour Straits and the Island of Timor* [1793]. Sydney: Hordern House.

Harris, James, Hatch, Henry John and Foster Turner Wiseman, James. 1870. *The Paglesham Oyster: containing tales of fact, fiction and romance*. Rochford: unknown publisher.

Historical Records of Australia, Series I: Governors' despatches to and from England. Frederick Watson, ed. 1914–25. Sydney: Library Committee of the Commonwealth Parliament.

Historical Records of New South Wales. Frank Murcott Bladen, ed. 1892–1901. Sydney: Government Printer.

Hooper, Robert. 1799. *A Compendious Medical Dictionary. Containing an Explanation of the Terms in Anatomy, Physiology, Surgery, Materia Medica, Chemistry, and Practice of Physic. Collected from the Most Approved Authors*. London: Murray and Highley.

Old Bailey Proceedings Online (www.oldbaileyonline.org, version 7.2).

Parker, Mary Ann. 1795. *A Voyage Round the World in the Gorgon Man of War: Captain John Parker. Performed and Written by His Widow; For the Advantage of a Numerous Family*. London: John Nichols.

Scott, Geoffrey and Pottle, Frederick A., eds. 1934. *The Private Papers and Journal of James Boswell, 1789–1794*, vol. 18. United States of America: privately printed.

Scott, James. 1963. *Remarks on a Passage to Botany Bay, 1787–1792: A First Fleet Journal*. Sydney: The Trustees of the Public Library of New South Wales in Association with Angus and Robertson.

Thomson, Basil, ed. 1915. *Voyage of H.M.S. Pandora, Despatched to Arrest the Mutineers of the Bounty in the South Seas, 1790–91, Being the Narratives of Captain Edward Edwards, R.N., the Commander, and George Hamilton, the Surgeon*. London: Francis Edwards.

Tobin, George. 2007. *Captain Bligh's Second Chance: An Eyewitness Account of His Return to the South Seas by Lt. George Tobin*. Roy Schreiber, ed. London: Chatham Publishing.

Wharton, W. J. L., ed. 1893. *Captain Cook's Journal During His First Voyage Round the World Made in H. M. Bark* [sic] *Endeavour, 1768–71*. London: Elliot Stock.

Whately, Richard. 1832. *Thoughts on Secondary Punishments, in a Letter to Earl Grey*. London: B. Fellows.

Secondary sources

Anderson, Clare. 2001. 'Multiple Border Crossings: "Convicts and Other Persons Escaped from Botany Bay and residing in Calcutta"'. *Journal of Australian Colonial History*, vol.iii, no.2, pp.1–22.

Anderson, Clare. 2009. 'Discourses of exclusion and the "convict stain" in the Indian Ocean, c. 1800–1850', in *The Limits of British Colonial Control in South Asia: Spaces of disorder in the Indian Ocean region*. Ashwini Tambe and Harald Fischer-Tiné, eds. Abingdon: Routledge.

Atkinson, Alan. 1997. *The Europeans in Australia – A History, Volume One: The Beginning*. Oxford: Oxford University Press.

Australian Dictionary of Biography (http://adb.anu.edu.au/).

Biographical Database of Australia (http://www.bda-online.org.au).

Cameron, Michaela Ann. 2015. 'Charlotte', The *Dictionary of Sydney*, http://dictionaryofsydney.org/entry/charlotte/.

Bateson, Charles. 1985. *The Convict Ships, 1787–1868*, second edition. Glasgow: Brown, Son & Ferguson.

Blount, Charles. 1952. 'Bentham, Dumont and Mirabeau, an Historical Revision', *University of Birmingham Historical Journal*, vol.iii, pp.53–167.

Brady, Frank. 1984. *James Boswell: The Later Years, 1769–1795*. New York: McGraw-Hill Book Company.

Brunon-Ernst, Anne. 2013. *Beyond Foucault: New Perspectives on Bentham's Panopticon*. Abingdon: Routledge.

Causer, Timothy. 2010. '"Only a place fit for angels and eagles": the Norfolk Island penal settlement, 1825–1855'. PhD thesis: University of London.

Carter, Sebastian. 2013. *The Rampant Lions Press: A Narrative Catalogue*. New Castle, Delaware: Oak Knoll Press.
Christopher, Emma. 2011. *A Merciless Place: the Lost Story of Britain's Convict Disaster in Africa*. Oxford: Oxford University Press.
Christopher, Emma. 2007. '"The Slave Trade is Merciful Compared to [This]": Slave Traders, Convict Transportation, and the Abolitionists', in *Many Middle Passages: Forced Migration and the Making of the Modern World*. Emma Christopher, Cassandra Pybus and Marcus Rediker, eds. London: University of California Press.
Clayton, Peter. 2015. 'Victor Crittenden 1925–2014', *Australian Academic and Research Libraries*, vol.xlvi, pp.56–7.
Cobley, John. 1970. *The Crimes of the First Fleet Convicts*. Sydney: Angus and Robertson.
Cook, Judith. 1999. *To Brave Every Danger: The Epic Life of Mary Bryant of Fowey*. Truro: Truran Books.
Currey, Charles H. 1963. *The Transportation, Escape and Pardoning of Mary Bryant*. Sydney: Angus and Robertson.
Duffield, Ian. 2005. '"Haul away the anchor girls": Charlotte Badger, tall stories and the pirates of the "bad ship *Venus*"', *Journal of Australian Colonial History*, vol.vii, pp.35–64.
Duffield, Ian. 2013. 'Cutting Out and Taking Liberties: Australia's Convict Pirates, 1720–1829', *International Review of Social History*, vol.lviii, pp.197–227.
Ekirch, Roger. 1987. *Bound for America: The Transportation of British Convicts to the Colonies, 1718–1775*. Oxford: Clarendon Press.
Elliott, Brian. 1966. 'Antipodes: An Essay in Attitudes', *Australian Letters*, vol.vii, p.51.
Erickson, Carolly. 2005. *The Girl from Botany Bay*. Hoboken, NJ: John Wiley & Sons.
Farram, Steven. 2007. 'Jacobus Arnoldus Hazaart and the British interregnum in Netherlands Timor, 1812–1816', *Journal of the Humanities and Social Sciences of Southeast Asia and Oceania*, vol.clxiii, pp.455–75.
Foucault, Michel. 1991. *Discipline and Punish: The Birth of the Prison*. Alan Sheridan, ed. and trans. London: Penguin.
Flynn, Michael. 1993. *The Second Fleet: Britain's grim Convict Armada of 1790*. Sydney: Library of Australian History.
Frost, Alan. 2012. *Botany Bay: The Real Story*. Collingwood, Vic.: Black Inc.
Frost, Alan. 2012. *The First Fleet: The Real Story*. Collingwood, Vic.: Black Inc.
Gascoigne, John with Curthoys, Patricia. 2002. *The Enlightenment and European Australia*. Cambridge: Cambridge University Press.
Gillen, Mollie. 1993. *The Founders of Australia: a Biographical Dictionary of the First Fleet*. Sydney: Library of Australian History.
Griffin, J. P. 2008. 'Changing Life Expectancy Throughout History', *Journal of the Royal Society of Medicine*, vol.ci, p.577.
Hägerdal, Hans. 2012. *Lords of the Land, Lords of the Sea: Conflict and adaptation in early colonial Timor, 1600–1800*. Leiden: KITLV Press.
Hirst, J. B. 1983. *Convict Society and Its Enemies*. Sydney: Allen and Unwin.
Hirst, Warwick. 2003. *Great Convict Escapes in Colonial Australia*, revised edition. Sydney: Kangaroo Press.
Hughes, Robert. 1987. *The Fatal Shore: A History of the Transportation of Convicts to Australia 1787–1868*. London: Collins Harvill.
Hume, L. J. 1973. 'Bentham's panopticon: An administrative history—I', *(Australian) Historical Studies*, vol.xv, pp.703–21.
Ihde, Erin. 2008. 'Pirates of the Pacific: The Convict Seizure of the *Wellington*', *The Great Circle*, vol. xxx, pp.3–17.
Inglis, K. S. 2006. *This is the ABC: The Australian Broadcasting Commission, 1932–1983*. Melbourne: Black Inc.
Jackson, R. V. 1993. 'Theory and Evidence: Bentham, Collins, and the New South Wales Penal Settlement', *Australian Journal of Politics & History*, vol.xxxix, pp.318–29.
Karskens, Grace. 2005. '"This Spirit of Emigration": the Nature and Meanings of Escape in Early New South Wales', *Journal of Australian Colonial History*, vol.vii, pp.1–34.
Karskens, Grace. 2009. *The Colony: A History of Early Sydney*. Crows Nest, NSW: Allen and Unwin.
Keneally, Thomas. 2006. *The Commonwealth of Thieves*. London: Chatto & Windus.
King, Jonathan. 2004. *Mary Bryant: Her Life and Escape from Botany Bay*. Pymble, NSW: Simon and Schuster.

Levell, David. 2008. *Tour to Hell: Convict Australia's Great Escape Myths*. St Lucia: University of Queensland Press.
Lever, Susan. 2008. 'Masculinity, Guilt and the Moral Failures of the Body: Nick Enright's Screenplays', in *Nick Enright: An Actor's Playwright*. Anne Pender and Susan Lever, eds. New York: Rodopi, pp.47–60.
Matthews, Kate. 'Curator's Notes: *The Incredible Journey of Mary Bryant'*. *Australian Screen*, http://aso.gov.au/titles/tv/incredible-journey-mary-bryant/notes/.
Maxwell-Stewart, Hamish. 2010. 'Convict Transportation from Britain and Ireland, 1615–1870', *History Compass* vol.xi, pp.1224–7.
Maynard, John and Haskins, Victoria. 2016. *Living with the Locals: Early Europeans' Experience of Indigenous Life*. Canberra: National Library of Australia.
Milne, Alexander Taylor, ed. 1962. *Catalogue of the Manuscripts of Jeremy Bentham in the Library of University College, London*, second edition. London: Athlone Press.
Morris, Norval and Rothman, David J., eds. 1995. *The Oxford History of the Prison: The Practice of Punishment in Western Society*. Oxford: Oxford University Press.
Morriss, Roger. 2015. *Science, Utility and Maritime Power: Samuel Bentham in Russia, 1779–91*. Farnham: Ashgate.
Nash, M. D. 1989. *The Last Voyage of the Guardian, Lieutenant Riou, Commander, 1789–1791*. Cape of Good Hope: The Van Riebeeck Society.
Nicholas, Stephen and Shergold, Peter M., eds. 1988. *Convict Workers: Reinterpreting Australia's Past*. Cambridge: Cambridge University Press.
Oxford Dictionary of National Biography.
Pottle, Frederick A. 1938. *Boswell and the Girl from Botany Bay*. London: William Heinemann.
Pybus, Cassandra. 2006. *Black Founders: the Unknown Story of Australia's First Black Settlers*. Sydney: University of New South Wales Press.
Rawson, Geoffrey. 1938. *The Strange Case of Mary Bryant*. London: Robert Hale.
Ritchie, John. 1970. *Punishment and Profit: The Reports of Commissioner John Bigge on the Colonies of New South Wales and Van Diemen's Land, 1822–1823; their Origins, Nature, and Significance*. Melbourne: Heinemann.
Ritchie, John. 1976. 'Towards Ending an Unclean Thing: The Molesworth Committee and the Abolition of Transportation to New South Wales, 1837–40', *Australian Historical Studies*, vol. xvii, pp.144–64.
Semple, Janet. 1993. *Bentham's Prison: A Study of the Panopticon Penitentiary*. Oxford: Oxford University Press.
Schofield, Philip. 2006. *Utility and Democracy: The Political Thought of Jeremy Bentham*. Oxford: Oxford University Press.
Schofield, Philip. 2009. *Bentham: A Guide for the Perplexed*. New York: Continuum.
Smith, Keith Vincent. 2016. 'Carangarang', The *Dictionary of Sydney*, http://dictionaryofsydney.org/entry/carangarang/.
Smith, Keith Vincent. 2013. 'Woollarawarre Bennelong', The *Dictionary of Sydney*, http://dictionaryofsydney.org/entry/woollarawarre_bennelong/.
Steadman, Philip. 2012. 'Samuel Bentham's Panopticon', *Journal of Bentham Studies*, vol.xiv, http://discovery.ucl.ac.uk/1353164/.
Tench, Watkin. 1793. *A Complete Account of the Settlement at Port Jackson, in New South Wales*. London: G. Nicol and J. Sewell.
Townsend, Norma. 1977. 'The Molesworth Enquiry: Does the Report Fit the Evidence?', *Journal of Australian Studies*, vol.i, pp.33–51.
The UCL Bloomsbury Project, http://www.ucl.ac.uk/bloomsbury-project/.
Winfield, Rif. 2007. *British Warships in the Age of Sail, 1714–1792: design, construction, careers, and fates*. Barnsley: Seaforth.

Fiction

Becke, Louis and Jeffery, Walter. 1896. *A First Fleet Family: A Hitherto Unpublished Narrative of Certain Remarkable Adventures Compiled from the Papers of Sergeant William Dew of the Marines*. London: T. Fisher Unwin.

Becke, Louis and Jeffery, Walter. 1898. *The Mutineer: A Romance of Pitcairn Island*. London: T. Fisher Unwin.

Durand, John B. 2005. *The Odyssey of Mary B*. Elkhorn, WI: Puzzlebox Press.

Hausman, Gerald and Hausman, Loretta. 2003. *The True Story of Mary Bryant: Escape from Botany Bay*. New York: Orchard Books.

Pearse, Lesley. 2003. *Remember Me*. Leicester: Charnwood.

Rey, Jo Anne. 2005. *The Sarsaparilla Souvenir*. Bloomington, IN: XLibris Corporation.

Sheehan, Laurie. 2006. *Mary Bryant, The Convict Girl: the real story....* Kinloss: Librario.

Veitch, Anthony S. 1980. *Spindrift: the Mary Bryant Story: a Colonial Saga*. London: Angus and Robertson.

Wertenbaker, Timberlake. 1988. *Our Country's Good*. London: Methuen.

Index

Page numbers in *italics* denote an illustration, n indicates an endnote

Abbot, Charles (Baron Colchester) 64, 166n372
Addington, Henry (Viscount Sidmouth) 62, 165n358
Allen, William
  conviction and transportation 17–18, 155n104
  family 46
  maritime experience 17–19
  Memorandoms, authorship of 70
  post-release fate 46
  released from Newgate 43–5
  return to England and committal to Newgate 36
Alt, Augustus 11–12, 153n63
Anderson, Andrew 17
Anderson, Clare 51
Anderson, Sir John 64, 166n373
Arscott, John 150n15
Askew, Richard (Private) 12, 153n68

Badger, Charlotte
  conviction and transportation 161–2n287
  seizes the *Venus* brig 50
Baker, James (Private) 12, 153n68
Baron, John, Reverend
  biography 160n238
  reports on Mary Bryant's conduct in Fowey, and transfers Boswell's allowance to her 41–2, 160n238
Batavia (Jakarta)
  convicts escape to Batavia 50
  The Bryant party's passage from Kupang 32, 123, 145, 170n488
  history of 170n490
  ill-health and death of Bryant party members 32–3
  paintings of *33*, *34*
Beccaria, Cesare 65, 166n379
Becke, Louis (author) 47, 52–3
Bennelong
  family's accident in William Bryant's fishing boat 20
  portrait *21*
  see also Carangarang
Bennett, Henry Grey 67, 166n387
Bentham, Jeremy
  'A Picture of the Treasury' 62–3
  'A Plea for the Constitution' 63–5, 68

David Collins as source of information on New South Wales 63, 66, 165n366
  'First Letter to Lord Pelham' 59, 62–6
  Memorandoms, absence of evidence of his acquiring 58, 71
  Newgate Gaol, links to 58
  panopticon penitentiary scheme 59–63, *61*
  Panopticon versus New South Wales 49, 58–9, 63–6, 67
  portrait *58*
  predicts an increase in convicts escaping from New South Wales 49–50
  'Second Letter to Lord Pelham' 62–3, 64–5
  theory of punishment 65–6
  transportation and New South Wales, critique of 2, 59, 63, 65–8, *67*
Bentham, Samuel
  biography 164n334
  originator of the 'central inspection principle' 59
  portrait *60*
Bigge, John Thomas 50, 161n283
Bird, James 7, 151n39
Bird, Samuel
  conviction and transportation 7, 151n38
  death 34
  maritime experience 19
Bligh, William
  1st breadfruit voyage (1787) 10–11
  2nd breadfruit voyage (1791) 24–5
  at Kupang (1792) 24–5, 29–30, 32
  biography 153n56
  Bounty mutiny 10–11
  portrait *10*
  William Bryant's lost journal 25, 29, 70
  see also Bounty mutineers
Blount, Charles
  discovers *Memorandoms by James Martin* in the 1930s 68–9
  edition of the *Memorandoms* (1937) 70–1
Bond, Nicholas
  biography 159n213
  presides over the surviving Bryant party members' court hearing 36, 46, 125, 147
Borrit, James Punt
  convictions and transportations 162n295
  escapes from Norfolk Island 51

181

Boswell, James
    biography 159n218
    lobbies on behalf of the surviving escapees 36–7, 43–5, 46, 48, 49, 53, 160n238, 160n247, 160n250
    portrait *38*
    possible souvenir from the surviving escapees *49*, 161n281
    sexual habits 42–3
    support for Mary Bryant after her release 40–42, *42*
    unsuccessfully defends John Reid (1774) 43
Botany Bay *see* New South Wales; First Fleet
Bounty mutineers
    captured by the crew of the *Pandora* 30–1, *31*
    returned to Britain: 32, 33–4
    see also Vessels, HMS *Gorgon*
Bowring, John 62
    biography 165n349
Bow Street police office
    surviving Bryant party members' hearing 14, 22, 36, 125, 147
    see also Bond, Nicholas
Broad, Dolly
    reunited with sister Mary Bryant 40, 160n232
    see also Mary Bryant; Elizabeth Puckey
Broom, Samuel (*alias* John Butcher)
    conviction and transportation 18–19, 155n113
    released from Newgate 43–5
    return to England and committal to Newgate 36
    wrongly believed to have returned to New South Wales as a soldier 46–8, 161n270
Broughton, William (Captain)
    biography 154n77
    returns the Turwood party from Port Stephens to Sydney 12
Brown, James (Private) 12, 153n68
Brunon-Ernst, Anne 60–1
Bryant, Charlotte Spence
    biography 171n502
    birth 4
    death: 35–6, 125, 147
    see also Mary Bryant; William Bryant; Emanuel Bryant
Bryant, Emanuel
    biography 155n102
    birth 17
    death 33, 123, 125, 145, 147
    see also Mary Bryant; Charlotte Spence Bryant; Emanuel Bryant
Bryant (née Broad), Mary
    conviction and transportation 3–4
    estrangement from husband imagined by modern writers 17, 29–30, 157–8n187
    fictional accounts and television adaptations of her life 52, 55–8, *57*, 163n300
    historical accounts of her life evaluated 52–5
    marriage to William Bryant 11
    pardoning and release from Newgate 37–9, *39*
    return to England and committal to Newgate 36
    return to Fowey after release 40–42
    signature *42*
    speculation as to fate after returning to Fowey 45–6
    see also William Bryant; Charlotte Spence Bryant, Emanuel Bryant
Bryant party, escape and voyage to Kupang
    at the Gulf of Carpentaria 28, 109, 117, 143
    at Lady Elliot Island 27, 103, 105, 137, 139
    at Moreton Bay ('White Bay') 27, 97, 135
    at Port Stephens 25, 85, 131
    departure from Port Jackson 22, 81, 129
    encounters with Indigenous Australians and Torres Strait Islanders 24, 25, 26, 27, 28, 83, 85, 87, 89, 91, 97, 99, 131, 133, 135, 137, 141, 143
    endure storms and heavy seas 26, 27, 91, 93, 95, 97, 99, 101, 103, 109, 111, 113, 133, 135, 137
    expertise and skills 19
    in Arnhem Land 117, 143
    find coal at Glenrock Lagoon ('Fortunate Creek') 24–5, 83, 131
    party's preparations to escape 22
    physical description of the party *24*
    plans delayed 17, 20
    reach Kupang 28–9, 121, 123, 143, 145
Bryant party, members
    see William Allen; Samuel Bird; Samuel Broom; Charlotte Spence Bryant; Emanuel Bryant; Mary Bryant; William Bryant; James Cox; Nathaniel Lillie; James Martin; William Morton
Bryant party, recapture and return to England
    commital to Newgate Gaol 36, 125, 147
    identification and arrest at Kupang, conflicting accounts 29–30, 31–2, 121, 123, 145, 157–8 n187
    passage to Batavia 123, 145
    passage to Britain aboard HMS *Gorgon* 34–6, 123, 125, 145, 170n494
    passage to the Cape of Good Hope 33–4, 123, 145
Bryant, William
    biography 150n21
    conviction and transportation 4–5, 150n22
    death 33, 123, 145
    lost journal of the party's escape 25, 29, 30, 40
    marriage to Mary Broad 11
    working of fishing boats in New South Wales and abuse of his position 11–12, 20, 22
    see also Mary Bryant; Charlotte Spence Bryant; Emanuel Bryant
Bunbury, (Sir) Thomas Charles
    biography 165n367
    supporter of Bentham's panopticon scheme 63–4
Burn, David 10, 152n52
Butcher, John (soldier of the New South Wales Corps)
    Samuel Broom mistaken for in historical accounts 47–8

Caesar, John 'Black'
  biography 152n45
  punished for absconding 8
Camden, Calvert and King (merchant and slaving company) 16, 154n94. *see also* Second Fleet
Campbell, James (Captain) 18, 155n111
Cape Arnhem and Arnhem Land
  Bryant party at 28, 117, 143, 169n473, 170n474
Cape of Good Hope
  First Fleet at 1, 79, 129
  Guardian broken up at 15
  passage of the Bryant party to 34, 123, 145
  Bryant party transferred to HMS *Gorgon* at 34, 123, 145
Cape York Peninsula
  Bryant party at 28, 109, 141, 169n465
Carangarang
  biography 156n130
  family's accident in William Bryant's fishing boat 20
  see also Bennelong
Cavendish-Bentinck, William Henry Cavendish (Duke of Portland) 165n359
Christian, Fletcher 11, 153n57. *see also* William Bligh; HMS *Bounty*; *Bounty* mutineers
Christopher, Emma 6
Clark, Ralph (Lieutenant)
  biography 159n210
  death of Charlotte Bryant 35–6
  passage to Britain aboard HMS *Gorgon* 35, 170n495
  television portrayal 56
Collins, David (Captain)
  arrival of the Second Fleet 15–16
  biography 152n43
  convict escapes 7–8, 37
  food shortages in New South Wales 14–15
  portrait *8*
  recapture of the Bryant party at Kupang 30
  reports of the Bryant party's intention to abscond 14, 20, 23
  Turwood party's escape 12–13
  William Bryant's abuse of role in colony's fishing enterprise 11–12
  William Bryant's attitude towards his marriage 17, 29
Connoway, George
  conviction and transportation 14
  escapes from Sydney with the Turwood party 12–13
convict absconding
  examples of 7–11, 12, 14, 49–51
  factors in success 12, 13–14
Cook, James (Captain)
  biography 152n55
  climate of Batavia 32
  exploration of the Pacific 10, 167n410
Cook, Judith
  assumptions about Bentham's acquisition of the *Memorandoms* 58
  To Brave Every Danger, evaluation 53–5, 156n132, 156n138, 157–8n187
  To Brave Every Danger, fictionalisation of aspects of the Bryant party's escape 14, 20, 29, 54–5

Cormick, Edward
  biography 152n42
  hanged for absconding 7–8
Courtenay, William, Viscount
  biography 167n408
  property stolen by James Martin 2, 77, 129
  see also James Martin
Cox, James (*alias* Rolt or Rott)
  conviction and transportation 5–6
  drowned or escaped in the Straits of Sunda 34, 158n205
  leaves behind a letter in Sydney after escaping 23
  Mercury mutiny and recaptured in Devon 6–7
  mistaken identity in historical accounts 151n26
  see also Convict transports, *Mercury*
Cox, John Matthew (*alias* Banbury Jack)
  biography, and James Cox mistaken for in historical accounts 151n26
Crittenden, Victor
  edition of the *Memorandoms* (1991) 69
Currey, Charles H.
  The Transportation, Escape and Pardoning of Mary Bryant 53

Day, John
  conviction and transportation 162n297
  escapes from Norfolk Island 51
Dew, William (Sergeant) 52
Dharug people 9, 152n48
Duffield, Ian 50, 52
Dukes (Lukes), Richard (Private) 12, 153n68
Dundas, Henry (Lord Melville)
  biography 159n219
  lobbied by Boswell on behalf of the surviving escapees 36–7, 44, 45, 46–7
Dundas, Lady Jane
  biography 160n249
  lobbied by Boswell on behalf of the surviving escapees 44, 160n250
Dutch East India Company (VOC) 32, 170n478

Easty, John (Private)
  on the Bryant party's escape 22–3, 37
Eden, William, Baron Auckland 64, 166n373
Edwards, Edward (Captain)
  biography 158n188
  given command of HMS *Pandora* to track down *Bounty* mutineers 30
  journey to and arrival at Kupang after wrecking of the *Pandora* 31–2, 121, 145
  takes command of the Bryant party at Kupang 33–4, 123, 145
  wrecking of the *Pandora* 31
Ellerington, William
  Neptune's first mate 17
  tried for murder 17
  see also Second Fleet, ships, *Neptune*; Donald Trail
Eora people
  encounters with Europeans 1, 20, *21*, 167n410

Erickson, Carolly
　The Girl from Botany Bay, evaluation 29, 45, 46, 53, 55, 163n311
Evans, Thomas
　brings a charge of murder against Donald Trail and William Ellerington 17

First Fleet
　members of the Bryant party transported by 2–7
　other convicts transported by 150n15, 152n45, 152n48, 153n65
　picture of 2
　voyage to Botany Bay and relocation to Port Jackson 1, 11, 16, 56, 77–8, 129, 167n412, 167–8 n414, 168nn416–21
First Fleet, ships
　Alexander 7, 151n39, 152n42, 152n45, 152n48, 167–8n414
　Borrowdale (store-ship) 167–8n414
　Charlotte 3, 4, 5, 7, 77, 129, 150nn15–16, 167n412, 167–8n414
　Fishburn (store-ship) 167–8n414
　Friendship 167–8n414
　Golden Grove (store-ship) 167–8n414
　HMS *Sirius* (escort) 2, 150n16, 153n65, 167–8n414
　HMS *Supply* (escort) 2, 22, 153n65, 167–8n414
　Lady Penrhyn 167–8n414
　Prince of Wales 167–8n414
　Scarborough 150n15, 151n26, 153n65, 153n68, 167–8n414
A First Fleet Family (novel) 47, 52, 55, 163n306
Forde, Thomas Brownlow (Reverend)
　biography 164n330
　corresponds with Bentham 58
Foucault, Michel 60

Gascoigne, John 67
Glenrock Lagoon
　Bryant party finds coal at 24, 83, 131, 168n425, 168n428
Graves, Thomas (Admiral)
　biography 155n107
　commander-in-chief of North American squadron 18
Grey, Henry George (Earl Grey)
　supposes it to be impossible to escape from Norfolk Island 51
Grosvenor, Robert (Viscount Belgrave)
　biography 165n345
　objects to Bentham's panopticon scheme 61, 62
Gulf of Carpentaria
　Bryant party cross 28, 109, 111, 117, 141, 143, 169nn471–3

Hagerty, Catherine
　conviction and transportation 162n288
　seizes the *Venus* brig 50
Haly (Elley), Jane
　assaulted by Donald Trail 17
　conviction and transportation 155n99

Hamilton, George (surgeon)
　biography 158n190
　identification of the Bryant party at Kupang 31–2
　passage from Batavia to the Cape of Good Hope 33–4
　passage of the *Rembang* from Kupang to Batavia 32–3
Hawkesbury River 14, 48, 152n48, 159n223
Hayden (*alias* Shepherd), Mary
　biography 150n16
　conviction and transportation 3, 54
Heath, John (judge)
　biography 151n32
　tries the *Mercury* mutineers 6–7
Hines (Haines), Luke (Private) 12, 153n68
Hirst, Warwick
　Great Convict Escapes in Colonial Australia 24, 25, 27, 53, 168n425, 168 n431, 169n444, 169n456
Hulks
　as part of British penal policy 4–5, 5, 65, 150n24
　Captivity 48
　Ceres 152n42
　Dunkirk 3, 5, 7, 14, 150nn15–16, 167n411
　Fortune 18–19
　Justitia 7, 19
　Lion 18, 19
　Stanislaus 18
Hungry Ones, The (TV series) 56–8, 57
Hunter, John (Governor)
　biography 152n46
　portrait 9
　seeks to prevent convict absconding 8–9, 14
Hunt, Joseph (Private) 153n68

Incredible Journey of Mary Bryant, The (TV series) 56–8
Irish convicts, escape attempts 8–9

Jeffery, Walter (author) 47, 52–3
Johnson, Richard (Reverend)
　biography 154n92
　describes the arrival of the Second Fleet 15–16
Jones, Thomas (Private) 12, 153n68
Joseph, John (cook) 17

Karskens, Grace 10, 12, 13
Keneally, Thomas 47
Kestle, Mr 40, 41
King, Jonathan
　Mary Bryant: Her Life and Escape from Botany Bay, evaluation 45, 47, 55
Kupang, Timor
　Bryant party at 11, 29–30, 121, 145
　history of 170n478
　see also William Bligh; Edward Edwards; vessels, non-convict, HMS *Pandora*

Lady Elliot Island
　Bryant party at 27, 103, 137, 169n456
Lakeman, Agnes
　assaulted and robbed by Mary Broad, Mary Hayden, and Catherine Prior 3, 54

184　INDEX

Laurence, French (politician) 64, 166n373
Lee, George
   conviction and transportation 14
   escapes from Sydney with the Turwood party 12–13
   hijacks the *Cumberland* 14, 159n223
Levell, David 9
Lillie, Deborah
   implicated, with her husband, in a burglary 48
   marriage to Nathaniel, and family 161n277
Lillie, Nathaniel
   conviction and transportation 19, 155n117
   marriage to Deborah, and family 161n277
   Memorandoms, authorship of 70
   post-release fate and possible later reconviction 46, 48
   released from Newgate 43–5
   return to England and committal to Newgate 36
Long, Charles (Baron Farnborough) in parentheses 62, 165 n351

Macquarie Harbour (Van Diemen's Land)
   convicts escape from 50–1
Martin, James
   conviction and transportation 2–3, 167n407
   family 49
   Memorandoms, authorship of 70–1
   post-release fate 49
   released from Newgate 43–5
   return to England and committal to Newgate 36
   television portrayal 57
Mary Bryant (Nick Enright musical) 56
Mauritius, convicts escape to 51
Memorandoms by James Martin
   Blount edition 68–9
   Crittenden edition 69
   original manuscript 69–71
Molesworth, Sir William
   biography 166n390
   parliamentary reports on transportation 67–8, 167n393
Moore, George (merchant) 6, 151n30
Moreton Bay (White Bay)
   Bryant party at 26, 97, 135
   penal station opened 50
Morton, William
   conviction and transportation 16, 155n120
   death 34
   maritime experience 19, 22–3
Moutray, John (Captain)
   biography 155n105
   commander of the *Ramilies* and loss of a merchant fleet 18

Nepean, Sir Evan
   biography 159n221
   lobbied by Boswell on behalf of the surviving escapees 37, 43, 44
   role in the release of Allen, Broom, Lillie and Martin from Newgate 45
New Caledonia
   convicts escape to 51
Newcastle (Coal River)
   penal station opened 50

Newgate Gaol 36, *37*, 43–5, 58
New South Wales
   British arrival at 1, 168nn419–21
   condition of prisoners arriving by the Second Fleet 15–17
   contact with Indigenous Australians 1, 12, 20, *20*, 24–8
   food shortages 14–16
   punishment of convicts 7–8, 12, 14
   skills and trades of convicts sent to 11–12, 19, 22–3
   soldiers hanged for stealing provisions 12, 153n68
   Turwood party escapes from 12–14
   see also Botany Bay; First Fleet; Port Jackson
New Zealand
   convicts escape to 50, 51
Norfolk Island 7, 22, 68, 69, 150n16, 151n26, 153n65, 155n99
   convicts escape from 10, 50, 51, 152n53, 162n295
   penal station opened 50
North America
   transportation to 4, 6, 151nn30–1
North, Lord Frederick 6, 151n29

Old Bailey
   surviving Bryant party members brought up at 36
   trial of James Bird 151n39
   trials of James Punt Borrit 162n295
   trial of George Connoway and George Lee 14
   trial of James Cox 5–6, 151n26
   trial of John Matthew Cox 151n26
   trial of John Day 162n297
   trial of Mary Desmond and Mary Butler 151n39
   trial of Jane Haly (Elley) 155n99
   trial of John Turwood 153–4n72
   trial of William Vine 162n296
   trial of John Watson 154n74
   trial of Sarah Young 156n144
Onrust Island (Honroost, Pulau Kapal) 34, *34*, 158n205

Paget, Joseph
   conviction and transportation 153n65
   informs on William Bryant 11–12
panopticon, *see* Jeremy Bentham; Samuel Bentham
Parker, John (Captain) 159n208
Parker, Mary Ann 159n208
Parsons, William
   biography 160n244
   doggerel about Boswell and Mary Bryant 42–3
Pedder, William
   conviction and transportation 163n298
   escapes from Norfolk Island 51
Pelham, Thomas (Lord)
   biography 166n368
   Bentham's critique of transportation addressed to 59, 63–5, 66

Phillip, Arthur (Governor)
    aware of the Bryant party's intention to abscond 20
    biography 149n2
    commander of the First Fleet 1, 168n419
    food shortages in New South Wales 15
    maltreatment of convicts transported by the Second Fleet 15–16
    physical description of the Bryant party 24
    portrait 3
Pitt, William 165n357
Port Dalrymple (Van Diemen's Land)
    convicts escape from 50
Port Jackson, see New South Wales
Port Macquarie
    penal station opened 50
Port Stephens
    Bryant Party at 25, 85, 131, 168n431
    Turwood party live among the Worimi people at 12–13
Potemkin, Grigory Aleksandrovich (Prince) 59, 164n335
Pottle, Frederick
    Boswell and the Girl from Botany Bay, evaluation 45, 53
Prior (Fryer), Catherine
    conviction and transportation 3, 150n15
Puckey, Edward
    seeks legal advice from Boswell regarding an inheritance 40–2
Puckey (née Broad), Elizabeth
    apparent inheritance due to her family 40–2
    Boswell sends news of her sister, Mary Bryant 40

Rawson, Geoffrey
    The Strange Case of Mary Bryant, evaluation 52–3
    The Strange Case of Mary Bryant, fictionalisation of aspects of the escape 52–3, 150n22
Reid, John
    unsuccessfully defended by Boswell on a charge of sheep-stealing 43
Romilly, Sir Samuel
    biography 166n374
    revises 'A Plea for the Constitution' for Bentham 64
Rose Hill
    Turwood party abscond from 12
Ross, Robert (Major) 150n16, 170n495

Salmon, George (merchant) 6, 151n30
Scott, James (Private)
    on the Bryant party's escape 156n136, 158n205
Second Fleet
    arrival at Port Jackson 13–14
    maltreatment of convicts transported by 15–17, 154n90
    members of the Bryant party transported by 17–19
    other convicts transported by 13–14, 151n39, 153–4n72, 154nn74–75, 155n99, 156n144
    supplies for the colony sent out in 15

Second Fleet, ships
    Justinian (store-ship) 15
    Lady Juliana 15, 156n144
    Neptune 13, 14, 15–17, 19, 151n39, 155n99
    Scarborough 14, 15, 18, 19
    Surprize 13, 15, 156n144
Semple, Janet 62
Senegambia, convicts transported to 4–5
Smit, Detmer 22, 168n424
Spencer, George (Earl Spencer)
    biography 165n344
    objects to Bentham's panopticon scheme 61
Stewart, Eliza
    marriage to Private John Butcher 48
    see also John Butcher (soldier of the New South Wales Corps)
Sutton, Joseph
    conviction and transportation 13, 154n75
    death 12
    unsuccessfully attempts to stow away on the *Neptune* at Port Jackson 14
Sydney 8, 9, 12, 14, 17, 24, 37, 47, 48, 53, 59
    paintings of Sydney Cove 13, 23
    see also New South Wales

Tahiti
    HMS *Bounty* at 11
    HMS *Pandora* at 30, 121, 145
    HMS *Providence* at 24
    Turwood party thought to have sailed for 12
Tasman, Abel Janszoon 170n484
Temple, William Johnson
    biography 160n234
    makes enquiries for Boswell in Cornwall about raising a subscription for Mary Bryant 40
Tench, Watkin (Captain)
    Bligh's journey to Timor after the *Bounty* mutiny 11
    biography 153n59
    identification of the Bryant party at Kupang 35, 70
    portrait 35
    travels to England aboard HMS *Gorgon* with the surviving Bryant party members 34–6, 170n495
Thurlow, Baron Edward
    biography 160n236
    refuses to give money to Boswell for Mary Bryant's subscription 41
Timor, see Kupang
Tobin, George (Lieutenant)
    biography 157n154
    William Bryant's lost journal 25, 30
Torres Strait Islanders
    encounters with the Bryant party 28, 109, 141
Trail, Donald
    biography 154n94
    maltreatment of convicts transported by the *Neptune* 16–17
    trial for murder 17
Transportation Acts
    of 1717 (4 Geo. I c. 11) 4
    of 1768 (8 Geo. III c. 15) 6

Turwood (or Tarwood), John
   conviction and transportation
      153–4n72
   hijacks the *Cumberland* 14, 159n223
   leads an escape party from Port Jackson
      12–14
Turwood party, members, *see* George
   Connoway; George Lee;
   Joseph Sutton; John Turwood;
   John Watson

Van Diemen's Land
   convicts abscond from 50–1
   First Fleet passes by 1
Vessels, convict transports
   Boddingtons 47
   Hyderabad 51, 162n295
   Mangles 51
   Mercury 6–7, 151n31
   Pitt 164n164
   Swift 6, 151n30
   see also First Fleet, ships; Second
      Fleet, ships
Vessels, non-convict
   Ann and Elizabeth 40
   HMS *Bounty* 10–11. *see also* William Bligh;
      Bounty mutineers
   Cumberland 14, 159n223
   HMS *Gorgon* 30, 34–6, 47, 52–3, 123–4,
      145, 158n205, 159n208,
      170nn494–5
   Guardian 15
   HMS *Helena* 6–7
   Hoornwey 33–4
   Horssen 33–4
   HMS *Pandora* 30–1, *31*, 32, 33, 121,
      145, 158nn188–90. *see also Bounty*
      mutineers; Edward Edwards; George
      Hamilton
   HMS *Providence* 12, 24, 25
   HMS *Ramilies* 18
   Rembang 32, 170n488
   Vreedenberg 33, 170n493
   Waaksamheyd 22, 156n135
   Wellington 51

Vine, William
   escapes from Norfolk Island 51
   conviction and transportation 162n296

Wanjon, Timotheus (Governor of Kupang)
   arrests the Bryant party 29, 32
   arrival of the Bryant party at Kupang 29
   biography 157n149
   shows William Bryant's lost journal to
      William Bligh 24–5
Watling, Thomas
   conviction and transportation 164n328
   introduced as a character in *The Incredible
      Journey of Mary Bryant* 56
Watson, John
   conviction and transportation 154n74
   escapes from Sydney with the Turwood
      party 12–13
Whately, Richard (Archbishop) 67, 166n388
White, John (surgeon)
   biography 153n66
   gives evidence in William Bryant's trial for
      stealing government fish 12
White, Joseph
   asks Nepean's opinion on whether Allen,
      Broom, Lillie and Martin should be
      released from Newgate 45
   biography 160n255
Wilberforce, William 64, 166n371
Wilson, Jacqueline Z.
   criticism of *The Incredible Journey of Mary
      Bryant* 56
Wilson, John (Bun-bo-e)
   biography 152n48
   conviction and transportation 152n48
   employed as a guide on expedition to the
      interior of New South Wales 9
Worimi people
   Bryant party encounter 85, 131
   Turwood party live among 12–13

Young, Sarah
   biography 156n144
   conviction and transportation 156n144
   letter from James Cox 23